THE POLITICS OF POVERTY

THE POLITICS
OF POVERTY

DAVID DONNISON

Martin Robertson · Oxford

First published in 1982 by Martin Robertson & Company Ltd.,
108 Cowley Road, Oxford OX4 1JF.

Reprinted 1982

British Library Cataloguing in Publication Data

Donnison, David
　The politics of poverty
　1. Poor – Great Britain
　I. Title
　305.5'6'0941　　HC260.P6

　ISBN 0-85520-480-X
　ISBN 0-85520-481-8 Pbk

Typeset in 11/12pt Sabon by Oxford Verbatim Limited
Printed and bound in Great Britain by Book Plan Limited, Worcester

Contents

Preface   vii

The Civil Service Hierarchy   xi

1   *The Meanings of Poverty*   1

2   *The State and the Poor*   9
The social security system   9
The Supplementary Benefits Commission   13
Ideas and origins   18
Winds of change   22

3   *Picking Priorities*   27
The opening moves   27
Towards a strategy   40
Launching the review   49

4   *The Political Environment*   61
On the defensive   61
The unemployed   67
The employed   75
The Labour movement   84

5   *Issues and Interests*   89
Discretion, rights and welfare   89
Saints and sinners   100
As husband and wife   107
Women's rights   116
The poverty lobby   126
The academics   134

6 *Reform*   140
   Reviewing the scheme   140
   Open government   147
   The approaching election   153
   New regime   160
   Changing the law   167
   What was achieved?   178

7 *Unfinished Business*   184
   Housing costs   184
   Fuel costs   193
   The quality of service   198
   Watershed   206

8 *Conclusions*   214
   The politics of poverty   214
   Policies   225

Sources quoted   233

Index   235

Preface

I accepted the invitation to become chairman of the Supplementary Benefits Commission in 1975 because it would give me an opportunity of learning about Britain's oldest and most basic social service: the social assistance scheme to which nearly one-tenth of our citizens turn for at least a part of their incomes. With the help of my colleagues on the Commission, I hoped we might also be able to change things a bit.

For five years the job also gave me an opportunity of learning about my own country. From Stornaway to Southampton, from Margate to Belfast and from Sunderland to Camarthen I visited the homes of people living on supplementary benefit, and talked with the people who work in social security offices. I worked very closely with our officials at headquarters. I met the CBI and the TUC, and talked with directors in boardrooms and shop stewards in trades councils, with social workers, housing managers, gas and electricity board staff and local government councillors. I met regularly with Ministers and shadow ministers, and also with back-bench MPs, journalists of every kind, and the spokesmen of claimants' unions and the pressure groups. I went down coal mines and visited factories. I talked with thousands of people at public gatherings and, through radio 'phone-in programmes, in their own homes. I also visited social security offices in other countries. And between us, by 1980, we had learnt a good deal about poverty and shifted an apparently immovable system: not much, but enough to make some changes and to learn what more should be done.

While the story was fresh in my mind and the lessons to be learnt from it still urgently important, I wanted to tell how it all happened, what parts were played by those involved – from claimants to Ministers – what poverty means in Britain today, and what we should be doing about it. So I wrote this book at speed, mainly on holiday, at week-ends and overnight, while doing another job. My main source for it has been my own memory, and the notes which I dictated while working at the SBC. These notes were not a journal, nor were they intended as the basis for a book. They were records of meetings and visits, and occasional private reflections about what was happening, where we were going and what we should be doing. I have also consulted speeches and articles I wrote and the annual reports we prepared during these five years. But I have not gone back to the files: there was not time.

The book begins, in Chapter 1, with a discussion of the meanings of poverty. This is basic to all that follows. To define poverty is to take a standpoint about our duties and rights as citizens, about the role of the state, and much else besides. Chapter 2 introduces the main institutions I shall be writing about, the assumptions on which they were founded, and the ways in which these assumptions are changing. Social reform is a process, not an event: a kind of drama. Chapter 3 deals with the first act of this drama, describing our attempts to pose questions and pick priorities for a review of the supplementary benefit scheme. Chapter 4 deals with the political environment in which we were operating. It describes our growing obsession with the unemployed – the silent poor – and our search for allies in a campaign for more effective action on their behalf. In the second act of the drama reformers look for solutions to the problems under discussion, and for the groups and interests most likely to gain a hearing in the debate. Chapter 5 discusses some of the issues explored at this stage, some of the movements which gained a hearing, and the role of the academics. In act three of the drama the reformers have to assemble a set of proposals around which some agreement can be mobilised. Then, in act four, the proposals for change which survive this process are formally registered and approved. In this story that meant getting a Bill through Parliament. These two acts and the changing political environment in which they unfolded are described in Chapter 6, which concludes with an attempt to assess what was achieved. I offer no final verdict. Changing the law provides no more than a licence for those who then have the crucial task of putting reforms into practice. I cannot trace that fifth act of the drama because it was only beginning as I left the scene. But in Chapter 7, entitled 'Unfinished Business', I say something about the sixth act which may follow: the possibility of keeping the impetus for reform rolling and using more of the ideas hammered out in the course of earlier debates. Finally, in Chapter 8, I draw conclusions from the whole experience, first about the politics of poverty – the drama and the actors who played a part in it – and finally about the policies to be followed in this field.

I want to thank a lot of people for the help they have given me, usually unwittingly, in writing this book. First of all, the customers of the supplementary benefit scheme whom I met at home and across the counters of social security offices almost every month for five years: 'I have a colleague with me today. Do you mind if he comes in with me?' was the formula visiting officers adopted, and no-one ever refused me. Staff in well over 100 of our local offices taught me a great deal, often in robust and cheerful argument derived from their own daily experience. Next I want to thank my colleagues on the Commission and our closest advisors, some of whom I have consulted about the first draft of this book. They were a marvellous team to work with, but they are in no way responsible for the use I have made here of their advice. I learnt something from nearly all whom I encountered in our work, and not least from our harsher critics. I have drawn freely and without acknowledgement on the ideas of academic colleagues. Ministers, Labour and Conservative, were unfailingly kind and courteous, even when they disagreed with us. Among them I particularly want to thank Sir Keith Joseph who appointed me deputy chairman of the Commission in 1973, and Barbara Castle who invited us to present the independent Reports to Parliament which were the starting point of the story. She it was who appointed me chairman. I am grateful to Paul Barker, editor of *New Society*, for advice about my first draft and for encouraging me to publish early versions of some of my chapters in his magazine. I owe a similar debt to the *Three Banks Review*, which published an earlier version of one of my chapters. I am grateful to Hector Breeze, Punch and Private Eye for allowing reproduction of the cartoons on the cover and page 110, and to

David Austin and Private Eye for the reproduction of the cartoon on page 68. I want to thank all those who helped me with the typing of successive drafts: particularly Sue Davies in London, Margery Russell in Glasgow, and May McKenzie and her colleagues in Canberra.

Finally, and most important of all, I want to thank Kay Carmichael, deputy chairman of the Commission, who has talked with me about every chapter of the book. To her I owe more than I can say.

David Donnison
University of Glasgow
August 1981

The Civil Service Hierarchy

From time to time throughout this book civil servants are described by their ranks. For readers unfamiliar with this system it may be helpful to study this list of the main grades in the administrative hierarchy, together with the equivalent army ranks. The salary scales shown beneath are for civil servants only: army salaries are higher.

Permanent Secretary	Field Marshall
Second Permanent Secretary	General
Deputy Secretary	Lieutenant General
Under Secretary	Major General
Assistant Secretary	Brigadier
Principal	Colonel
Senior Executive Officer	Lieutenant Colonel
Higher Executive Officer	Major
Executive Officer	Captain
Clerical Officer	} No recognised equivalents
Clerical Assistant	

Salary Scales from 1st April 1981

Head of the Civil Service	£35,845
Permanent Secretary	£33,170
Second Permanent Secretary	£30,495
Deputy Secretary	£26,215
Under Secretary	£21,935
Assistant Secretary	£17,685 – 20,895
Principal	£11,372 – 15,010
Senior Executive Officer	£9,232 – 11,265
Higher Executive Officer	£7,467 – 9,184
Executive Officer	£4,069 – 7,247
Clerical Officer	£2,594 – 5,102
Clerical Assistant	£45.42 – 78.26 weekly

For those working in London all grades below Deputy Secretary receive an addition of £1,016 (in inner London) or £424 (in outer London).

CHAPTER 1

The Meanings of Poverty

"Tell me, Professor Donnison" said the BBC interviewer, "*very* briefly: is there any real poverty in Britain today? Or is it all just relative – keeping up with the Joneses?" I groped for the few words our twenty remaining seconds would permit, a flood of images flowing through my head. As chairman of the Supplementary Benefits Commission I had been meeting social security claimants every month in their homes and across the counters of social security offices. In crude statistical terms they represented the poorest tenth of the population.

If 'real' poverty means hardship and misery, then many of these claimants were definitely not in it. Courage and luck, family and friends, subsidised housing and supplementary benefits, were keeping their heads above water. A widow, for example, ageing but chirpy, in a snug council house on the fringe of a small midlands town: she was getting a little lame, but she was growing cabbages in the back garden, roses in front, and was visited several times a week by her children and grandchildren. She was neither in hardship nor in misery; and she would certainly not have described herself as 'poor'.

The inner city shelters many other people with equally low incomes who keep their heads above water. A West Indian woman with two lovingly tended children, living in a newly converted council flat in Hackney, was among them. With a frilly-quilted double bed and a wardrobe already installed, and most of her rooms carpeted and curtained, she had asked us for a grant to buy curtains and floor coverings for the remaining rooms. The 'liable relative' responsible for maintaining her had disappeared from the scene. But she was cheerfully determined to devote the next stage of her life to raising the youngsters: a more important and demanding job than the better-paid work to which she'll eventually return. The state gets a bargain by paying her to do it.

But there are many other kinds of cases. Social security officials deal with a lot of people who are contending with crises in their lives which could turn into lasting misery and hardship. Take a man in his fifties – my own age. He had worked for many years as a moulder, re-treading motor tyres in a small factory in the Potteries. The elderly capitalist who owned the firm had let it run down and then closed the works, giving his people only two weeks notice. This claimant turned to us when his insurance benefit ran out. Standing with his wife amidst brass ornaments and holiday mementoes assembled over a lifetime, they wondered whether he would ever work again. Both were still in a state of shock and grief. Grief of more familiar kinds constantly assailed me on my visits. Widows I recall, giggly and inconsequential in face of a loss too appalling to comprehend, unable to concentrate for more than a few moments at a time on the questions we had to ask; deserted wives, numbed by varying mixtures of rage, relief, guilt, and fear for the future; and their children too, who would run to their mothers for reassurance as we entered, and peer up at us.

These people received weekly payments which generally ensured that they could keep a roof over their heads and get enough to eat. Supplementary benefit is roughly double the real value of the national assistance which similar people would have had in 1948. But whenever you begin to grow convinced that everyone in 'real' need claims the benefits to which they are entitled, you run across someone who doesn't. A spiky little widow in Islington, for example: the state had owed her money for years – nearly £4 a week when we found her – because she kept herself to herself and didn't want to be bothered by officials. Provided we do our best to help people to claim their rights, we must recognise that they also have a right to do without us. We had come to see her because she had been struggling for nine months to pay off an electricity bill a few shillings at a time, which dragged her living standards still further down. Coaxing her to accept a supplementary pension was like persuading a fierce and frightened animal to take food. She eventually agreed when we said that we could settle the rest of the electricity bill right away. The taxpayers had owed her much more than that for a long time. She seemed to have no close family or friends, but got by with the help of a day centre where she was given hot meals.

There are other people – some in working families, and others living on social security benefits – who suffer poverty which is certainly 'real'. I think particularly of bleak housing estates on the fringes of Merseyside and Clydeside, but every big city and many small ones have similar neighbourhoods; streets daubed with graffiti, and littered with rubbish drifting in the wind; undernourished people hurrying by, clutching plastic clothing around bodies which are painfully thin or bulge mis-shapenly; houses in which you sit shivering in your overcoat to interview pallid women, and set out gratefully to warm up, walking through snow or wintry rain; unpaid fuel bills; rent arrears; children with running noses; the sour smells of condensation and dirty laundry.

Why are these people so plainly in old-fashioned, miserable poverty when others in the same streets, with incomes no higher, are not? 'Mismanagement', some say. Many dull their appetites with cigarettes, cups of tea, biscuits and sticky buns. Some – poorly fed and ill-clad – burn far too much electricity keeping themselves warm. But their problems are unlikely to be solved by lectures on domestic science.

Much of this poverty Britain has created for itself. We have too often consigned poor and vulnerable people to high-cost environments. There richer people could manage very well, but the poor, who cannot afford it, find that they *have* to have central heating – the most expensive forms of it moreover, because all the flats have electric night storage (or underfloor or ceiling) heaters, and there are no open fires. They really *need* a refrigerator because the flats are warm and shops are distant. They need a washing machine and clothes drier, too, because there's no launderette and no garden in which to hang out the laundry. They need to have a car or to use taxis, because to take their children to the shops by the failing bus service is difficult and expensive. Since they can't go out much and don't read a lot they really need a television set too. But they can't afford these things. (And we on the Supplementary Benefits Commission refused to make special grants for them because we would then have had to do so for every claimant which would have been administratively and politically impossible.) So they run up debts for rent, hire purchase and fuel. And once in arrears they are locked in, because the housing department never gives transfers to tenants who are behind with the rent.

What they are locked into is a neighbourhood with so many lone parents, large families and handicapped people that the fit adults among them get dragged down – by exhaustion, loneliness, depression. . . . A social security visiting officer could work for a whole day in the same few streets: he has so many customers there. Windows, trees and hedges are broken even before the vandals arrive. The grass cannot bear the constant wear of running feet.

Those who can escape to something better do so. Those completely engulfed by arrears and those whose children become too troublesome to the neighbours are evicted to similar roads on some other estate. Others simply melt away, defeated. The turnover of people is therefore so high – half today's residents may be gone within a year – that it becomes very difficult to make friends or to organise people to help each other. There is no community.

The unrebated rents and rates of housing in these neighbourhoods are often higher than those of much nicer estates nearer the middle of town. These payments are all related to valuations made for rating purposes. And on council estates the valuers believe new housing must be worth more than old, and flats must be worth more than houses of similar sizes. Differences in the reputation, accessibility or quality of the neighbourhood which are notorious to everyone else in the city are completely disregarded.

The poor can get rent and rate rebates, if they are working. If they are not, the supplementary benefit scheme can pay the whole of their rent and rates. If they get a chance of going back to work, or of moving from a low paid to a better paid job, they lose these subsidies and may end up no better off. They are in a poverty trap.

As a society, we could do something about most of these problems. Competent housing management would not allow council housing to become even more elaborately divided than private housing has ever been into neighbourhoods of varying reputation and quality. The poorest people would not be compelled to live in high-cost environments. Rents and rates do not have to be completely unrelated to the demand for housing. The consignment of the most vulnerable people to stigmatised ghetto neighbourhoods has rarely been a deliberate policy. But for public housing authorities which, since the Housing (Homeless Persons) Act, are no longer permitted to turn people out and leave them to fend for themselves, the threat of banishment to these neighbourhoods has become a means of disciplining the poor rent payers and the difficult tenants. So ghettos have been allowed to develop. In some ways they suit housing managers rather well.

As standards improve, the least popular houses are bound to grow increasingly hard to let. Instead of using them as dumping grounds for the impoverished whose rents will be paid with their supplementary benefit, the housing authorities could recognise that some of these houses are over-priced. They could reduce rents and rates here, and raise those of the most popular houses. They could also extend the range of people to whom they are prepared to let their housing.

After that we come to more fundamental questions. We do not have to accept high unemployment as inevitable – like bad weather – or deliberately increase it, as current policies do. If we can find money to give away in order to keep pensions and tax allowances – mostly for childless people – moving upwards in line with inflation, then we could have found money to maintain or improve the real value of child benefits. The fact that we chose to do one and not the other is a policy, not an oversight. We could change it.

A definition of poverty also defines our obligations to our fellow citizens and the responsibilities of government. Thus poverty has meant different things at different stages of Britain's history, as living standards, social obligations and the role of government have evolved. All these meanings still lurk in the words we use to talk about it.

During the nineteenth century the concern of the state was to prevent destitution – hardship, misery and starvation: that was what poverty meant. In Ireland, which still contained one-third of the population of the United Kingdom, people did die of starvation on a horrifying scale. The English, who so often talk of the industrial revolution as a time of general progress and growing prosperity, have eliminated Ireland and much of Scotland from their memories.

Early in the twentieth century people began to re-define the responsibilities of the state. Poverty came to mean a living standard which fell below a tolerable minimum. Seebohm Rowntree was most precise about it, calculating the incomes which households of various kinds required to maintain physical efficiency. This became the language of the Labour movement, of Beveridge and of the reforms introduced during and after the second world war to provide a 'national minimum' – a floor to living standards below which no-one need fall. This concept of minimum standards or 'subsistence poverty' is what most people have in mind today when they talk about poverty and the poor. It suits liberals who want to help the poor without upsetting other people or abandoning their own privileges. With a poverty line of this sort and continuing economic growth, we could in time raise everyone's living standards to a point at which even the poorest are lifted out of poverty, without affecting relativities and relationships between the different social classes in society. The same thinking can be applied on an international scale, suggesting that poor countries will – and can only – climb out of poverty by following in the industrial footsteps of richer countries.

But that road is long and terribly slow. Even in favourable economic times the earlier stages of industrialisation, which may last for several generations, are apt to make the poor poorer if nothing is done to prevent that. (As we ought to know, for that is what happened in Ireland.) And what should we do, now that we are entering a period when the nation's living standards are not rising, and may indeed fall for years to come? Do we abandon altogether the attempt to reduce poverty?

In practice it is clear that we do not really have any fixed idea of a tolerable minimum. We often do better for the poor than that. In Britain the real incomes of the poorest people, living on means-tested social assistance, have for many years moved upwards in step with those of wage earners. Thus, if there's a floor it does not stay put at a fixed level: its value is a social convention, subject to political decisions. It has to be. For if we stuck to the standards of Beveridge's day and only paid people enough to keep a small fire burning and buy the cheapest food from the corner shop, in a world where open fires, corner shops and cheap food are all disappearing, some really would starve. The frail conventions on which we rely to keep poor people docile would then disintegrate. How political these judgements are can be seen from the fact that we fix higher minima for some people than for others, with no regard to their needs. The long-term rates of supplementary benefit which are paid to all pensioners and to younger claimants after one year, but never to the unemployed, are about 25 per cent higher than the short-term rates. Although the Supplementary Benefits Commission had a lot of research done on this question, no-one was able to find any difference in claimants' needs which would justify these differences in income. On top of these differences we then load regular discretionary additions to benefits which – although described as 'heating additions' – really amount to sympathy payments for most pensioners and for all claimants with children under five. The national minimum is a myth.

Poverty is a word that is used in at least three different ways. Each poses questions which every society should be prepared to answer. The first usage poses questions about hardship, misery and 'destitution poverty' – conditions which are still occasionally to be found, among low-paid workers as well as people out of work. The second usage poses questions about the incomes, wealth and real living standards of different kinds of people: the answers will not provide a scientific measure of 'subsistence poverty', for that cannot be clearly defined, but they will show whose living standards are lowest and may suggest the reasons for these patterns. The third usage poses questions about inequality, exclusion, discrimination, injustice and 'relative poverty'. If this third concept of poverty is to have any practical cutting edge it calls for nothing less than a new morality.

I believe that poverty means a standard of living so low that it excludes people from the community in which they live. We explained that definition and its implications for our service in the Supplementary Benefits Commission's Reports to Parliament.

To keep out of poverty [we said in our Report for 1978], people must have an income which enables them to participate in the life of the community. They must be able, for example, to keep themselves reasonably fed, and well enough dressed to maintain their self-respect and to attend interviews for jobs with confidence. Their homes must be reasonably warm; their children should not feel shamed by the quality of their clothing; the family must be able to visit relatives, and give them something on their birthdays and at Christmas time; they must be able to read newspapers, and retain their television sets and their membership of trade unions and churches. And they must be able to live in a way which ensures, so far as possible, that public officials, doctors, teachers, landlords and others treat them with the courtesy due to every member of the community.

This book deals with the main British service concerned with poverty, and describes an attempt to review and change its principles and practices. It is about poverty policies and the politics of poverty. The next chapter explains the setting for these events, briefly introducing the services to be discussed and the ideas on which they were based.

CHAPTER 2

The State and the Poor

The Supplementary Benefits Commission (the SBC) is dead, and before long only the historians will remember it. To explain what it was and why it's still worth writing about I must briefly describe the whole social security system and the small but controversial part of it which was presided over by the Commission.

The Social Security System

'Social Security' is the name a lot of people use for supplementary benefits. But, properly speaking, *all* the cash benefits distributed through the Department of Health and Social Security (the DHSS) together make up the social security system. That system began as poor relief, distributed by the local poor law authorities. Back to Elizabethan times and even earlier, the parish had a duty, enforceable by the justices of the peace, to support paupers who would otherwise be destitute. Later, under the new poor law introduced in 1834, this duty was taken over by unions of parishes for which boards of 'guardians of the poor' were elected – the first agency specialising in poor relief. The paupers still had a local court of appeal against the relieving officers' decisions in the justices of the peace, who had to bear in mind that if too many people came too close to starving there would be riots – as from time to time there were. The people helped by this system had to show that they were in need and were entitled as local citizens to their neighbours' help. (If they could not claim 'settlement' in the area, they were sent back to the parish they came from.) They had to pass a crude kind of means test – calculated in loaves of bread – and the relief they were given kept them alive at a standard which was intended to be worse than the lot of the lowest-paid labourers. From the start this service was concerned both with people's welfare (preventing them from starving) and with controlling their behaviour (preventing disorder, and encouraging paupers to earn their own living). It still is. The international term for this kind of scheme is 'social assistance'.

In nearly every other country social assistance is still administered, as it used to be in Britain, by local government – although the national taxpayer has usually had to shoulder most of its costs. In some countries social assistance is used to top up low incomes of all kinds, whether they come from wages or from other sources. But one of the main purposes of Britain's new poor law of 1834 was to impose the labour disciplines required for an industrial economy in which most people were going to have to work full-time in factories and mills. Thus people in full-time work were denied poor relief, no matter how low their wages might be. They still were until recently when family income supplement was invented to help low wage earners with children to support. From 1834 too, the central government intervened (at first through a Poor Law Commission, later through the Local Government Board) to supervise and regulate the work of the local poor law authorities.

Since then the history of social security has been the story of successive schemes devised to lift one group after another out of social assistance. The main steps in this story have been: the development first of old age pensions (non-contributory, and later contributory), then of other insurance schemes for the unemployed, the sick and the disabled, and of allowances for their dependants. In parallel with these came the growth of employers' obligations to compensate workers suffering from industrial accidents and diseases. Then, after the second world war, came family allowances (now renamed child benefits) for children, with a premium recently added for one-parent families. For the first time a major cash benefit was being distributed to large numbers of families with a breadwinner at work. More recently a growing range of benefits has been created for the mentally and physically disabled: these benefits are more generous for insured workers than for housewives and those who have never been able to work.

Meanwhile, because wages took no account of the worker's family responsibilities, and because low-paid workers were excluded from social assistance and child benefits were low, a host of new means-tested benefits grew up, sometimes for the 'working poor' only, and sometimes for people on social assistance as well. I have already mentioned family income supplement. Others, outside the social security system, were: legal aid, under the Lord Chancellor's Department; free school meals and transport, and clothing and uniform grants from the education authorities; rent rebates and allowances, grants for the insulation of homes, and other help from the housing authorities; remission of health service charges, help towards the cost of travel to hospital, and free milk and vitamins from the DHSS; and the cost of travel to visit relatives in prison, paid for by the Home Office.

If people are poor, it might be better just to give them money and leave them to decide whether they want to spend it on school meals, getting a divorce, or visiting their relatives in hospital. But that policy is very expensive if pursued far enough to meet all these needs, as the Conservatives found when they tried to work out a tax credit scheme for this purpose. Although they are cheaper, these means-tested benefits nevertheless have a lot of disadvantages: they are complicated, difficult to understand and fail to reach many of the people who should get them. Family Income Supplement (FIS) was an attempt to follow the alternative policy: a simple cash benefit, simply administered. But it remains a small benefit, going to only 85,000 of the 7¼ million families with children.

Social assistance is still the basic safety net, guaranteeing a minimum income for those who are not lifted out of it by other schemes. In Britain it has since 1966 been called supplementary benefit – because in most cases it supplements other kinds of income (usually a pension) bringing these incomes up to the levels prescribed and annually revised by Parliament for households of various kinds.

The same process of lifting people out of the poor law has been going on in other fields besides the cash benefit services. The poor law used to provide most of the state's child care services, most of its hospital services, a good deal of schooling, and – in the old workhouses – a lot of housing. Services specially designed for poor people always tend to be poor services. They provoke resentment among the poor and against the poor. They divide society, creating second class citizens who get second class treatment. That's why so many of these have been taken over by specialist departments which provide housing, medical treatment, education and so on for the whole of the population.

Meanwhile, alongside all these services, two other systems of support have developed on a comparable scale, regulated by Parliament and sustained by the taxpayer. Employers provide a growing range of benefits – pensions, cars, health services, subsidised meals and much else – which are partly paid for by the state because their cost is deducted from company profits before they are taxed. Their pension schemes are the biggest element in this occupational welfare system.

The other welfare system is provided by the Treasury which in all sorts of ways reduces the income taxes which are now paid by nearly all wage earners. Tax allowances are given to married men, to taxpayers with children or adult dependants, to people paying mortgage interest, and to many others. These are the Treasury's 'social services' – a fiscal welfare system. They escape the controls imposed by the Treasury on all other social services because they are regarded not as public expenditure but as taxation. This is no small matter. The net value of tax forgone in respect of mortgage interest alone amounted in the years 1979–80 to nearly £1,500 millions, which was more than half the total sum distributed in supplementary benefit.

The occupational and fiscal welfare systems confer their biggest benefits on the rich, because employers are more generous to their top people and tax reliefs are worth more to those who pay a lot of tax. Thus these systems make a less direct impact than other benefits on social assistance for the poor. Yet there are frontiers at which these systems too overlap with the supplementary benefit scheme and become entangled in it. This does not complete the list of major schemes of cash grants and benefits and tax reliefs. Housing subsidies, rate rebates and grants for students are some of the others which impinge on the supplementary benefit scheme in various ways, making it difficult for administrators of one scheme to decide how to take account of other sources of help, and for the citizen to decide which benefits would be the 'best buy' for him.

The supplementary benefit scheme and its place within the wider social security system can be summed up in a few figures. The whole social security system administered by the DHSS distributed over £15,000 millions in 1978–79. This was one tenth of the nation's gross national product, and one fifth of total public expenditure. Retirement pensions, amounting to £7,600 millions, or 50 per cent of this bill, were much the biggest element in this system. Other major elements were child benefits (£1,800 millions) and insurance benefits for sickness (£1,500 millions) and unemployment (over £600 millions). Supplementary benefits distributed £2,500 millions in 1979. That amounted to nearly 15 per cent of all social security benefits. Of the claimants who got this money, 60 per cent were pensioners (nearly all of them had a retirement pension as well), 20 per cent were unemployed, 11 per cent were lone parents, and 7 per cent were sick or disabled. The small FIS scheme distributed only £24 millions.

The Supplementary Benefits Commission

Why was a separate Commission required for one relatively small part of this enormously complex pattern of payments? The SBC's origins go back to the Poor Law Commission, appointed in 1834 to set up and supervise the new poor law authorities. In those days the local ratepayers met the costs of poor relief, but the central government kept an eye on this politically sensitive service. And it did so in great detail. Before the end of the century it was laying down exactly how many ounces of meat the paupers in the workhouse were to have each day, and the precise ingredients of workhouse cocoa (partly to make sure that supplies were not side-tracked into other people's pockets). In 1934 the depression was bankrupting the most impoverished local poor law authorities (by then they were the Counties and County Boroughs since the abolition of the guardians). Others were threatening to bankrupt themselves by paying more in relief to the unemployed than the central government had prescribed. Parliament set up the Unemployment Assistance Board to provide a national, uniform system of relief for unemployed people who had run out of insurance benefits. It was concerned, as ever, partly with welfare (guaranteeing a minimum income even in the poorest areas) and partly with control (preventing disorder and excessive payments).

In 1940 and 1941 this Board's responsibilities were extended to supplement old age pensions and to cover needs arising from the war, and it was renamed the Assistance Board. After the war, in 1948, the local authorities' remaining responsibilities for relieving the poor were taken over by the newly formed National Assistance Board. Eighteen years later, in 1966, the NAB was replaced by the SBC. All these bodies served Great Britain only: parallel developments took place in Northern Ireland throughout this period.

Since the second world war, governments have usually said they wanted to reduce the need for social assistance. Aneurin Bevan, the Minister of Health introducing the Bill which set up the NAB, told Parliament that the work "to be left to the Assistance Board after the whole of the needs have been met by all the other measures – insurance allowances, old age pensions, sickness benefits – will be very small indeed. Only the residual categories will be left". But the one million people receiving national assistance by the end of 1948 had grown to over two million when the SBC took over in 1966, and to over three million when the SBC closed down in 1980. Together with their dependants there were by then nearly 5 million people depending on social assistance, and these numbers are now steadily rising.

This growth has created a much larger social assistance scheme supporting a much larger proportion of the population than can be found in any other country. This is due partly to changes in Britain's population and economy. Nearly all the people who turn for help to social assistance – the old, one-parent families, the unemployed, even students – have been growing in numbers faster than the rest of the population. And more of them have gained confidence to seek their rights from the scheme: the 'take-up' of benefits has gradually improved. A national scheme, constantly exposed to national political pressures, has had to grow more uniformly and generously and offer more assured rights than its counterparts administered by local government in other countries. Thus our safety net is stronger. It has to be. For other benefits – pensions, insurance benefits for the unemployed, the sick and injured, and child benefits for larger and poorer families – are generally less generous in the United Kingdom than they are in neighbouring European countries.

The Unemployment Assistance Board began in 1934 as an independent statutory authority, employing its own staff, presenting its own annual reports to Parliament, and fixing its own benefit rates in consultation with a Government which in the early days felt compelled to push the Board's rates up lest they provoke serious disturbances. Its chairman – a former Minister of Labour – was paid £5,000 a year: big money in the 1930s (150 per cent more than his salary as a Minister). At every stage since then the Board's successors have been incorporated more deeply into the workings of their parent department and their legal powers have been reduced. By the 1970s, the SBC's staff all belonged to the DHSS; they produced, till 1976, no annual reports; Parliament fixed the rates of benefit on the recommendations of the Government; and the chairman (usually a retired trade unionist) was paid four-fifths of an assistant secretary's salary for a job which was expected to be part-time.

Unlike its predecessors, the UAB and the NAB, the SBC no longer managed its own service, and had no authority to tell other people how to do so. The only executive power it retained was its responsibility for the discretionary parts of the system. The Commission could use 'positive' discretion to make extra grants, increase weekly benefits, and waive the normal rules (the obligation of unemployed people to show that they were seeking work, for example) for claimants who had special needs or problems. It could also use 'negative' discretion (to reduce benefits for unemployed people classed as having 'voluntarily' quit their jobs, for example). It could pay part of the benefit to a third party (to a landlord if the claimant was badly in arrears with his rent, for example). And it could set aside some of the benefit as savings for claimants who were constantly in debt. The discretionary extra payments were troublesome to administer, but small in value, amounting only to about 5 per cent of all the money distributed in supplementary benefit. These small payments had by 1975 spread all over the system, and were still growing fast: nearly 50 per cent of claimants got some weekly addition to their benefits, and over a million discretionary lump sum grants were made each year.

In the early 'seventies the Commission's eight members were a distinguished group. Their chairman was Lord Collison, a farm worker who had become head of his trade union and chairman of the TUC; a compassionate and unfailingly courteous man. He devoted most of his time to the Commission. The other members had full-time jobs and were expected to devote much less time to it. Professor Richard Titmuss (philosopher and friend to half the social reformers of his day) was deputy chairman. There were two other university teachers of social administration, a social worker, the head of a major charity concerned with old people, a trade unionist and a business man – each of them deeply involved in public service of various kinds. Together they ensured that the Commission's discretionary decisions passed through a humane and exceedingly expert mill. They gave a good deal of private advice to civil servants and Ministers – much of it individually from Titmuss – and they published a Handbook and five occasional papers on special topics. The chairman, who had come to the job when staff morale had been badly shaken by local outbursts of anger from claimants' representatives and the radicals of the late 'sixties, visited nearly every local office in the country and exchanged encouraging words with everyone working on supplementary benefits.

Whatever private pressures they may have exerted, and whatever private disagreements they may have had, the Commission in public defended virtually every feature of the scheme: its proliferating discretionary benefits (their own remaining *raison d'être*), its secret codes of instructions for staff, its 'wage stop' which for low-paid workers with several children reduced benefits to a level no higher than the wages they might earn in work, the refusal to publish most of the SBC's own research findings, and the bureaucracy's defensive attitude towards external research workers, journalists and activists of all kinds. Usually the Commission avoided public contributions to debate altogether, preferring to respond individually, humanely and privately to cases as they arose – to the flow of problems referred for advice by staff in the front line, letters from MPs (the chairman answered about 4,000 a year), protests from pressure groups and the like.

The Commission's officials preferred to work in this way. They had to serve their Ministers and a semi-independent Commission. That would become a tricky job if the Commissioners were ever to begin flexing their muscles and disagreeing publicly with the politicians. The leading DHSS officials had made personal friends of the Commission, but the deputy secretary who led them was suspicious of Ministers (some of whom returned the sentiment) and preferred not to cross the Thames and go down to the centre of DHSS power at Alexander Fleming House if that could be decently avoided. In the ranks below him were good, conscientious people – mostly in their fifties, and nearly all of them men. (Most of the people supported by supplementary benefit and most of the rank-and-file staff administering it are women.) These officials had extensive experience of the service, going back in many cases to national assistance and even to the poor law. Cautious but humane response to daily events was their job, calling for lots of hard work but little innovation.

The Commission could exert a good deal of influence if they were determined to do so. But they could only make decisions about the 'discretionary benefits' which together accounted for only one pound in every £20 paid out. They could do no more than advise about the rest of the system. The staff, who were all DHSS civil servants, were ultimately accountable to the government, not the Commission.

The most important attempts to get new things going in the social security system had for years been concentrated elsewhere, around Alexander Fleming House and in offices in John Adam Street where the Department's crack troops laboured through nights and weekends to mount new schemes for pensions, child benefits, tax credits, benefits for one-parent families and the disabled – each one usually shot from under them in the dusty aftermath of successive general elections. Meanwhile in Carey Street the SBC's headquarters became as peaceful as the grave a few minutes after 5 p.m. each day.

Ideas and Origins

I should explain how I got involved in the social security services. Richard Titmuss, deputy chairman of the SBC, died in April 1973. Soon afterwards Sir Keith Joseph, then Secretary of State for Social Services, asked me if I would take his place. The job would only demand one-fifth of my time. I knew very little about social security. In 1956 I had come from Manchester to work with Titmuss and the talented team he was then assembling at the London School of Economics. There he offered us an open field of study, not a specialised discipline fenced off from its neighbours – a field in which any discipline we were capable of learning could be brought to bear on a lot of important questions. These questions dealt with the relationships between different social groups and classes, the distribution of opportunities between them, and the part played by government in shaping the character of a society. He was concerned as much with status and power as with income and wealth. "How can we create a fairer and a more caring society?" "Do social policies, invented to set injustices right, end up by building new injustices into our institutions and even justifying them?" These were recurring themes.

Richard Titmuss gave us the courage of our convictions. While so many of our colleagues in the universities strove earnestly to wring the life blood of social commitment out of their work, writing increasingly technical papers for increasingly expert academic audiences, he never doubted that the university should be involved in trying to make the world a better place. The moral purposes of education were for him as important as its scholarly and scientific purposes. No one had taught him otherwise; for he had first entered the university as one of its professors, and his only degrees were honorary ones, awarded later for distinguished scholarship.

But you do not devote much time to studying social security if you work for thirteen years alongside Titmuss, Brian Abel-Smith, Peter Townsend, Tony Lynes and others – the finest team of researchers in that field then to be found anywhere in the world. My own research, teaching and participation in public affairs (for us the three always developed together) dealt with other fields – housing, town planning and education in particular. So when I received Sir Keith Joseph's invitation I wrote to him outlining some of the questions I would particularly like to explore if I joined the SBC (questions about the take-up of social security benefits and the representation of claimants, for example). He invited me to see him. We had last worked together in 1964 when he had been Minister of Housing and Local Government and I had served on his Central Housing Advisory Committee. He pressed me to take the job, but was cautious about my questions. The Commission's chairman and chief officials were even more welcoming – and even more cautious about the questions. So I decided to have a go. The distribution and redistribution of income have always lain at the very centre of social policy. Where better to start learning about them than among these talented experts?

For two years I served my apprenticeship, attending the Commission's monthly meetings, visiting social security offices, reading and talking whenever I could get away from my main job as Director of the Centre for Environmental Studies. I had a few advantages which were useful in this work: some training in the analysis of social problems and policies, some knowledge of the ways in which other countries tackle the same problems, and some experience of government committees and the civil service. (I had served on the Milner Holland Committee on rented housing in London, the Plowden Committee on primary schools, the Public Schools Commission and other bodies, and had helped to write their reports.) I also had a circle of friends in research, teaching, journalism, the pressure groups and various branches of central and local government who could offer advice and intelligent criticism as my ideas developed. But a way of seeing is also a way of not seeing. I was handicapped by the blinkers worn by this circle of people.

Looking back on that time with hindsight, the early 1970s stand out as the end of a way of seeing things which began in the 1930s when I was a child, flowered in the 1940s when I was a sailor and a student, flickered briefly into life again in the 1960s when I was a professor, and is now over. The debate about social security policies was for many years shaped by the assumptions of that time.

People who worked in groups such as the 'Titmuss school' at

the LSE found that they had joined a much larger movement of progressive social democrats sharing similar concerns and assumptions. As the research arm of this movement they inherited a tradition of laborious investigation in the pursuit of social reform which went back to the early Fabians and the blue books of Victorian England. They were able to play a part in changing the world: members of our own group had helped to reorganise the nation's pension schemes, secondary schools, rent Acts, mental health and social work services, and – more dramatically – the social policies of Mauritius and Tanzania. That was not just because they were able, hard-working people, but because they found among the leaders of the professions, bureaucracies and political movements of their time people who shared their tradition and their concern. By and large, we relied on the following assumptions.

- The growth of the economy and the population would continue. That, by itself, would not solve any problems; but it provided an optimistic setting for debate. The pursuit of social justice could be carried forward by engines of economic growth which would produce the resources to create a fairer society without anyone suffering on the way.
- Although inequalities in incomes would persist, their harsher effects could be gradually softened by a 'social wage' (consisting of social services distributed with greater concern for human needs) and by the growing burden of progressive taxes, taking more from the rich than the poor, which were required to finance the social services.
- Despite fierce conflicts about important issues (comprehensive schools, pensions, rent controls and so on) the people with middling skills and incomes – 'middle England' you might call them – would eventually support equalising social policies and programmes of this kind. Trade unions and the Labour movement would usually provide the political cutting edge for reform; and the Conservative governments which followed them would accept most of its results.
- Therefore government and its social services, accountable to this central consensus, were the natural vehicles of

progress. Among their generally trusted instruments were the doctors, teachers, town planners, nurses, social workers and other public service professions. The pretensions and powers of these professions should be critically watched, but progressive governments were expected to recruit more of these people – and generally did so. (And we earned our bread by training them at places like the LSE.)

– 'Social' policies dealt with the redistribution of the fruits of economic growth, the management of the human effects of growth, and the compensation of those who suffered from them. Thus social programmes were the concern of 'social' departments of government responsible for health, welfare, social security, housing, education and social control. The economy itself could be left to the economists and the departments of government concerned with economic management.

– Although economic crises, political accidents and sheer ineptitude would often compel governments temporarily to abandon these aims, over the longer run they would all try to increase industrial investment and improve Britain's lagging productivity, to secure some broad agreement about the distribution of incomes, to get unemployed people back into jobs, to free poorer people from means tests by giving them adequate benefits as of right, to give children a better start in life and more equal opportunities for the future, and to provide better care and support for the most vulnerable people and for families living on low or modest incomes. 'Middle England', we assumed, would not tolerate any radical departure from those aims. A government which allowed – let alone encouraged – a return to the high unemployment, the social conflicts and means tests of the 1930s could not survive.

This was the framework of assumptions within which most political debate took place. We did not regard it as a particular culture: it seemed the natural order of things. But in fact it *was* a culture: a culture originally derived from progressive thinking of the period before the first world war, gradually fashioned into a central consensus by the experience of depression and two world wars, and made economically feasible by the long post-war boom in the advanced economies of the world.

Winds of Change

Had we been more perceptive we would have noted the changes which were already eroding the economic and social structure on which this consensus rested. The advanced economies – and particularly the weaker ones like Britain's – faced a growing crisis as, one after another, their traditional industries were overhauled by the third world, and competition for the raw materials on which they depended grew fiercer. As the trading advantages afforded by empire and its aftermath gradually disappeared, Britain's ill-equipped and obsolete industries had to catch up with their foreign competitors or go under in a world in which trade was no longer expanding. Those that survived closed their uneconomic plants and replaced traditional skills with more advanced machinery, ending up with fewer but more highly paid workers who had reasonably secure jobs and better pensions and fringe benefits – the Weinstock way in General Electric. Firms unable to reduce their labour costs in this way had to force down real wages instead. Many of them relied increasingly on women, immigrants and unorganised workers – the Grunwick way. Those which did neither tended to go under if they were exposed to foreign competition – as much of the textile industry did. Or they sub-contracted more and more of their work abroad – as the printing and publishing industries do. Meanwhile, there was lots of growth too – in central and local government, the health services, the universities, banking, insurance and financial services for instance. These growing industries offered reasonably secure jobs, even if the wages were sometimes low; and their pensions, sick pay and other fringe benefits were generally good.

Thus the population was being more deeply divided into a majority in the core of the labour force with secure jobs and improving occupational benefits, and minorities on the fringes who were the people most likely to be unemployed and to depend on the 'welfare state'. The minorities included large proportions of young school-leavers, unskilled workers, older workers with obsolete skills, women, lone parents, blacks – a varied assortment, each of them minorities within their own groups, and difficult to organise into any collective political force.

The trade union movement had shifted its centre of gravity since the 1930s. The solidarity of the working class – always precarious – had disintegrated. Many of the best organised workers (such as the printers and the miners) and the most rapidly growing unions (representing teachers, local government staff, civil servants, health service and technical workers) got better pensions and sick pay from their employers than they would ever get from the 'welfare state'. Very few of those who belonged to trade unions expected to be unemployed. Their leaders might still make radical speeches, and believe what they said; but they were elected for their militancy, not their radicalism, by members who cared more about their next increase in wages than the 'social wage' provided by the state.

Meanwhile families were growing smaller; people were postponing parenthood till later in life and having fewer children; and there were more and more old people. Only one-third of British households now include dependent children. The education, health and welfare services, on which families depended most heavily, constantly tended to rise in price by comparison with the prices of consumer goods. Teaching, curing and caring for people demand a lot of skilled labour: they could not be mass-produced from an automated assembly line. Partly to meet these rising costs, workers were drawn into the tax net at lower and lower levels of real wages, and compelled to pay higher and higher rates of tax. But the social wage which their taxes bought for them often seemed a poor return. Many of them would have rather spent the money on television sets, freezers and cars which in real terms were growing cheaper over the years.

Thus the old symbols and the loyalties which they evoked were losing their potency. The solidarity of the working class was degenerating into sectional militancy. The unions themselves were therefore dismissed, even by their own members, as insatiably self-seeking. The inflation they helped to generate compelled them to battle ever harder to push their members' pay ahead of it. The family – meaning parents with dependent children – was a dwindling political minority. The 'welfare state' seemed to cost more and more. Radicals prepared to defend the social services and the people who rely on them found that middle England was no longer behind them. Workers in the secure core of society were making their own deals with their employers and the government which gave them private welfare states of their own, better than anything the social services provided.

However callous previous regimes may have been, they knew that in the last resort the nation depended for its survival on the capacity of ordinary people to bear and raise healthy sons who would be willing to turn out and fight for King and country when called to the colours. From time to time that knowledge led to real advances in social policy and the living standards of working people. But with the spread of nuclear weapons and the ending of conscription sheer canon fodder has been devalued, and one more motive for building a healthy and united nation has been lost.

More recently the rejection of Keynesian economic policies has had a rather similar influence. The controversy between spokesmen of this tradition and spokesmen of monetarist economics has been presented as a dispute about economic management. But it is much more than that. For Keynes presented in economic form an essentially moral doctrine expressing the conviction that the progress of the nation depended on the welfare and living standards of every citizen. His economic doctrine may have to be modified, but to abandon the broader social responsibility it expresses and the search for a political consensus which can be built on it amounts to a decay in public morality. Our present leaders have made it clear that they are prepared to accept rising unemployment, lengthening waiting lists for housing and medical treatment and other signs of social neglect, in the hope that they will bring inflation under control and increase the sum total of the nation's wealth – with scant concern for the way in which that wealth is distributed or the people who suffer on the way.

That is how I see it now. But these ideas were only dimly forming in my mind at the end of 1974 when my friend Brian Abel-Smith, policy adviser to Barbara Castle in the newly formed Labour Government, suggested I might consider succeeding Lord Collison when he retired from the chairmanship of the SBC the following year. The idea had never occurred to me. Some of my friends would think I had sold out to one of the more conservative branches of the bureaucracy. I had no formula to bring to the job – only a feeling that social assistance had been allowed to run on without any major shake-up since 1948, and that times had changed since then. I had seen enough to know that the scheme was growing increasingly unmanageable. But to get any changes made we would need the Secretary of State's support and a way of presenting uncensored ideas to the public and provoking a debate. For the Commission itself had no power to change the main features of the scheme. We only had authority over its discretionary elements which were chicken feed when compared with the main flow of benefits.

So I wrote to Brian Abel-Smith saying that I would be prepared to take on the chairmanship if Barbara Castle publicly invited the Commission to make an annual report to Parliament and gave me an assurance that although this would be prepared in consultation with Ministers, it would not require their approval. Our predecessors, the National Assistance Board, had produced annual reports – rather dull ones – so she could present this proposal as the revival of an earlier practice.

I then consulted the deputy secretary who was the SBC's chief adviser. He was utterly opposed to annual reports, and tried to deter me from seeking the chairman's job. Months went by, and I thought the whole idea was off. Other candidates were considered. The Treasury opposed annual reports: me too, probably. So did Brian O'Malley, the Minister of State for Social Security, who was busy getting the new pensions Bill through Parliament at this time. Then I was offered the job informally, in a letter sent by Brian Abel-Smith, provided I accepted that published reports from the Commission would all need Ministerial approval, as they did at that time. I replied that on those terms I was not interested.

Finally I met Barbara Castle in her room at the House of Commons on 31 January 1975. Later a formula was worked out which I was happy to accept. Announcing my appointment to the House of Commons on 2 May 1975, she said 'I . . . propose to restore the practice of a separate Annual Report by the Commission in which, in addition to the usual statistical material, they would be free to comment on developments and express views about priorities.' In a private letter she gave me all the assurances I needed.

What an old-fashioned, Victorian act, I reflected: to take on monstrous responsibilities for the poor, armed with nothing but the obligation to write a 'blue book' – an official report which very few people would read.

CHAPTER 3

Picking Priorities

Barbara Castle had given us an opportunity to rethink poverty policies which might open up possibilities for reform. Reform is a process, not an event – a drama that leads through successive scenes in which many actors play a part. Often the action is disrupted or the cast dispersed before any effective conclusion can be reached. Even when something is achieved the outcome can rarely be foreseen or planned in detail from the start. This chapter presents the first act of the drama in which the problems to be tackled were formulated. That goes a long way to settle what the drama is to be about, which in turn helps to decide who is likely to play a part in it. If the story seems confused this is not just because I can only tell the bits of it I saw or heard about. It is also because none of us at first had any clear idea where we were going, and because a lot of people didn't much want to go anywhere. Which makes it a fairly typical account of the workings of government.

The Opening Moves

After working as the very part-time deputy chairman of the Supplementary Benefits Commission for two years I came for the first time as chairman, on 1 October 1975, to devote most of my energies to the job for the next five years. The first days – indeed the first hours – anyone spends in a job of this kind are vital: not for anything he can achieve in so short a time but for what the experience does to him.

The headquarters of the Commission, on which one-tenth of the British people depended for at least a part of their incomes, stood appropriately in Carey Street, where the old bankruptcy court used to be, in a discreet, grey, six-storey block between the Law Courts, the Royal College of Surgeons, the London School of Economics and the lawyers' offices of Lincoln's Inn. Its presence was not revealed to passers-by, or mentioned in the London telephone book. I went in, showed my pass to the uniformed men at the desk, and ascended in the lift to the chairman's office on the fourth floor. It was a big room, carpeted from wall to wall, with highly polished reproduction furniture, a big rubber plant, a big settee, and a big red chair behind one of the biggest desks I've ever seen – two grey telephones and one red one on it. On one side of the room there was a gleaming nine-foot table. Laid out along it were all the daily newspapers and the main weeklies. On the other side, through a glass wall, a large balcony faced south towards the Strand. Opening off this room were others in which staff of the Commission's private office worked. From them emerged Mrs Anna Lowe, secretary to the Commission, who brought coffee and biscuits and kindly welcoming courtesies. Greetings over, I asked whether there were files or incoming letters to deal with. No: my predecessor, Lord Collison, had cleared up all out-standing work before leaving. I read the papers, drank the coffee, explored the room, and had another cup.

The newcomer to this kind of job knows that those who surround him with all this luxury and deference are showing their respect for his office and the institution over which he presides, not for him personally. (He is the same person as he was yesterday: I had ridden to work as usual on my bicycle and locked it to the railings outside.) Their behaviour warns him that he should be cautious about tampering with any institu-tion that attracts so much respect. Politicians who are account-able to movements whose members may not feel at all respectful towards the bureaucracy find it easier to resist these unspoken pressures. (They may succumb to their Party's pressures instead.) But some of the supposedly independent people ap-pointed to lead 'quangos' such as this Commission quickly lose, or never acquire, the capacity to be shocked and enraged by the stupidities and cruelties to be found in any big bureau-cracy. If they are not shocked they cannot put things right. Their only hope is to expose themselves constantly to the experience and feelings of rank-and-file staff and the more vulnerable of their customers. That helps to remind them – and senior officials themselves are apt to forget it – that the ample resources and the intelligent, caring people surrounding them at headquarters are not entirely typical of life in the front lines where the public meet the service.

On my first day I had expected that there would be piles of urgent papers, senior officials anxious to settle critical questions or at least to explore their new chairman's mind on key issues, and a pace of work for which my academic career had not prepared me. Deep, unhurried, Edwardian peace was not what I had expected to find at the heart of one of the most controversial bureaucracies in the land. At 3 p.m. I was to meet our top men – a deputy secretary and two under secretaries (very experienced officials, paid a good deal more than most professors). Perhaps things would start to happen then.

I already knew and admired these three men. The 'dep. sec.' – Chief Adviser to the Commission – was a cultivated, elegant, gentle man, and an old friend of my own mentor Richard Titmuss. The under secretaries were contrasting characters. One, full of suppressed aggression, sardonically witty, had had a rough time during the war as an extreme young pacifist. In more recent years his radical energies had been diverted into channels outside his profession: voluntary social work, top class photography, and driving like Jehu. The other, a more reflective man, spoke several languages and had written a novel under a pseudonym. I had sent them a long letter, suggesting about a dozen things we should discuss – questions of policy to be explored, and practical initiatives we might try out. The three men assembled punctually and greeted me warmly. With them came twenty-six year old Alice Perkins, previously private secretary to Brian O'Malley, Minister of State for Social Security. She was to be my personal assistant.

What, I asked, were the main things we should focus on for the next few years? We could only tackle a few of the larger issues outlined in my letter, and there might well be other more urgent problems we should work on. "I think you will find, chairman", said our Chief Adviser gently, "that this is not really a very helpful approach. In practice the priorities pick themselves." We talked for about two hours as they led the conversation through a succession of technical issues, each too complex for me to follow for long. Every practical suggestion I made was resisted. I proposed new ways of conducting meetings, which, I knew from experience, tended to ramble rather indecisively through a pile of papers without distinguishing the few issues which we were empowered to decide from those on which we could only offer advice or seek information. All these ideas were opposed.

Tony Lynes, a talented and very experienced member of the small team of policy advisers recruited from outside to work with Barbara Castle, was an old friend of mine, and particularly expert on supplementary benefits about which he had written a widely used Penguin book. Since I would be consulting him from time to time, I suggested we should give him an office near mine, and invite him to Commission meetings. That was fiercely opposed too: "We do not want a ninth member of the Commission." The other main source of independent advice which I wanted was a regular seminar to which we would invite administrators and researchers – outsiders along with insiders from various other departments. "I hope you do not mean this seriously, chairman" said our Chief Adviser. "Who on earth would come? How could hard-pressed officials take on such a burden? Confidential thinking would be leaked, and we would all be made fools of." I suggested some of the people who might attend: insiders such as Barbara Adams (head of the Social Research Division at the Department of the Environment), Ian Byatt one of the top economic advisers at the Treasury), John Boreham (then in charge of social statistics at the Cabinet Office) and their colleagues. The Commission's officials appeared to know none of them. As for academics and other outsiders – they were regarded as a menace.

The only other meeting I had that day was with Bert Jarmany, our press officer, to discuss how we would handle the media and use such contacts as I already had there – mainly among journalists specialising in housing, town planning and education (fields I knew better than social security). Each of us cautiously explored the other's responses. I was delighted to find a press man who really cared about the people who depend on social security, and he to find a chairman who really wanted to meet journalists and contribute to public debate. The Commission had so few powers to do anything: our influence would therefore depend heavily on gaining a hearing through the media.

At the end of the day, alone in my room, I pondered about this vast organisation, its twelve regional offices, the 30,000 staff who distributed supplementary benefit through nearly 500 local offices, and the people – nearly 5 million of them – whom it supported. The whole system was so complicated: I would never understand it at all. Could one person make any impact on it? Had I been crazy to accept the job? It took a week or two for the implications of the day to seep corrosively through my mind. Our chief officials – such able and nice men – had in effect gone on strike. They seemed determined to oppose everything I wanted to do, and to exclude me from the inner councils where policy was made. It dawned on me much later that it was anxious incomprehension rather than deliberate obstruction that I faced. And there was *no* inner council; *no* regular policy-making process. Responding to events, "the priorities picked themselves". Meanwhile, I resolved to call my own meetings and seminars, and to write my own papers. Amateurish though they might be, they would show that the policy bus had left. Officials might run after it and jump aboard if they wished. If not, I would press on as best I could with whatever help I could get.

We eventually did all the things I had proposed – even finding a room across the corridor from mine for Tony Lynes and getting him to all Commission meetings. But it took a good deal longer to ensure that he got all the Commission's papers – and much longer to arrange the more political of the meetings I had called for: with the TUC, the CBI, the back-bench committees of MPs interested in social security on both sides of the House of Commons, the Association of Directors of Social Services, and the civil service trade unions. (I knew senior officials had already been swopping memos discussing how I could be prevented from meeting the unions.)

Barbara Castle's promise that we could publish an independent annual report subtly changed all sorts of things. She had said nothing about our right to publish anything else; hitherto, public pronouncements from the SBC had been rare and carefully vetted. But there would be little point in censoring something in April if we were entitled to publish it in September in our report to Parliament – *and* to explain why we had been compelled to wait so long before saying it. (We could not publish our Reports before September because statistics for the previous year could not be assembled sooner.) Thus the opportunity we had been given might open a much larger door. But tact would be needed. Barbara had taken a calculated risk, overriding a good deal of opposition from her colleagues and senior officials. Her confidence in us deserved respect. If we were to contribute effectively to public debate, we would inevitably disagree with Ministers from time to time. To make sure we did not stumble into unnecessary conflicts we had to get our communications with politicians into working order. So I had private talks with Norman Warner, head of Barbara's private office, with our Ministers' policy advisers, and with people from the Prime Minister's Policy Unit at 10 Downing Street, the Treasury and the Central Policy Review Staff – the Cabinet's 'think tank'. Most of these were old friends. We were not a mafia – we could not fix things among ourselves – but we could at least make sure that our organisations and their political leaders did not trip over each other accidentally.

It was to be the Commission's Annual Report, not mine, and all the Commissioners must feel that it spoke for them. If important things we wanted to say were suppressed, there would in the last resort be nothing to do but resign. That would be an empty gesture unless we all went together. So I had to keep much closer to them than my predecessors had done – and play a part in picking successors to the five Commissioners who were due to be replaced in December and January.

We would have to win the confidence of the media. I began with my friends – the correspondents and leader writers who wrote about social policies in the posh papers. Over the next year I invited all the specialists working in our field, followed by the editors of all the main newspapers and some of the radio and television people, to talk over lunch in my office. The point of these encounters was not to get a 'good press', but to convince my guests that problems of social security were as urgent and interesting to their readers and audiences as many other topics to which they devoted more space, and to focus their attention upon issues more significant than the stories about 'sex snoopers' investigating claimants' love lives which seemed to be the standard social security news item at this time.

I talked with the Department's economists and with officials responsible for training social security staff. Then I began touring our headquarters, trying to understand what the 150 people working there were all doing. I also set up a regular programme of meetings with the SBC's Inspectorate – not in fact 'inspectors' at all, but a small research and intelligence unit whose members are recruited from local social security offices. Although their research was good, it was never published. They were our only instrument for finding out things not revealed by the Department's regular statistics, and the only people at headquarters whose work brought them constantly into contact with claimants and the staff of social security offices all over the country.

I was visited by the under secretary in charge of head-quarters staff who was responsible for security in the DHSS – the guardian of the Department's secrets. He was a gentle, courteous man, slightly embarrassed by his colleagues' expectation that he should tie me down with the usual civil service rules which would prohibit me from publishing anything over my own name or without permission from the top. I signed a declaration under the Official Secrets Act for him, and said I would consult Ministers about anything I proposed to write or say in public. (Which meant in practice that I would show it to their advisers.) If they objected, I would consider their advice but could not promise to accept it. Indeed, I already had a short book review and a longer article on 'Equality' for *New Society* which I would treat in this way. "That's alright", he said quickly. "They must have been written in your private capacity, before you became chairman." "No", I replied, spotting the trap, "they were written this month" – which was true.

On 16 October I held my first meeting with the heads of various branches of the Department who would be contributing to our Annual Report, and took them through an outline of its contents, prepared with the help of Alice Perkins my personal assistant who would edit it. I explained that these Reports should become a vehicle on which they could load their own ideas about the future – a way of educating the public about problems in our field and the action which should be taken to solve them. They were polite but sceptical, wondering how far this thing would go before it all blew over. No-one volunteered any ideas. I realised how important it was on such occasions to be able to quote Barbara Castle's invitation to the Commission to write the Report, announced to Parliament the previous May, five months before I came on the scene: this was not just the whim of a new chairman. I wondered whether I could ever persuade these men to pick up the ball I had thrown to them and run with it. But for the first time I felt I was convincingly running a meeting of officials which I had myself called together.

I was invited to meet the Department's second permanent secretary – one of the two knights at the head of this bureaucracy. He looked after the social security side of the DHSS. We discussed potential replacements for the Commissioners who were retiring, and for the deputy secretary who was our Chief Adviser. He was due to retire too before long. I made clear whom I wanted – not quite forcefully enough, perhaps. The two under secretaries, next in line to our Chief Adviser, were also due to retire within nine months. Their successors would be appointed by the Department, not by the Commission. But it was important to establish that the Commission's chairman would be consulted about such matters.

My first monthly meeting with the Commission, as its chairman, on 15 October, followed a new pattern: we planned the agenda with officials beforehand; a line was drawn across it separating things which had to be discussed from papers which could simply be noted; a lunch arranged for the Commission and its officials gave us all opportunities for informal talk; we held a private meeting afterwards, without officials; and later I checked over the minutes of the meeting while they were still in draft.

One of the proposals we discussed at this meeting came from Michael Young, chairman of the National Consumer Council. He wanted us to set up local consultative committees representing staff and users of all the social security schemes administered through our local offices – a proposal I had discussed with Sir Keith Joseph when he first asked me to become deputy chairman of the Commission. The Department had suggested that Michael should discuss the idea with the manager of our Walthamstow office. Exposed to Michael's enthusiasm, he had come back saying he would like to try out the Consumer Council's idea himself. (Would he be hung by the thumbs from the top of Alexander Fleming House, I wondered?) The more sardonic of our under secretaries gently derided the proposal, but we asked him to consult Staff Side – the Department's trade unions – and see what progress he could make with it.

Twice a year the Commission published a useful but uncontroversial news sheet, mainly for social workers and pressure groups, called SBC *Notes and News*. Since it already existed, this seemed the least provocative way of presenting something I had long wanted to publish: quarterly figures showing changes in the real value of our benefits. As Barbara Rodgers, one of the Commissioners, said, we were supposed to be "guardians of the minimum income". For this we would need graphs, comparing changes in the value of benefits with changes in prices and average earnings. We would also have to gain a much wider circulation for *Notes and News* and publish it four times a year. Again one of our under secretaries opposed the idea, and when the Commission resolved that we must try it he sought by sleight of hand to make it a twice-yearly, not a quarterly, publication. We stuck to our guns. The next step would be to take the proposal to Barbara Castle, who would clearly be advised to reject it. Yet this seemed to be exactly the kind of thing she had asked us to do. It would, if necessary, be a resigning issue for me.

Towards the end of the month I spent four days visiting social security offices in Aberdeen, Inverness and Glasgow, and the Scottish central office in Edinburgh, travelling with Kay Carmichael, our deputy chairman – fey, fierce and delightful: a Scottish socialist, feminist, nuclear disarmer, prison reformer, and much else. On my return I dictated a note for officials saying that henceforth on such trips I should visit claimants with a visiting officer in the normal course of his work and "should always meet Staff Side representatives" wherever I went. I should "try to get the press and radio along to feature the local manager and one or two of his staff, together with me. That means we must have something to *say*. We should also meet some local authority people – ideally the Director and Chairman of Social Services. I should try to visit a local university or polytechnic to give a seminar to which our staff and other outsiders must be invited". If invited to supper afterwards, I must remind my hosts to invite social security officials too: they could not be relied upon to remember. Noting some first thoughts about policy, I said "I am increasingly convinced that the SBC may in its Annual Report want to argue for a gradual reduction of discretionary extras of various kinds", and explained why.

As on so many other occasions during those first months, Alice Perkins accompanied me. She was already the best kind of courtier: very able, acutely sensitive to human feelings and to every political nuance in the corridors of power, she had entered the service in order to make the world a better place and was completely unselfseeking. Whenever I felt most depressed about civil servants, I reflected that they had been capable of recruiting and training her, and sending her to me when I most needed her. With most of the Commission and our three top officials on the brink of retirement, I had to think policy out for myself: but Alice could tell me so much about people and the workings of power – and do it without ever denigrating those whom she so aptly described.

After a seminar at the University of Glasgow we had supper with Professor Tom Wilson in his big house in Professors' Square. Meanwhile down in London, the Commission's next Chief Adviser was being chosen. Alice, who had kept in touch with Norman Warner, sensed that things were going wrong. She managed to link me up late at night by telephone from the Wilsons' house to Barbara Castle who was in the thick of strife over doctors' pay, between meetings with the British Medical Association and Harold Wilson. Barbara told me that the Department's top men had said that I would not mind which of the leading candidates became our Chief Adviser. I said this was nonsense: I had made it clear that I wanted Geoffrey Otton, a deputy secretary who had come recently to the DHSS, bringing with him the children's service from the Home Office. "You were very tough before agreeing to take on your job" she said, "and you must go on being tough. If I back you on this you must not let me down." I promised I would not waver, and she promised we'd be given Geoffrey. We had a chance of doing something at last. Disarmingly, deceptively debonair and carefree, Geoffrey Otton was to become the tiger in the SBC's tank.

My next visit out of town took me to Ulster to meet the Supplementary Benefits Commission for Northern Ireland and their principal officials at Stormont. If we were to make changes in the British scheme we had better keep in close touch with the Ulstermen whose social services had for so long marched in step with our own. They were saddled unwillingly with the Payments for Debt Act, originally prompted by rent strikes and civil disobedience. It compelled their DHSS to deduct from claimants' benefits the money which they owed to agencies of the State for any reason. They were running, in effect, a small branch of the Inland Revenue. How do you deal with a mother's claim for a grant to help her buy clothes for her children if that 'exceptional need' is largely due to the fact that you are taking a lot of her income away for arrears of rent, rates and fines? This was a road down which we had ourselves already started by making direct payments to landlords and fuel boards for rent, gas and electricity, and many were pressing us to go further along it. We must resist them.

The small team of Ulster officials whom we met included, along with one or two hoary old reactionaries, some marvellous men – in touch with their smaller society in a way Whitehall never can be. A great case for devolution. I stayed the night with Maurice Hayes who knows everyone – poets, politicians and paramilitaries of all persuasions. Paddy Devlin came to supper, his coat so stuffed with armament that I could scarcely lift it on to the peg. He had been chairman of the Committee responsible for social services in the power-sharing executive demolished eighteen months earlier, and unlike most Ulster politicians he really knew what he wanted to *do* with the power for which he had been battling. A robust radical with a Brendan Behan style, he was convinced that the SDLP could strike bargains with the Unionists through Craig. The rest of us were less optimistic, foreseeing a long and bloody period of direct rule. Would that he had been right!

A few days later I was off again to one of the northern industrial cities with Michael Meacher, MP, one of our Parliamentary Secretaries. Graham Woodman, an assitant secretary from our headquarters, came with us. We visited a reception centre: one of a score of such centres which the SBC provides for men 'without a settled way of living' – a responsibility originally inherited from the local poor law authorities. This centre operated in a war-time hostel, left stranded in one of the city's less fashionable suburbs. It was shining clean but utterly impersonal and rather isolated from the rest of the world, like a little army barracks. Indeed, the staff running it seemed to model the place on their happier memories of the army. They were given a brief training for their job by the civil service, but they did not visit old people's homes, mental hospitals or other places where similar work is being done, or see the point of doing so. The food was good, and a doctor called regularly.

Even if they slept rough from time to time, most of the men using this centre had lived in and around the same city for many years. They were local citizens, with as much right to the help of the local housing, health and welfare services as anyone else living there. They were getting excellent physical care, but on terms which must have made it harder rather than easier for them to get jobs or council flats, or to find their way back into the settled community. The central government had no business to be providing this service: it was only making it easier for local authorities to evade their duties.

We ended up, late at night, in an abandoned Catholic primary school where a voluntary group to which we made a grant offered more primitive food and shelter to a much larger number of men and women – some 200 souls, ranging from migrant Irish builders' labourers to alcoholic dossers and damaged old ladies. It was less comfortable than our little barracks, and far less hygienic; but less isolated from the rest of the world. It was in the centre of town for a start. The place was run very competently by an eccentric man who lived on supplementary benefit. He was helped by another claimant – a woman with lots of children who had once been a teacher. The project got most of its income not from our grant, but from the few shillings levied each night on everyone who slept there. It was our local office's job to ensure that users of this hostel who were not working got proper board and lodging for a payment which was handed over to the hostel manager. If necessary our staff could pay the money direct to him. That was the way to fund such an enterprise: make it accountable to its customers, not to the government. What the project now needed was more support from the local authority: ordinary housing for their long-standing residents, a decent lodging house for transients, and grants to provide better wash places, more heating and some decent beds and bedding in the derelict old school. People there were sleeping in battered old arm chairs and on the concrete floors, and the place was bitterly cold. The reception centre we maintained out in the suburbs and the grants we gave to this voluntary project could not have made it easier to get the local authorities to assume their proper share of these responsibilities.

It was great to find in Graham Woodman a civil servant who seemed perfectly at home in the middle of the night, introducing a Minister and the chairman of the SBC to this bizarre but creative scene and the remarkable people who presided over it. Better still, he was doing it for a purpose: to show us what could be done, and to win our support for the longer-term policies which would ultimately get central government out of this business and place on the local housing, social service and health authorities the responsibilities which they ought to bear, with help from voluntary workers.

Next week we held the first of the monthly seminars which were to run for five more years. Ministers' policy advisers, administrators, economists and social scientists from various departments of government and from the academic world all turned up. Soon they were to be joined by people from the pressure groups. We had a lively discussion about plans for the Commission's first Annual Report, followed by informal talk over sherry in my room.

A few days later Michael Partridge came over from the Regional Directorate which manages the network of local offices throughout the country. We had lunch and talk. At last: a senior administrator fizzing with ideas about things we should *do*. Alice was delighted to show me that such people existed. I think she was also introducing Michael in the hope that he might later be induced to come and work with us and that I might ask for him. Things were beginning to look up.

The weeks which followed were filled with talk, travel and reading: meetings with Ministers (occasionally), with officials (constantly – ranging from local offices to 'the top of the office'), with the press (increasingly), with pressure groups and welfare rights workers (kept anxiously at arm's length by the bureaucracy for so long), and with academic and professional gatherings at which I could try out the ideas gradually taking shape in our minds. I sought a meeting with the chief officials who were experts about the deployment of staff, and asked what it cost, in money or in man-hours, to administer benefits of various kinds. They had no idea. Lack of imaginative vision I had expected, but the lack of basic managerial techniques amazed me. (Things have improved a lot since then.) None of them seemed to know how business is conducted in banks, building societies, supermarkets and other organisations which serve millions of customers and handle vast amounts of money.

But the service had its strengths too. If I dictated ideas for a speech, an article or a letter – no matter how hastily – even the sceptics would turn to at any time of day, night or weekend and supply figures, check facts, explain the law, and improve my argument and style, all without the least concern for personal recognition: so different from the competitive, dilatory, opinionated academic world in which I had been reared. To work comfortably in the public service, the outsider has to learn to love quite a lot of his officials. To work *effectively* there, he must neither dominate nor be dominated, but create relationships which enable him and them to do more than either could have done without the other: a sort of marriage. Publicly questioning long-established policies and procedures is a political act. Barbara Castle had given us an opportunity to do that and we had to seize it. But following up the questions by analysing problems, formulating solutions and comparing their costs – these are jobs which officials generally do best.

Towards a Strategy

With help from civil servants I was by the end of 1975 beginning to understand supplementary benefits well enough to formulate strategies for the future. The scheme had originally been devised to support what was expected to be a small and dwindling minority of people facing unusual hardship. But the failure of insurance benefits and child benefits to grow as they had been intended to do, coupled with people's increasing willingness to demand their rights, had inflated social assistance into a massive scheme on which nearly one-tenth of the British people depended for at least a part of their income. Meanwhile, a lot of other services had grown up around this scheme, creating muddle and injustice on its frontiers. Some of the neighbouring services had made special arrangements to help the poorer people they dealt with. The housing and rating authorities had devised rebates of various kinds to protect poor tenants and rate payers, for example. But there was often great confusion between these complex and ill-coordinated schemes, and even more between each of them and the supplementary benefit scheme. The average widow with a small pension had no idea whether she would be better off on a supplementary pension or with rent and rate rebates: she often ended up getting the wrong benefit or none at all. Other services made arrangements to help the poor, and sensibly used the supplementary benefit scheme as a device for picking some of the people who would get this help. Home helps and school meals were usually provided free if the customer was living on supplementary benefit, for example; and legal aid was distributed through the Law Society to people whose incomes were assessed by supplementary benefit staff. But some services tried to shuffle off their responsibilities for the poor on to the DHSS. There were education authorities, such as Birmingham, which told parents who were unable to pay for the school uniform and sports kit demanded by their own schools that they should ask their social security offices for grants to buy them. Too often poor people were caught in the cross-fire of frontier warfare between bureaucracies, and ended up getting the wrong help or none at all.

Some services made no proper provision for the poor. Student grants, distributed through education authority means tests, were worth less in real terms than they had been when I had been a student in the 1940s. Thousands of young people therefore claimed supplementary benefit each vacation, which meant that they were expensively means tested all over again by a service which was poorly equipped to administer what amounted to a small addition to student grants. In other fields the social security service was less generous. A single-handed East-end mother I met whose son was charged with being involved in an affray at Southend was supposed to come to court with him. Indeed, he was entitled to have her at his side. But neither the SBC nor the courts would pay their fares to Southend. Meanwhile, if she found a job which barely enabled her to dispense with supplementary benefit and support herself, the Inland Revenue would charge her the high emergency tax rate for months and make time-consuming difficulties about maintenance payments and tax allowances for her children before giving her the tax advantages to which she was entitled. It was no wonder that many women in this position preferred to stay on supplementary benefit or to conceal their earnings.

Wherever you looked, there were no common principles or practices to protect poor people who were the bewildered victims of these frontier problems. Had the DHSS and other services recognised their obligation to ensure that all who were entitled to their help were getting their rights, these problems would have been more quickly solved. But in the DHSS, as in other Departments, there was no branch – indeed, no official of any kind – whose job it was to worry about 'take-up' or to report regularly on the Department's success in fulfilling its legal obligations to get benefits to the people who were supposed to have them. (There were hundreds, however, whose job it was to make sure that people did not get away with money they ought *not* to have.)

There was a benign side to this system too. But it was going wrong. Steadily growing use had been made of the SBC's powers to add discretionary payments to weekly benefits and to give people single payments for special needs. One Government after another had encouraged the Commission to use their ingenuity in distributing the relatively small sums the Treasury permitted the DHSS to spend in this way. Social workers, welfare rights workers and pressure groups grew increasingly expert at demanding new discretionary benefits, and extracting these payments from social security offices and the appeal tribunals. As a result, more than half the claimants on the books were being treated as 'exceptions' to the normal rules. These numbers had roughly doubled in three years.

Since the Commissioners themselves could not run around the country handing out these extra payments and sorting out the frontier problems of the service, they had to make rules to guide the staff who did the job. And since the public were rightly critical if the rules were secret or administered in widely varying ways from place to place, growing efforts had been made to give the staff instructions about every kind of case and to publish these instructions. As a result, the book of rules which in 1948 every NAB officer had been able to carry around in his pocket had grown into several massive volumes, so often amended and so complicated that even the staff could not understand them. In the more hard-pressed offices they were no longer using them: local rules of thumb took their place.

All these trends were still flowing strongly – growing frontier problems, growing numbers of discretionary payments and growing complexity interacting to lead the system to chaos. Together they produced bewilderment, incomprehension, poor take-up of benefits, enormous variations in practice from place to place, and a growing sense of injustice and hostility afflicting claimants, staff and the public at large. They distracted pressure groups and the public from real issues – basic problems such as the adequacy of the scale of rates fixed by Parliament to support families and children – and focused contention instead upon small claims, technical trivia and mere folklore. We received hundreds of letters that year prompted by the story that claimants (usually 'a black man') were getting large grants to buy television sets (usually 'with doors' or 'with legs' – 'so it counted as furniture'). No such grant was ever paid. (We looked into every case with a shred of evidence to support it.) But to demonstrate that did nothing to halt the circulation of a myth which has now taken its place alongside those about Russians marching through England with snow on their boots to join the western front in 1915, the council tenants who were said in the 1930s to put coal in their baths, and more recently the school girl – usually 'a comprehensive school girl' – who made her mother pregnant by stealing her contraceptive pills and replacing them with asprins. All equally implausible.

Meanwhile, at a more fundamental level, the system was tottering. In many offices – particularly in small northern towns and country districts – it worked very well. But in inner city neighbourhoods and other hard-pressed areas, where the customers' problems were most harrowing and experienced officials were scarcest, the staff had somehow to protect themselves from the potentially limitless demands which limitless flexibility might impose on them. If every claimant were to ask for every discretionary extra payment available – and then exercised his rights to appeal – the system would simply collapse. Only by deterring claims could staff keep the pressures of work under control: hence the complaints from claimants who could not get through to their social security office on the telephone – and were then told that their files had been lost, or (quite untruthfully) that a giro cheque was already in the post to them; hence the leaflets which were not available unless you waited for hours in a queue and knew what to ask for; hence squalor and discourtesy. It was not really the fault of the local staff: the Commission and headquarters officials, nagged by the pressure groups, had asked for all this by promising the public more than the most hard-pressed offices could be expected to deliver.

Those offices which distributed a growing mass of discretionary payments could no longer exercise the humane and discerning judgment, matching benefits to the infinite variety of human needs, which theory and the training courses assumed. Instead, they invented their own rules of thumb. They had to: it was the only way to cope. "Has she had a grant during the last six months? Is she asking for more than twenty pounds? If not, give her the money: we've no time to make a visit". In less generous offices the local limits might be twelve months and ten pounds. In effect, they were handing out lump sum payments every six (or twelve) months. But claimants did not know they could get them because these rules were secret. They also varied enormously from place to place, and from one kind of customer to another. Claimants at some offices had ten times (in Scotland, *twenty* times) more chances of getting exceptional needs payments than claimants in other offices in the same regions. Unemployed claimants, who were generally the poorest of all, were less likely to get discretionary extras than pensioners or lone parents – and less likely to win their cases when they appealed to the tribunals.

In so far as it did produce the goods for them, this system compelled people to let officials into their homes to inspect their poverty: the worn out underclothes of an impoverished woman, the wear and tear inflicted by a lame man's caliper on his threadbare trousers, or the extra laundry costs of an incontinent old lady. Some of these indignities might be unavoidable in a social assistance scheme dealing with every predicament of the poor, but to multiply them needlessly – instead of ensuring that every claimant had a sufficient income and letting him spend it as he chose – was degrading alike to the customers and to those who served them. It was at this time that one of our most remorseless critics – leader of the National Council for One-Parent Families – complained on a BBC programme about our policies on sanitary towels. "We think this is a special need" the transcript read. "We've helped mothers in three different offices. One office allowed her extra money because it was a special need, the other office refused the extra money, the third is still pondering it. In other words it is up to the individual office and officer to use their discretion, and if they don't use their discretion, then it is the right of the person concerned to go to an appeal tribunal". We were drifting into degrading nonsense if being a woman was to become an 'exceptional circumstance", and if claimants and their families (the majority of whom *are* women) were to be nagged by pressure groups into asking civil servants for the money to buy such intimate necessities.

Meanwhile, ticking away beneath these trends, lay another time bomb. More and more appeals were going to the tribunals, and the tribunals were becoming more and more like little courts: not very good courts, some of them. They dealt with more cases than any other kind of tribunal to which the citizen takes his grievances, and they were free to exercise in their own way any discretionary powers which the SBC had. Being at the bottom end of the tribunal trade – some of them dispensing jungle justice with scant consistency or explanation – they found it difficult to recruit enough good members. The Government was clearly going to accept most of the recommendations made in a very good official report by Professor Kathleen Bell which in 1975 called for more legally qualified chairmen, training for tribunal members, an upper-tier of 'super-tribunals' to which further appeals could be made, and much else. In future the tribunals' decisions would be more carefully reasoned; and they would be more frequently quoted by more plentiful and better organised advocates representing appellants. These decisions, though binding on all the parties in each case, were not regarded as precedents to guide decisions on similar cases in future. But as the appeals procedure became increasingly 'judicialised' and more of the tribunals' decisions were appealed to the higher courts, the whole system was beginning to acquire the force of precedent. If that went further, staff would not know whether to seek guidance from the SBC or from their local tribunal, and each tribunal's policies might be different. The courts were pretty inconsistent too. We had to get the tribunals in better shape to give more consistent and more clearly reasoned decisions. To deal with appeals from the tribunals we needed lawyers who specialised in social security work. And if they were not to wreak havoc between them we had first to wring a lot of discretion out of the system, and thus ensure that everyone could work to the same clearly understood rules.

These were the main features of the diagnosis we formulated. The strategy to which it pointed would create a simpler and more comprehensible scheme, paying adequate basic rates, and offering fewer discretionary extras. The stress would be on rights, higher rates of 'take-up', prompt and courteous service. And we did not have much time in which to act. Staff cuts were on the way. Complexity, discretionary benefits, time-consuming direct payments of benefit to landlords and the fuel boards, claims from students, and a whole plague of other burdens were all steadily increasing. So were the numbers of customers. Pretty soon the more hard-pressed offices would be having to make their own simplifications in order to cope with the work. Thus reform of some sort was on the way for sure. We had perhaps a couple of years in which to achieve some nationwide agreement which would lead to constructive and orderly changes. After that it would be too late.

In January and February 1976 I tried out these ideas – first in the journal *Social Work Today* (in reply to five open letters from key members of the Child Poverty Action Group), then in a seminar with an expert group at the National Institute for Social Work, and finally at a public lecture at the University of Edinburgh which was published in the *Journal of Social Policy*.

Our officials, shocked at first by my habit of calling press conferences for these major statements, were beginning to enjoy the campaign. They distributed copies of my reply to the CPAG in a circular to staff working on supplementary benefits in every local office in the country.

But although everyone was dissatisfied with supplementary benefits there was no coherent pressure for reform. Thus to get anything done would call for monstrous effort and the recruitment of some unlikely allies. The implications of this strategy for the whole style of the service and its relationships with outsiders were as important as specific proposals for reform. I tried to explain the new world in which we were all operating in the closing paragraphs of my reply to the pressure groups in *Social Work Today*.

Finally, if I may turn the tables on you, I want to say what we expect of you and the poverty lobby. Some of you (and I am not thinking particularly of the four to whose letters I am replying) have not noticed that times are changing. You are (forgive me) the slightly ageing spokesmen of a tradition which flowered in the mid-sixties, when Tony Smythe was transforming the dusty old National Council for Civil Liberties into a force to be reckoned with; Tony Lynes, pedalling on his bike between his flat, the LSE and Westminster, was creating in the Child Poverty Action Group a new kind of pressure group; and at Shelter that dazzling 25-year-old, Des Wilson, had the mass media eating out of his hand and the sixth formers of the nation on the march.

Since then, many of the first crying scandals – the easier targets for indignation – have been put right. I am not complacently suggesting that all is well. But now that the Parliamentary Commissioner provides some opportunities for appealing against officials' decisions, furnished tenants are not *automatically* excluded from rehousing, homeless mothers and their children can often get shelter somewhere without being separated from their husbands, and (belatedly, you may think, but at last) the wage stop has gone, the problems to be tackled are becoming increasingly complex. So are the solutions.

Meanwhile, everyone has learnt the techniques your predecessors had to invent for themselves. Spokesmen for the victims of muscular dystrophy and thalidomide, for autistic children, battered wives, small businessmen, hunted foxes and slaughtered seals, for a half-a-dozen groups of the elderly, and airport and motorway protesters by the score, all compete with each other for the attention of governments and for time on the screens and wavelengths. And the public (sadly, for many of those are important and urgent causes) is getting a little bored by it all.

That public was in a radical frame of mind in the mid-sixties . . . It is now in a very different mood. People fear inflation and economic collapse, and tax thresholds have fallen to a point at which everyone knows he is helping to support the poor – and many resent it.

From these developments I draw several conclusions – not all of them glum. Commissions, politicians and officials should feel less defensive about pressure groups than they used to be. They are part of the every-day scene, and we can often learn a lot from them. They share and support our own concern for poor people in a world where that concern is scarcer than it used to be. They can do a lot of good; and they are rarely strong enough to do serious harm.

Meanwhile life is going to be intellectually tougher for spokesmen of the poverty lobby . . . in a world no longer instinctively on their side . . . Indignation and noise no longer cut much ice: there are twenty other lobbies which can outbid you in that kind of currency.

Remember that the goodwill of officials – particularly the most junior ones – is always valuable to your clients; and there is no end to the good you can do if you don't mind who gets the credit . . . those who would rather write to the newspapers, the Chairman and the Secretary of State than gain the help of local staff, and those whose letters are generally insulting and unfair soon become known for being more interested in expressing their feelings than in helping the poor . . .

. . . don't waste too much time on us and the officials of the DHSS. Get in among the industrial and political movements of Left and Right alike, wherever the ordinary people of this country are to be found, and convince them of the justice of your cause – *our* cause, too. Those letters which arrive by the hundred each month, complaining that we hand out too much in social security benefits and support too many layabouts and scroungers, rarely come on headed notepaper from the leafy suburbs. Most of them are written by ordinary voters and taxpayers.

Along with my lecture in Edinburgh, this was given thorough coverage in the newspapers – *The Express, The Sun* and other populars as well as the *Financial Times, The Guardian, The Times,* and *The Economist.* The diagnosis stood up pretty well. The much bigger review of the scheme which was soon to be set in hand dealt with all these issues. We had failed to spot only two of the larger questions which that review was to deal with: how to give equal rights to married women who were their families' breadwinners, and how to devise simpler, better ways of supporting the steadily growing numbers of unemployed claimants.

Launching the Review

Anyone who advises the government works on the fringes of a court and its courtiers. There were very few things the Commission could decide for itself: benefits which fell within our own discretion amounted to only 6 per cent of all the money we handed out. Whatever else we achieved depended ultimately on a reputation for gaining the ear of Ministers and the senior officials who advised them. If people ever concluded that Ministers would not listen to us we might as well shut up shop and go home.

Sir Patrick Nairne came in October 1975 from the Ministry of Defence to be the Permanent Secretary, or head, of the DHSS and its 100,000 civil servants. He visited me in my office on 30 October: a spare, military figure, trained to wield and to accept authority. Like most of the top brass, he had other talents besides those his job called for: he painted – and occasionally exhibited and sold – water colours of professional standard; and he wrote with a most elegant hand. Although I sensed he would have preferred to run a different department, he was working with obsessional drive, a massive capacity for soaking up detail, and instant, total loyalty to the DHSS and whatever Ministers it might have. I talked with him very frankly about our staffing problems.

I returned just after Christmas to find our new Chief Adviser in post. Already the building felt different. Geoffrey Otton's light was still on at 6 p.m. each evening. (But he kept up his singing in a local choir too.) The senior officials in our headquarters, together with others working most closely with the Commission, met him once a week to discuss current problems and priorities. Before long, more papers about questions of policy, saying more challenging things, began to flow across my desk. Devoted to his profession and without ideological hang-ups of any kind, Geoffrey Otton is one of the great courtiers. He gets out and learns from junior staff, welfare rights workers, academics – anyone who seems to know what's going on. He clarifies, simplifies, and writes beautifully. He sharpens people up, more by example than by criticism; never humiliates them and never pulls rank. He overcame the opposition of senior officials in the DHSS, the Treasury and elsewhere – all the fearsome old dinosaurs – partly by knowing his job so well, and partly by imparting his own buoyant confidence that things can be changed: a great enabler. But in 1976 Geoffrey had just arrived from quite different fields to join the tight little gang of able but battle-scarred men who had been running the social security system and advising Ministers about it for fifteen years or more. You have to earn whatever influence you wield in that company.

At the beginning of February I met Alf Morris, Minister for the Disabled, and soon afterwards Brian O'Malley. Much of politics is about important trivia. Among the topics I discussed with each of them was the announcement they would make about the appointment of five new members of the Commission – and in particular Carmen Holtham, our first immigrant Commissioner, a magistrate and organiser of a citizens advice bureau. Should we say that she came from Jamaica and was black? If she was content with that, I wanted to do so. Both Ministers insisted that we must not publicise these facts. (Alf said it would be rather like saying that the Commission had a physically handicapped member: how our liberals reveal themselves!) Next day, 6 February, I agreed with Barbara Castle that we would publish a brief biography, with a photograph, for each new member. An acceptable compromise. The other four newcomers were Dr Bernice Tanner, a general practitioner working in Notting Hill; Ted Brown, Director of Social Services in North Yorkshire; Arthur Stabler, a Labour councillor from Newcastle; and Brenda Dean, shortly to become Secretary of the Manchester Region of SOGAT, the printers' union.

It was a bitter winter, and Ministers were much concerned about fuel bills and the plight of pensioners. 'Couldn't we find some way of giving them woolly blankets?' Barbara asked. I said stern things about simplifying an excessively complicated scheme and leaving people to spend their money in their own way. If the Government wanted to help pensioners they would have to increase pensions.

On 1 March, I had my first meeting with the Health and Social Services Group of back-bench Labour MPs in a committee room at the House of Commons. One member said that many of his constituents thought that decisions about our benefits were made by officials without the help of rules of any kind. It was encouraging to find MPs pressing for clear statements to be given to every claimant showing how their benefit was worked out, and for the publication of the secret Codes which guide staff in administering the scheme. Brian O'Malley had clearly won their respect for his detailed grasp of the Pensions Bill which he had just piloted through the House. He had told me a few days previously that once this Bill was out of the way he looked forward to working more closely with us. I looked forward to that too: but it was not to be.

On 25 March I was lecturing on a course for recently promoted under secretaries at the Civil Service College out in the suburbs at Sunningdale. Sir Claus Moser, the Government's Chief Statistician, and other senior officials were contributing too. We talked about Harold Wilson's resignation, a day or two earlier, and the battle for the leadership of the Labour Party. The abler mandarins were depressed by the prospect that Callaghan would win. There was nothing ideological about that: they just felt he would be such a dull fellow to work with.

On 6 April I lunched with Sir Patrick Nairne at his club, the Oxford and Cambridge. People and jobs were to be our principal topics. One of a permanent secretary's most important tasks is to sense which sectors of the enormous front he commands are going to 'go live' in the next year or two, and get the best people into key positions there. Policy is usually formulated much lower down, among principals and assistant secretaries. Pat already knew that the whole supplementary benefit scheme would have to be overhauled. But before we could settle down to talk, Club officials told us to leave the bar and excluded us from the restaurant because I was not wearing a tie. (I had not owned one for years but no-one had objected on my previous visits to the place.) We found food and a bench in the canteen at the back of Club, where we continued our talk. But – along with Callaghan's arrival as Prime Minister – the incident seemed to symbolise the increasingly conservative climate of the times.

Later that afternoon I went to see Barbara Castle in her room at the House of Commons. She arrived in tears. Callaghan had just announced Brian O'Malley's death from an altogether unexpected heart attack. All along the corridors she had had to run the gauntlet of Members commiserating with her. She had been out early in the morning to see Brian's wife Kate, at the hospital and was now clutching a plastic bag full of little delicacies 'to tempt that poor woman's appetite'. But she switched briskly to my agenda (it again included the question of publishing figures on the real value of benefits in a new version of SBC *Notes and News*). Then she turned to a constituency problem which she wanted me to sort out (a tricky case of a widower's benefits which I promised to look into). Meanwhile, at his desk, Norman Warner was with cold ferocity 'phoning Tony Crosland's office at the Department of the Environment (which controls transport) to get them to permit Brian's driver (withdrawn during the night, the moment he died) to take Kate O'Malley and her daughter home to Mexborough – pausing in the midst of this to fend off Michael Foot who, I guess, was trying to rally the Left before Callaghan took decisions about his new administration. I ended up helping Barbara to wrap up the parcels her own driver was taking to Kate. All within thirty minutes. And Barbara herself did not know whether she still had a job in the Government.

Next day I was back at Sunningdale for a big conference between senior social security officials and researchers from universities, research institutes and government departments: the first of its kind. We discussed research needs and priorities. Pat Nairne, Geoffrey Otton and all the top brass were there. Some of the more critical academics began to grasp the managerial and political problems of the service as Leslie Trew, Director of the Regional Organisation, talked about staff shortages and cuts, militant trade unions and the growing pressures on local offices. Over the bar, Leslie himself heard Adrian Sinfield, a sociologist then at the University of Essex, remark that appeals to the tribunals in Colchester were taking three months to deal with. He said he would sort that out. Something new was happening.

Then, as word went round the conference that Barbara had been sacked, the principal courtiers filtered away, inviting me to come back with them to Alexander Fleming House. There a wake was being held. Barbara, surrounded by her outside advisers, staff of her private office and all the top people in the Department, was throwing a party. Over the drinks she made a brief speech, stressing that the Prime Minister was entitled to pick his own team, but making it clear that she was sorry to leave them, with so much work unfinished. She was *not* going to the Lords. She would be on the House of Commons Committee dealing with private beds in NHS hospitals – and would clearly give her successor hell if he weakened in dealing with the doctors.

With five of our eight members newly appointed, we had a new Commission. Two new under secretaries would be joining us later. They and our new Chief Adviser, Geoffrey Otton, were convinced that the whole supplementary benefit scheme would have to be re-examined. Thus we had the makings of a working team.

There had not been a really thorough overhaul of social assistance policies since the National Assistance Board was set up nearly thirty years earlier. By now the scheme was supporting three times the number of people who had depended on it in 1948. Meanwhile, all sorts of new and overlapping services had grown up around it – new kinds of housing subsidy, new grants for deprived children and their families, new benefits for the disabled, and so on. Our Commission's first Annual Report was shaping up in ways which made it clear that the SBC would be asking a lot of fundamental questions about the scheme. It would be far better to take these on board the ship of state and make a proper job of them.

But how? Reforming a major part of the social security system takes longer than the lifetime of any government which sets its hand to the task. If the impetus for reform is washed away by general elections which bring new governments to power, the DHSS finds it difficult to recover a momentum for change. That is partly because it runs the social security services itself instead of working through an independent system of local government, and partly because it has been less prepared to take outsiders into its confidence and create a wider, national movement of the kind which escorts education and housing Ministers. As a result, the handful of able under secretaries and assistant secretaries whom the Department calls upon to lead any team working on major reforms of the system are a war-weary crew. That is not just a figure of speech: when Crossman's virtually completed pension scheme was sunk by the Conservative victory of 1970, one of his officials killed himself. The next pension scheme and the tax credit scheme almost launched by the next government had been sunk in turn by the 1974 election. The child benefit scheme was now struggling uncertainly towards birth. And the new pension scheme which Brian O'Malley had just got through Parliament was built on twenty years of hard labour and bitter disappointment. Meanwhile the economic weather was worse than ever. Rescued from their latest crisis by the International Monetary Fund, the government were being compelled to impose cuts in public expenditure and staff, and depended for their survival day by day on the precarious support of Liberal and Nationalist members of Parliament.

If we were to get anything done about supplementary benefit we would have to pick limited targets. There was no point in calling for massive expenditure, or a new Beveridge report reviewing the whole social security system. The prospect of such a report would be seized upon by the Treasury and its Ministers to put the new pension scheme and other hopeful developments on ice for years to come by arguing that nothing should be done until this report had been completed and thoroughly debated. We would have to create a small team of officials committed to bringing about reform – a team sufficiently expert and respected to mobilise support among their colleagues within the bureaucracy. They would also need wider public support to sustain the impetus for change beyond the next general election. Public support might gain for their proposals the approval of Ministers and of leading Opposition spokesmen. But if the issue became identified as the property of one political party that would compel other parties to reject whatever solutions were proposed. It was not going to be easy.

Geoffrey Otton took the lead in planning what came to be called the review of the supplementary benefit scheme (deliberately keeping a low profile, 'review' was always written with a small *r*.) The proposal was for a reappraisal of the administration of the scheme – there were plenty of good reasons for that – with an assurance that new developments costing extra money or staff were not contemplated. This seemed such a modest piece of good housekeeping that it was approved at equally modest levels in the Treasury and Civil Service Department hierarchies. Both Departments must agree before any public service can be re-examined. (If they refused, our Ministers would have to talk to their Ministers and try to win their support for the proposal.)

Our Ministers were consulted about these plans and brought together for a meeting with about fifteen of their senior officials and political advisers on 5 May 1976. Officials spoke in that taut, condensed fashion, using the simple words, short sentences and confident tone which seasoned courtiers adopt on such occasions. In twenty minutes we got all that we were asking for.

At the Commission's monthly meeting on 21 July I felt for the first time that we were beginning to take an effective, collective line of our own. We had been urging for years that all claimants should be given, as a matter of course and without asking for it, a statement explaining how their benefit was calculated or why it had been refused. A small experiment had been mounted to see what could be done. Papers on this proposal had been delayed on one pretext or another for months; but at this meeting we were given one which rather unfairly criticised the research which Southampton University was doing on our experiment, and proposed that the whole project be abandoned forthwith. Officials supported their arguments with daunting estimates of the numbers of extra staff who would be needed to write on an extra sheet of paper for five million claimants a year. (Plainly bogus estimates: had carbon paper not been invented?) No mention was made of forthcoming developments, such as the staff cuts which were compelling us to reduce internal checks on payments and therefore making it all the more important that claimants should in future be able to check their benefits for themselves. We pursued officials fiercely on this. When they fell back on the argument that a new form of the sort we wanted could not be fitted into the claimants' files without changing all the filing cabinets in our 500 local offices I knew we had them on the run. No problem was too trivial to baffle these men when they did not want to act. We resolved to discuss the issue with the Southampton researchers in September, and called for papers which would show what could be done without extra staff or expenditure. I was beginning to realise how important were the visits I made to two or three local offices each month. Talking with the staff in two of the offices which were conducting this experiment, I had been told that 'written notices of assessment' (to use the jargon term for these forms) probably *saved* staff. If claimants understood more clearly how their money was calculated, they were more likely to produce the right information when claiming, and less likely to appeal against the decisions they were given.

We were also given a paper about translating our leaflets into minority languages – another thing for which we had been asking for some time. It was placed below the line on our agenda, suggesting that it could be approved without discussion. And it rejected the whole proposal. No mention was made of the translations which DHSS and other Departments had already arranged for leaflets dealing with medical care, rent rebates and other matters, or the translations of our own leaflets already being made by immigrant organisations and local community relations committees. It emerged in discussion that no-one had consulted the Community Relations Commission whose offices were only five minutes walk from our own. We called for firm proposals for translations at our next meeting. (It took a lot more time and a good deal of rage to get the job done, and even then part of the caption on the cover of the Gujerati leaflet was printed upside down. But eventually we made it.)

We also had a routine paper on error rates, giving estimates derived from samples of our files showing the proportions of claimants who get the wrong money (about 10 per cent), and the proportions of these claimants who get too much (about 30 per cent) and too little (about 70 per cent). From this paper there had been omitted the figures for the twelve different Regions – because their Regional Controllers did not like such comparisons being made, we were told. (They always show that, for various good reasons which affect all public and commercial services in much the same ways, the London regions make most mistakes, and the northern regions generally do best. Marks and Spencer would tell you the same story.) The Commission insisted that we got the missing figures at our next meeting.

Stan Orme, Minister for Social Security and (unlike Brian O'Malley his predecessor) a member of the Cabinet, joined our meeting for forty-five minutes. He promised that he would resolutely maintain the real value of social security benefits, and defend claimants against unjustified allegations of 'scrounging'. (Iain Sproat, an MP who was constantly making such allegations, was then given a credence by the media which he later deservedly lost.) We concluded with a private meeting, without officials, at which we decided to get together for a week-end somewhere out of London to discuss larger issues – particularly the contents of our next Annual Report, and the need for 'doomwatch' procedures to alert us to all the nastier things which could happen as unemployment rose and cuts were imposed during the coming months. We were beginning to act like a Commission.

The day before, our new version of *SBC Notes and News* had been published with figures and graphs comparing the movement of our main benefits with movements in prices and earnings. We presented this to a press conference, with an informal briefing for experts in the media and among the pressure groups beforehand, in what was now our normal way. We got good coverage in all the posher papers, from the *Daily Telegraph* upwards; but nothing in the populars. It was a start, but we would have to do better.

Our Annual Report for 1975 was going to describe the scheme and the people it served, providing information about many things never previously revealed – long-term trends in the real value of benefits, error rates, staff turnover, the number of appeals won and lost (showing, for example, that appellants supported by social workers or members of claimants' unions were more likely to win a better decision from the tribunals than those supported by lawyers) and much else besides. But the main purpose of the report was its opening chapter which presented the arguments for reviewing the supplementary benefit scheme. Alice Perkins, who edited the Report, had consulted each of the Departments which had an interest in its contents – Employment, Environment, Education and so on – seeking their help and meeting their objections wherever she could. The Treasury sent the longest list of comments and objections, many of them couched in tones of rather supercilious distaste.

"I am surprised", said the Treasury official in question during a final telephone conversation, "that civil servants should be associated with such stuff. It's like something out of *New Society* – a magazine I fortunately do not have to read". Some of their criticisms helped us to clarify what we were saying. For the rest, we stuck to our guns. We relied heavily on Barbara Castle's decision to 'restore' the practice of presenting an Annual Report, quoting her invitation in our opening pages. But if her successors were to keep the Reports going they would have to be convinced that they were, on balance, helpful. So the ultimate test we had to apply to each criticism was to ask whether its author would go so far as to persuade his Minister to object to our Ministers, and how our own would then respond. This ritual was re-enacted for every one of our five Reports. The Treasury never dissuaded us from saying what we wanted to say, but never relented in their attempts at censorship – focusing particularly on the chapters I wrote and maintaining to the end their disdainful tone.

Our first report was published on 15 September 1976. It was given good coverage and a pretty warm welcome by almost every paper, ranging from *The Sun* and the *Telegraph* to *The Guardian* and the *Financial Times*. Months later people were still quoting its figures and using its arguments. We were beginning to focus debate on the crucial issues.

The Secretary of State welcomed the Report, and announced as it was published that he was setting up a team of officials to review the whole supplementary benefit scheme. Alan Palmer, the assistant secretary who had been in charge of the most heavily-loaded branch in our headquarters, had already begun work as leader of this team of four or five younger officials who were to conduct the review. Alan, who had worked on social assistance for donkeys' years, knew more about the scheme than anyone else. In the job he was doing previously he had perfected a technique of protecting himself from new and heavier demands with a restrained melancholy which implied that one more burden laid upon his shoulders would drive him into a breakdown. But, as leader of the review, he blossomed into a very effective reformer. Able youngsters competed to get into his team. This was to be a recurring experience. The officials attracted to work with Geoffrey Otton and the SBC worked harder and more happily than ever before. Equally important, their colleagues elsewhere in the DHSS and in other Departments of Government noted the quality of the people who were joining us and knew that this was to be an attempt at reform which they would have to take seriously. You do not concentrate so many crack troops on one sector of the front unless a big push is coming.

Alan Palmer's team were to work to a steering group, chaired by Geoffrey Otton, on which every Department affected by the Review would be represented – normally by under secretaries. The Treasury, Civil Service Department, Education, Environment, Employment, Home Office, other branches of DHSS, and the Central Policy Review Staff – the Cabinet's small 'think tank' – were all there. Despite the protests of some officials, I was to be a member too, representing the Commission. The review team would discuss all their main analyses and proposals with the steering group and with the Commission. On the Commission we decided henceforth to begin all our monthly meetings with a progress report from Alan. But he and his team would ultimately report to Ministers who would have to decide what to do about any recommendations they made. In this way they should be able to go as far as possible in sorting out problems in advance with other branches of the bureaucracy before trying to gain the support of Ministers. Meanwhile the Commission would open up a wider public debate, mobilise support for change, keep in touch with the Opposition, and prevent promised options for reform from being suppressed before they had been properly discussed.

The officials at the top of DHSS who set up this procedure had invented a new way of inquiring into a public service. There are two conventional procedures for doing this: through an independent committee of some kind, or through an internal committee of officials. The independent people who sit on Royal Commissions and Committees of Inquiry can call for evidence, mobilise widespread concern, and thrash out problems publicly. But they take a long time to complete their work, they are disbanded on the day they report, and the few officials who work for them are then promptly moved to different duties. Lacking political 'clout', such bodies are too often used to delay action rather than to achieve anything. An interdepartmental committee of officials is better equipped to consult and coordinate plans with every branch of the bureaucracy and to move fast. But they cannot stir up public debate, their brightest ideas can be strangled at birth if they offend powerful Departments, and no-one is obliged to publish what they say. They are good at dealing with technical problems, bad when the problems are essentially political. We hoped that the review team and the Commission would together combine the strengths and avoid the weaknesses of each of these procedures. Like two players on the same side, we could pass the ball back and forth between us in the hope that one or other might eventually make a breakthrough. When the Treasury spokesman on the steering group said it would be undesirable to raise public expectations by publishing proposals for giving equal treatment to men and women, I could – and did – say that these would in any case be discussed by the Commission in its next Annual Report, so we had better give them the more expert treatment which Alan Palmer's team could bring to bear. But to make the partnership work would be a delicate operation. We would each have to collaborate closely with the other while retaining our independent freedom of action.

CHAPTER 4

The Political Environment

The first act of the drama was over. It had taken a year to pose questions about poverty policies and launch a public debate about them. Social reformers look next for answers and for the people who offer them, sizing up the strength and character of the interests at stake. The following chapter deals with this second act of the drama. But before getting into that I must explain the political climate in which we were operating. It was growing colder by the hour. During my first year as chairman of the SBC we had advanced into new territory and begun exploring it. But as the second year unfolded we were driven back to defend more familiar ground. Who exactly were we defending? And from whom? The first question was easier to answer than the second.

On the Defensive

In November 1976 I was spending a week-end in a council flat in one of the poorest of Glasgow's east end estates. When the council built it in the 1930s, in the depths of a depression, they were starting on the daunting task of clearing some of the most crowded slums in the western world. Gone were the hopeful days when they had built neat little houses with gardens under the Act named after their own John Wheatley, the housing Minister who had insisted that working-class people were entitled to the kind of houses which middle-class people had. Instead, under Chamberlain's meaner legislation, they ran up long grey slabs of tenements with two flats to each landing on their four floors. There were no gardens, no balconies, no trees, no shops or pubs – not a trace of style or human dignity anywhere: just mass produced dwelling units for the poor. And from the start poor people had lived in these streets.

Down the dusty vista visible from my window there was only one battered car to be seen. Litter scattered on the verges and around the backs of the tenements seemed never to be picked up. Windows on the stairwell had been broken, and the brass nosings to the concrete stairs had all been ripped off and sold to scrap dealers. Middle-class people never came down these streets. Many of the residents live on supplementary benefit. They depend for survival on the skilled working class and the lower middle class: corporation workmen, social security officials, clothing club agents, and shopkeepers who tide you over by selling goods on tick when your giro cheque arrives late. Any man wearing overalls or driving a van – symbols of power in this street – is apt to be stopped by women who run out to plead for repairs to windows, plumbing and heating systems. Round the corner, a couple of blocks away, is the compound where building materials are stored behind a high fence. Women cluster at the gates in the mornings to intercept the corporation workmen and ask them to fix things; or perhaps to do a 'homer' – a job for which they'll pay, knowing well that much of the work may be done with time and materials stolen from the council. For the same job, different prices will be charged: a declining tariff for employed people, people living on social security, and women on their own. The headlines they see in the *News of the World* on Sundays about 'social security scroungers' must convey for these people an oddly selective view of sin. Politics survive in a desultory way on these estates. But councillors are rare: if someone living here is elected to the council he is likely before long to get transferred to a nicer housing scheme.

As I gazed down the street I reflected that we must never rest content with perfecting the supplementary benefit system. Our ultimate aim must be to abolish it. Even when it works well, the lives of claimants in neighbourhoods like this will always be grey and anxious, with constant temptations to dishonesty. It must be possible to find work for those who can do it: you need only look down the road to see how much needs to be done before this could be a tolerable place for people to live in. If we took account of the value of their work to the community, and the tax and insurance contributions they would pay, it would cost little more – possibly less – to give people jobs than to keep them in idleness. And those who cannot work should be entitled to an income, without intrusive, degrading means tests, which does not depend on the discretion of officials.

Visiting social security offices at about this time in the north west of England, I had a glimpse of this world from the other side of the counter. I was talking with a group of staff drawn mainly from the old textile towns around Manchester. Their bosses – local and regional office managers in their fifties – had been polite but dour. Many of them saw the Commission as a bunch of social workers and trendies, lacking the moral fibre to stand up for hard work, thrift and moral rectitude: the permissive society incarnate. Younger staff – the women even more sharply than the men – attacked me with complaints about fraud, workshy claimants, feather-bedded claimants, cohabiting claimants, and women who will not go back to their husbands because we give them too much money. From radio 'phone-in programmes and from my own postbag I knew they spoke for many in the communities from which they came.

I'm not sure why these towns produce the most punitive attitudes towards the poor. Manchester and Liverpool are tinged with the same anger, but less deeply; Clydeside and Tyneside, with as long an experience of poverty and puritanism, are realistic and humane by comparison. The people of Bolton, Bury, Oldham and Rochdale are not cold or mean: any professional fund-raiser will tell you they give more generously than the more prosperous West Midlands. And if I'm ever knocked down far from home by a passing car I'd much rather it was in Blackburn than in Birmingham. If you do claim supplementary benefit in these towns you are more likely to get the right money promptly than in most places further south. That's partly because they take pride in their work and partly because there are fewer opportunities here for school leavers with 'O' and 'A' level certificates, so the public services get better staff who are more determined to hang on to their jobs.

Their intolerance towards claimants in general and the unemployed in particular may reflect the low wages paid for a century and more in cotton mills. (Why, they ask, should the unemployed get almost as much?) Working-class chapel religion, working-class home ownership and working-class Conservatism (surrounded by the improvident and fecund Irish) may be part of the story too. Or it may be the culture of declining small towns. Where everyone knows the reputation of every street, where the social hierarchy is more clearly marked (there's just one famous grammar school and one social security office) and where 'fiddling' and fraud are harder to conceal, the class war is fought out more starkly day by day across the counters of the public services. Whatever the reasons, the tone is unmistakeable.

Ordinary, unemployed couples with children tend to be the poorest of all those who live on supplementary benefit. That is partly because they are drawn to a greater extent from the least skilled and most impoverished families in the country (injury, sickness, widowhood, and divorce being distributed rather more randomly through the population) and partly because we keep them poorer by paying them less (they are never allowed the higher, long-term rates of benefit which all other claimants get). Unemployed claimants are also less likely than others to get discretionary extra benefits. And if they appeal to the tribunals they are much less likely than other appellants to win a favourable decision from them. That is probably not due to conscious discrimination against them. It is easier to find something 'exceptional', and thus worthy of extra help, in the needs of one-parent families, the sick, the disabled and the elderly. But the needs of the unemployed are the needs of a whole class – no different, in most cases, from the needs of low paid working families.

Richer and more confident people can generally get what they want from selective services which have a lot of discretion built into them. That's why middle-class people often defend discretion so fiercely. Listening to our young officials from Bolton and Bury, I reflected that we must always beware of exposing the poorest people of all to this kind of treatment; and particularly if they are unemployed. They, above all, need the protection of clearly defined rights and decisive government policies. But the rights of the unemployed were not at the forefront of our leaders' minds at this time.

During the summer I was invited to a splendid lunch by the British Institute of Management. Sir Frederick Catherwood, at the head of the table, presided over a large circle: among them a Labour and a Conservative MP, a famous trade union leader, managers and city gentlemen. Conversation over the cigars and brandy dwelt on the troubles of the British economy "now we are so deplorably dependent on short-term money from the Arabs". To put things right, drastic cuts must be made in local government spending – £1,000 millions, they agreed – to make room for more private investment. (A pretty accurate forecast, as it turned out, of what was to happen five years later.) Thinking that this was not going to be one of the occasions on which I would have to contribute to the talk, my mind wandered. Then suddenly our chairman turned to me and said "But we have the biggest spender of them all amongst us. Professor Donnison – I constantly hear how your social security system is abused. What do *you* think?" I woke up with a start in the silence that followed.

I said first that the cuts which they intended to make in the public sector must come largely from education because it accounts for more than half the local authorities' current expenditure. Most of those round the table, I pointed out, were past the age at which they had to worry about their children's education – and I doubted whether many of them had sent their children to state schools anyway. Before willingly accepting cuts imposed on the schools my own children were attending I would like to be sure that they knew how to invest this money more usefully. Wouldn't much of it go abroad, and into commercial property? (That was to be a pretty accurate forecast too.) When a big manufacturing enterprise such as British Leyland was plainly foundering, the investing institutions just abandoned the sinking ship: they did nothing to put things right. As for supplementary benefits – far from being the biggest public spender, it accounted then for only 13 per cent of the whole social security budget: roughly equivalent in value to tax relief on the insurance premiums and mortgage interest payments of people a good deal richer than our customers. I had no need to say more: indeed, it was difficult to get a word in edgeways.

On the streets it was clear which way the wind was blowing. When we first pressed Barbara Castle to let us publish quarterly figures showing changes in the real value of benefits we had assumed that people would be pleased to discover that benefits were keeping up with the movements of wages and prices. By the time we got the figures out it was clear that many would have been happier if they had been falling behind. When the upratings in social security benefits came round each year we had to prepare speeches, broadcasts and press releases to show that the great majority of claimants had always been much worse off than people in work, and still were.

There was little time now to float new ideas for reforming supplementary benefits. We had to spend so much of our energies trying to defend the existing scheme and the people who depended on it. My fullest defence of claimants and the benefits system was received in dead silence at the London Hilton by a conference of business men hoping to hear that social security payments were too high and that half the claimants were scroungers. But we reprinted and distributed this speech to each of the 65,000 staff working in local social security offices.

We had talks with Ministers about threatened cuts in benefits which they and their officials succeeded in fighting off at this stage, and about cuts in staff, the worst of which we also escaped, although reductions were made in the visiting of claimants, the checking of payments and other work. Stan Orme was doing a coolly resolute job coping with public hysteria about fraud. A particularly flagrant case was in the headlines in July 1977 – but it was not quite so spectacular as Mr Deevy, the enterprising con-man involved, would have had the world believe. After thorough investigation we could only discover about half the innumerable identities and addresses he claimed to have used in order to milk the system for himself and his imaginary families. He was as good at conning judges and journalists as social security officials.

We could not rest content with making speeches, bringing some realism into the biases of social security staff, and deflating stuffed shirts at dinner parties. Deeply rooted prejudice does not give way to rational argument. We needed hard evidence, a cogent philosophy and some supporting troops.

The Unemployed

Towards the end of 1976 we began thinking out what became, for the rest of the Commission's life, our main priority: policies for the unemployed. Our main priority and our main failure. Those who had set up the National Assistance scheme, on which our own was still largely modelled, had expected that the few people who would briefly be out of work would normally live on insurance benefits till they found jobs again. But the numbers out of work had risen, with only one short break since 1966; and they were out of work for longer and longer. Less than half of them were now drawing insurance benefits; more were living on supplementary benefit. Although they were still less than a quarter of the people on our books, they accounted for two-thirds of the claims we dealt with each year. Thus the quality of our service, the morale of its staff and its public reputation all depended heavily on our capacity for dealing with the unemployed.

We needed to know more about who was out of work, how much money they were getting, what they would earn in work, and how they felt about it all. Dr Bernice Tanner was the first Commissioner to press for this. She saw the human impact of unemployment in her surgery every day. We assembled the evidence gradually from other people's research and from several studies of our own, publishing the results in our Annual Reports. We were quite prepared to find that a lot of people were deterred from working by social security payments. (That would pose political problems, but it would not bother me personally: if there are not enough jobs to go round, it seems best to give the work to those who want it most.) But so far as supplementary benefit is concerned every single study confirmed that very few people (less than 5 per cent of unemployed claimants, less than 1 per cent of all claimants) get more when they are out of work than when they are working – provided that they claim when in work the rent and rate rebates, the family income supplement and other means-tested benefits to which low paid workers are entitled. It's the numbers of jobs available, not the level of benefits, which decide the numbers of people out of work.

Individual claimants may indeed be deterred from working

– usually by oddities in their own circumstances. I recall a smart young man in Bristol who seemed perfectly capable of getting a job. I could not understand why he had been out of work for so long in this prosperous city till he explained that he was fighting his divorced wife for custody of their children and needed the generous legal aid he was getting while he stayed on supplementary benefit. (Since then the extension of legal aid to more of the working population has solved this problem for many people.) Another man – a van driver, tiger-striped with tattoos and fiercely aggressive, surrounded by a big new television set, fridge and cooker, and getting behind with the payments on all of them – said there was no point in getting a job because if he did so the court would only increase the weekly payments he was making to his creditors and on fines for theft offences. (You may want him to work: but, with plenty of unemployed van drivers about, would you employ him? Or write a reference for him?) Then there was the builder's labourer in Essex with nine children who said he'd need at least £120 a week to make it worth his while to go back to work, and blamed it all on his wife and the Pope. (I blamed it on the low child benefits we pay for larger and poorer working families, and on government policies which were by then cutting out free school meals and other services for working families.) But ordinary unemployed claimants – a school leaver, an older man, or a couple with one or two children – were getting no more benefit in comparison with average wages than they would have got in 1948. What had changed since then was not the benefits but the demand for labour. The research showed, moreover, that people seek work for many reasons besides the wages it pays. Pride, comradeship, pension rights and many other factors motivate them. The men with larger families and higher benefits try just as hard to find work as anyone else; and when they get it they work longer hours than other people.

There were plenty of people drawing unemployment *insurance* benefits, together with earnings related supplements and private pensions, who were not in the least interested in finding work: they included retired civil servants, bank managers and the like. (The latest cuts will at least put a stop to that: and high time too.) But the editors and the MPs who hounded supplementary benefit claimants rarely worried about these people – any more than they worried about fraudulent employers when mounting campaigns against fraudulent claimants. That gave the game away. It was only the less skilled among the unemployed, living on the lowest benefits, about whom they got so angry. We were dealing with a serious political problem; but it was more a problem of comfortable people's prejudices about the poor than a problem of claimants' behaviour.(The same kind of thing happens in race relations: they also present serious problems – mainly about white prejudice.)

If people were simply and honestly concerned about the possibility that social security payments deter men from working, they would quickly recognise that if we are really paying the unemployed more than the wages they get from work it would be cheaper and more productive for us to give them jobs instead. They would then discover that it is only claimants with several children who can get anywhere near as much in benefit as they would earn from work when their wages are combined with family income supplement and other benefits to which the working poor are entitled. Therefore, if incentives to work are to be restored by cutting benefits, that must mean cutting benefits for children. But benefits for children are already too low in relation to benefits for adults. Moreover, three out of five of the children living on supplementary benefit are not children of the unemployed: they are in one-parent families. Their mothers are not expected to register for work at all. It is true that a lot of people get very little more money from working than they get on benefit. But it would be better to tackle that problem by raising the incomes of the working poor: enforcing minimum wage regulations — now widely disregarded – increasing child benefits, and ensuring that the low paid get any means-tested benefits to which they are entitled.

As for fraud, there was certainly plenty of it – arising mainly from the concealment of earnings. It is a serious problem, although it scarcely justified the overheated attention later focused upon it by Reg Prentice, the next Minister of Social Security. I shall have more to say about that in Chapter 7. Since you need skills, confidence and contacts to make a lot of money from concealed jobs, most of this fraud is committed by the working population, not the people on social security payments. But that is not the kind of fraud that editors believe their readers want to hear about. They benefit too much from it — as customers of the 'informal economy' if not as workers within it. (I challenged one journalist who was pursuing me about fraud to print his next claim for expenses on the front page of his paper.)

Since the vast majority of those out of work would rather support themselves, and would be much better off doing so, the Commission's first priority had to be to press for more jobs. That would call for changes in the management of the economy and in general economic policies both in Britain and in other countries — changes extending far beyond our powers. We could, and did, draw attention to these problems at every opportunity, but others would have to solve them. We constantly reminded people that those out of work were unwillingly conscripted into a growing army of the unemployed (it was Kay Carmichael's phrase in a broadcast) required by present policies in order to control inflation and make room for wage increases for the rest of us. Whenever they hear the familiar phrases used to announce the settlement of some major industrial conflict ("there is to be an increase in pay . . . and a productivity deal . . . but there will be no redundancies . . . overmanning will be reduced by natural wastage") people should recognize that the employers, the unions and the government are again planning to bring about more unemployment among next year's school leavers, and to consign more of this year's short-term unemployed to the ranks of next year's long-term unemployed. When those things happen they should not just be deplored with a lot of hand-wringing: they are deliberately planned — on behalf of the rest of us who have secure jobs. This was a very unpopular message. The Treasury always tried to censor it out of our Annual Reports.

Those conscripted into unemployment should be entitled to an adequate and simply calculated income without a lot of hassle. I do not understand why the incomes of unemployed manual workers excite such hysteria. If university teachers or the managers of failing enterprises are sacked we do not question their right to decent redundancy payments, or snatch the money away from them if they get another job the next day. And they have a good deal more responsibility for the fate of the organizations they worked for than the average unemployed worker. People out of work should be entitled without question to the minimum wage. If the country could not afford that, this might compel us all to manage our affairs in better ways – but in fact it can. If that is still politically unthinkable – and in the present climate it probably is – and most of the unemployed have to live on supplementary benefit, then arrangements for paying them should be greatly simplified and they should get the same public services and the same consideration as every other citizen. That means for a start that they should have the higher long-term rates of benefit on the same terms as other claimants. If they need help to find their way back into work, that should come mainly from the employment service and the job centres which everyone else uses, not only from social security offices which are less well equipped to help them. The DHSS's 'unemployment review officers' ' role should be to make sure that the unemployed get this help, not to substitute for it. If, after a long period at home, they need some training to prepare them for work, that too should come from the employment services which have long been running courses for people with special difficulties of this kind in their employment rehabilitation centres, not from a less well-equipped re-establishment centre run by less well-paid social security staff which must be regarded with some suspicion by most employers. Likewise, if poor people need selective help in paying their rents or their fuel bills, that should be arranged through the housing and fuel services in ways which treat equal needs equally, rather than through separate schemes for those in work and those out of work. These were the priorities we advocated, month in and month out, for the rest of the Commission's life. To whom could we turn for support?

We talked many times with Sir Richard O'Brien, chairman of the Manpower Services Commission, and his senior officials. From Richard himself we always got the most sympathetic hearing. Working parties of officials were set up to discuss problems which concerned his service and ours. I visited job centres in various parts of the country, and an employment rehabiliatation centre. But virtually nothing was done. The MSC was beginning to pour money into programmes for the unemployed – nearly all based on the assumption that a gap in the demand for labour had temporarily to be filled till the recession lifted and the economy returned to normal. That was the government's stance. It still is. But it is a long time since any properly informed person believed that story. We face more fundamental difficulties calling for more fundamental action.

The TUC and the CBI together dominate the Manpower Services Commission. The former is more interested in dues-paying union members than in the unemployed. The latter is more interested in the firms still struggling to survive than in those which have gone bankrupt. Both might feel threatened by more radical policies. Meanwhile unemployment goes on rising; and that means fewer union members, lower profits and more bankruptcies.

I met Len Murray and his staff at the TUC. They understood exactly what was wanted. "It's our job", he said, "to make unemployment too expensive for any government to tolerate much of it." But their movement had more urgent things to worry about and it was years before they took any action on behalf of the unemployed. (Now at last it is beginning.) We met regularly with the TUC's Social Insurance and Industrial Welfare Committee (could any title more clearly convey that their concern was for the people still at work?) but the really powerful figures on the Committee rarely showed up. We talked with social workers and their professional associations. But they are principally concerned with mothers, children, the aged, the sick and the handicapped. Members of the family who could go to work and the training and job opportunities they need in order to do so do not bulk large in social workers' minds or in the training they have been given.

We discussed these issues many times with Ministers and gained vigorous support from Stan Orme and David Ennals for getting the higher long-term rates of benefit for the unemployed. Their Conservative successors also accepted the case for this "in principle" and "when resources permit". But again nothing happened. There are no powerful groups outside government pressing for action on behalf of the unemployed.

A new and fuller edition of our Supplementary Benefits

Handbook which explains the whole scheme was being prepared for publication at the beginning of 1977, and I was asked to write a foreword to it. Casting aside the boring draft I was offered, I tried to say some of the things in this chapter, using Kay Carmichael's phrase about those "unwillingly conscripted into the army of the unemployed". David Ennals's press officer, Peter Brown, put this draft in one of the red boxes David took home for the weekend – underlining the offending phrase and adding a marginal note to say it must be deleted. David agreed. Although its foreword appeared over my name, the Handbook was, strictly speaking, published by the Department, not the Commission – for him, not for us. I said he was not obliged to have a foreword at all: I would happily scrap it and present the same arguments in our Annual Report instead. We ended up by amending a few words but retaining the crucial ones. Later they were used in many other places.

David was not out of touch with the Government or his Party in taking this line. Shortly after, on 18 February 1977, I attended a conference of LEFTA – a Labour Party association of economists and financial experts – which was addressed by Denis Healey and prominent back-benchers. While further increases in unemployment were never explicitly mentioned, the speakers made it quite clear that they were confidently expected and pretty complacently accepted. The day before I had a meeting with a prominent Labour back-bencher – chairman of the Parliamentary Party's Health and Social Services Group. He began by saying "I know you will disagree with me, but I should make it clear that I think it's a *good* thing that people are reluctant to ask for supplementary benefit. I want them to go on feeling they would rather not do so."

As for the unemployed themselves – they are the silent minority. At any public meeting or radio 'phone-in, I learnt to expect the voices of lone parents, widows, pensioners and the disabled. But the ordinary, unemployed family men – the people who were having the hardest time of all and whose claims accounted for so large a proportion of our work – never spoke up. We only learnt their views by going to interview them in specially planned surveys and by reading the work of other people who did this kind of research. True discrimination begins when its victims believe they deserve to be scapegoats. Things will not change until the unemployed themselves demand a hearing. In a confused and brutal way that is at last beginning to happen – in St. Pauls, Bristol, in Brixton and Toxteth and many other places where large numbers of young people know they have no hope of work, but know also that they have some support from angry communities which do not accept that they deserve to be scapegoats. Within a few weeks that violence has produced more action – wholly inadequate though it still is – than years of liberal argument and peaceful demonstration ever did. It is tragic that so many policemen have been injured and so many shop-keepers have lost their livelihood in the process. Pointless too, for they are not the proper target of all this anger. If the allegation that these riots were politically organized had been true, the rioters would have gone down Pall Mall to Smith Square – burning down the Reform Club, the Carlton Club, Transport House and Conservative Central Office instead of smashing up some of the poorest working-class neighbourhoods – and Britain might now be mobilising herself to respond more effectively to their demands.

Meanwhile, as the numbers out of work go on rising, we are laying waste the only real riches of this country: the capacity, the skills and the pride of our own people.

The Employed

For years the determination of so many powerful people to avert their eyes from what was happening and pass by on the other side of the road was propped up by a confused mixture of beliefs: the belief that we were only in a temporary recession; that the problem was an increase in the supply of labour (more married women at work, more school leavers) not a fall in the demand for it; that the oil boom would create a British 'miracle' before long; and that most of the unemployed were either unemployable or working secretly in the 'informal economy'. The economists I consulted were divided and reluctant to prophesy. To grasp what was really happening we had to get a clearer picture of what was going on in the world of work. (To understand the abnormal, always look first at normality: if you want to learn about crime, look first at the righteous. Likewise with unemployment.)

So we met the CBI at their headquarters and in their regional groups, and we started calling on factories and their workers whenever I went visiting social security offices. But first I consulted Ministers about this initiative. They were reluctant, fearing embarrassment of some sort. Thus are maintained the crippling barriers which in Britain divide the professions from commerce, and the social from the economic departments of government. They need not have worried: we were generously welcomed wherever we went, and no embarrassments followed.

Managers in CBI groups repeated the folklore about abuse of social security: "Why, my taxi driver told me on the way here; there are *hundreds* of men on the fiddle." They had a general feeling that the whole system was morally corrupting, too expensive, and employed too many civil servants. But they knew virtually nothing about supplementary benefit. Some of them thought we 'supplemented' the wages of full-time workers. They knew a lot about pensions and sick pay provided by employers however, and much of their anger about 'scroungers' and 'malingerers' was directed at the people who abuse their own schemes. Personnel managers were unwilling to help low paid workers to claim means-tested benefits which might raise their incomes well above supplementary benefit levels: "Our job is to get a fair wage for people, not tell them we pay them so little that they should claim free school meals, family income supplement, rate rebates and all that." Shop stewards said the same thing.

I repeatedly challenged those who insisted that over-generous benefits deterred people from working to say whether they had actually advertised jobs and failed to fill them when they knew that suitable unemployed workers were available. The only employers who seemed plausibly convinced that they had done so were public transport enterprises. (Why? Working hours are 'unsocial' in their industry, and conducting a bus on some routes is a demanding and even dangerous job: perhaps we don't pay people enough to do it?)

The most important lesson I learnt from these meetings was that scarcely any of the employers we met expected to have more people working for them five or ten years hence than they already had. Most of them knew they would have to invest in more labour-saving machinery and reduce over-manning if they were to stay in business. With greater confidence in their competitive capacity they might have called it 'under-production' rather than 'over-manning' – but none did. Women and part-time workers of all kinds were expected to bear a large share of the cut-backs in the demand for labour. Employers hoped to increase their workers' pay, and particularly their pensions, holidays and sick pay – the fringe benefits. But these advances were likely to be confined to the gradually dwindling numbers of people in the secure core of the labour force.

The CB. best represents manufacturing, construction and transport: the 'production' industries. Unless the service industries, public and private, can take up the slack, there will be more people out of work; and one-parent families, the elderly and the disabled will all find it harder to get part-time jobs. More and more will be turning for help to supplementary benefits.

Visits to individual enterprises threw more light on these patterns. Some of the smaller plants we saw were still growing – depending rather heavily on low paid women and on adaptable, mobile, semi-skilled workers willing to do different jobs without demarcation disputes. But the Shotton Steel Works, which I visited in May 1978, was typical of the faltering heartlands of British industry. Crowds of men were brewing up molten iron, fresh ore, limestone and scrap metal in thunderously blazing open hearth furnaces, using methods which went back to Vulcan. This was the biggest, and probably the most antiquated plant of its kind in Europe. Meanwhile, in a neighbouring hangar, one man in a white coat, seated at the console of his computer and assisted by four less skilled colleagues, spun cold steel strip through the rollers. Racing by, it emerged further on already coated in coloured plastic. The heroic but archaic steel makers would have to become like the cold rolling and finishing shops if they were to survive at all. Either way, most of the 10,600 people working at Shotton – 40 per cent of the male labour force in the surrounding districts – would have to go. (Two years later it happened.) The apprentice-trained craftsmen could probably get jobs elsewhere. So might the less skilled labourers if they moved far enough – there would be nothing for them in these parts. But the elite – the highly-skilled steel-makers who learn their craft on the job – were unlikely to find any other plant which could use their obsolete craft.

At British Leyland we talked with managers and shop stewards who argued among themselves over whether car-making would in the long run survive in Britain, or whether it would all go to Taiwan, Brazil, Nigeria. . . . They agreed that if it did survive it would be the complicated, luxury models and the military vehicles we would be making. The bonnets of the 4.2 and 5.3 litre Jaguars we saw inching their way down the track at Coventry were being packed as full of intricate machinery and electronics as aeroplanes.

Cammell-Laird is the biggest heavy industry and one of the main trainers of skilled manual workers on Merseyside. Their labour force, like Shotton's, had already fallen – down from 10,000 to 3,500 in a decade. They hoped to stay in business if the government ordered more warships. Tankers and freighters could now be more cheaply built in Japan and the third world. Here, as at Jaguars and Shotton, nearly all the workers were men. And white. The key people – the top earners and the shop stewards – were men of power in their communities: there were councillors, tribunal members, justices of the peace and elders of the church among them.

At Wills' marvellous new factory in Bristol – coolly elegant in its parkland – most of the workers were women. But here too everyone knew that they would have to get their numbers down to the lower manning levels already attained by their competitors on the continent. And, as more and more people recognise the dangerous character of their products, tobacco manufacturers face a declining demand. Yet there was no talk of switching to other products.

Workers and line managers in all these places were proud of the things they made: every car, every ship, every carton of cigarettes rolled off the line and sold was an achievement. Top management thought in terms of the return on capital. Increasing it was their kind of achievement. That might eventually mean extricating it from the plant and reinvesting it more profitably elsewhere – in an office block in Brussells, perhaps. Academic economists would have confirmed and blessed these moral values for them – all in the name of pure theory. The social elite of British business – in the City of London – devote their working lives to this philosophy. Rarely did I find the older, and commercially more successful, tradition which I met when I went to Japan. There, managers and workers said the main job of an enterprise was to keep its people successfully employed – all of them, for contracts last a life-time. The reality can be pretty exploitative: watch what happens to women and Korean immigrants. Nevertheless every enterprise had constantly to be searching for new markets, new demands and processes. What they had to offer was not just a product, a skill or a capital fund, but an adaptable, creative, well or-ganised team. Their success in the markets of the world is not simply due to hard work, high rates of investment and low defence expenditure: it is also due to a distinctive set of moral values – in many ways superior to those of western capitalism.

The subtle but profoundly important divisions within the working class emerged more clearly as we saw different plants at work. The wages of women turning out transistors in Brighton may be fairly low, but they account for a large share of the cost of the finished product: the firm cannot add much in pensions, holidays and sick pay if it is to stay in business. Moreover the women, who come and go fairly fast and don't have much time for unions, are unlikely to ask for fringe benefits. They prefer ready money. If a batch of radios goes wrong, it's cheaper to throw them away than unpick and rebuild them. Contrast C. A. Parsons' plant in Newcastle: producing turbo-generator sets for power stations, it is basically a 'jobbing' factory making ten or twelve machines a year – their technology less sophisticated than transistors. But each machine costs about £5 million. That man you see is tending a kind of lathe: a very big one, costing a million pounds. Suspended between its centres are 20 yards of steel which will become a turbine shaft. It weighs 150 tons and is worth £200,000 before he starts carving pieces off it. He'd better not drop it. He's more likely to be reliable if his grandfather and his uncle worked in the plant, and he hopes his son will do one day. Later, under test, these turbines revolve at 60 revolutions a second, the blade tips moving at the speed of sound. If things went wrong they would explode like a bomb. The men who run such tests are worth keeping in the plant. Since many of Parsons' 5,000 workers hope to spend a lifetime there, solidarity really means something to them. They belong to unions and press for better pensions, sick pay and other fringe benefits, gradually narrowing the differentials in rewards between manual and white collar workers. And since factory wages account for only 10 or 12 per cent of the cost of a turbo-generator (the rest is materials and overheads) Parsons can improve these benefits without seriously endangering profits. But even here the future is uncertain. Since the demand for power grows about twice as fast as the economy, anyone who can retain a share of the world market for turbines should have a prosperous future. The recent capture of the order for the great Drax B power station had staved off 1,500 redundancies, but Parsons will have to win a lot more orders to keep their 5,000 workers going. Their efforts to diversify into other products have not been very successful. Already the steel for their turbine shafts is imported from the USA and Japan, and their million-pound machine tools are made in Germany, Italy, Eastern Europe – anywhere but Britain.

Work in the foundries of these heavy industries is harsh and dirty. But no-one can doubt that the things they make are important. Every turbine blade is numbered and exactly weighed and measured: if one goes wrong later in India or the Argentine, an exact replacement can be flown out at once. It's not like wrapping iced lollies. There is a similar sense of participating in a shared mystery in the big new power station at Thurrock on the Thames estuary, where some of Parsons' turbines are operating. If you want to play God there would be no better place to start than at the vast banks of switches and dials in the control room where white-coated men watch over these monsters. Television screens overhead enable them to monitor the burners at the foot of each furnace (towers of flame, five storeys high) the state of each generator and the colour of the smoke emerging from the stacks high overhead. Whole cities live or die at the turn of their switches.

There is so much more to a decent job than money. That's why we found in our research that even the small minority of men who get a better income on supplementary benefit than they can earn for themselves often go back to work as soon as they get a chance to do so. That's why we should never rest content with buying redundant steel workers and ship builders out of their jobs with handsome redundancy payments. Many of these were great men within the working communities we are destroying. When the big closures came on the Clyde we were told that the price of public houses was racing up in anticipation of these payments and the way in which they would be spent in the bars. There must be more challenging things these men could do for the rest of their lives.

What about women? At Thurrock, as at Parsons, Cammell-Laird, Shotton and Jaguar, they were confined largely to the office and the canteen. At Parsons they had taken on one girl among forty-five apprentices recruited that year from 1,000 applicants. All agreed she was the best of the lot; and all confidently predicted she could never work alongside the men when qualified. At Jaguar and elsewhere the managers insisted there was no bar on women, but added that you need a union card to get in, "and we would no longer be managing this works if we disregarded union views about women". The shop stewards agreed. The first women to break through these barriers are going to have to be tough. The collapse of British manufacturing industry is making the task much harder for them.

The pride and comradeship of men who share a dark mystery was most powerful among coal miners. We visited a Yorkshire colliery. Two miles from the shaft bottom and 1,000 feet underground, we watched a pair of circular shears come roaring by, carving coal off an eight-foot seam in a whirl of dust and water-cooled teeth. The coal face is the front line. The élite who man it are visited several times a week by the colliery manager and backed up by ten times as many support troops in a highly disciplined, all-male army. That evening we met their union leaders at their club – the 'miners' welfare'. I talked briefly about the supplementary benefit scheme, the cuts in social insurance and strikers' benefits announced a few days earlier in the budget of 1980, and the government's failure to keep child benefits moving up in line with rising prices. They were very angry about the loss of money for strikers' dependants, but not particularly concerned about reductions in contributory benefits or the abolition of the earnings-related supplements – cuts sixty times bigger than the money lost to strikers' families. As for child benefits – no-one was much concerned. "That's just paying for other men's pleasure", some of them said. Male chauvinists, yes; but not just Alf Garnetts. They were intelligent and well-informed men. They made 1945 seem a very long time ago. Arthur Scargill will win their votes; but for his militancy, not his radicalism.

In Wales the NUM is still part of a wider social movement concerned about the country's future, and coal seams are thinner – making everyone's job more precarious. The men in a Welsh pit I visited were more radical than their Yorkshire colleagues. They still had a sense of what the welfare state was about. As trade unionists they spoke for their people not only as workers but also as neighbours, fathers of families and pensioners. But they, too, knew little about supplementary benefit. These miners had tough, but absolutely secure jobs. Neither pit will close till well into the next century. They have reasonably high wages (about £130 a week at the face in 1980, plus concessionary coal; less amongst the support troops). They had good sick pay and injury benefits, and pensions from the age of sixty-two. They will never have to seek means-tested social assistance.

Along with my own reading and research, these encounters taught me that Britain is not just passing through a temporary recession. With their profits steadily falling, many of her industries will only stay in business if wage costs can be reduced by replacing workers with machines, by closing older plants, or by replacing well-organized men with lower-paid women, blacks and other cheaper labour. If they cannot improve productivity and profits as fast as their competitors abroad, more and more of the work will go overseas, taking with it the jobs now done by British workers. The oil bonanza is another part of the disaster, postponing confrontation with these realities. It strengthens sterling, thereby putting more firms out of business, and pours money into the Treasury to pay the rising burden of unemployment benefits.

None of this is inevitable. At Greenock, in an underemployed region famous for its industrial conflicts, we saw the

IBM plant which has grown from nothing in thirty years, bringing thousands of jobs to the area – here and among sub-contractors. They had produced a changing array of tech-nologically advanced products (typewriters originally, visual display units for computers today) calling for constant retrain-ing and redeployment of workers. Management is intensive, labour turnover is low and demarcation disputes present no problems. The bosses are subject to the same annual reports on their performance as the least skilled workers. They also use the same canteen, get the same holidays, and receive the same proportion of their pay when off sick. They've 'gone Japanese'. We shall never get everyone into enterprises like these, creating for their workers a secure and private welfare state. IBM's sub-contractors form a protective shock absorber, taking up much of the fluctuations in demand for their products. And because it's a good place to work IBM's people are a select team: you have to get your 'O' levels to sweep the floor there. So the 'welfare state' and its social security services will always be needed. But we could create more enterprises like this. To do so will call for profound changes in Britain's industrial culture, among managers and workers alike.

Meanwhile, I reflected after such visits, most of the political war-dances going on to the Left and the Right were equally irrelevant to these problems. So were the stop-gap palliatives of the Callaghan Government and the Manpower Services Commission who were building a bridge into the fog, with no pier in sight on which to rest its further end. Nevertheless, for the time being, most workers felt perfectly secure. Unemploy-ment was concentrated mainly among those on the fringes of the labour market, among women, school leavers, blacks, the least skilled – the people who have less prestigious jobs, a less central place in their communities, and who are less likely to be active in trade unions and political parties. That was always so. And that was why a Labour *movement* was created: not just a collection of trade unions fighting for their own members but a party and a congress which can speak collectively for all – for workers and their families, and for people beyond working age and without work. What could be hoped for from that movement?

The Labour Movement

With a Labour Government in office I was often in touch with the political and Parliamentary end of the movement. There were no solutions in sight there: although in office they were not in power. But how about the industrial end of the movement, now being brought into much closer consultation with the government? We met officials and members of the TUC fairly often, and attended their annual conferences.

At Blackpool in September 1977 the TUC passed a resolution about extending insurance benefits to more of the unemployed to keep them off means tests. That was good news for us. But the resolution was moved by our own Brenda Dean of SOGAT – the youngest member of the Commission – and was right outside the general run of the debate. That focused, as usual, mainly on technical questions about industrial injuries, safety at work and other matters which concern workers securely employed in the better-organized industries. At the doors of the winter gardens the youngsters of the Right to Work March chanted and bawled in their luminous orange jackets, reinforcing the conviction of delegates that serious politics deals with the employed, not the unemployed.

The debate staged on the Grunwick strike was a great celebration of the traditional themes of working-class solidarity. All the old battle cries were rehearsed, and at the end of it the Grunwick pickets in the front row of the gallery – women and blacks among them – were invited to stand up while the delegates applauded. Soon afterwards they were abandoned by the movement and defeated – as many had foreseen they would be.

At Brighton next year, Terry Parry, in his annual report to Congress as chairman of the Social Insurance and Industrial Welfare Committee, commented briefly on the inadequacy of benefits for the long-term unemployed. It was the only reference made in a long speech to the issues which the SBC had been discussing for the past three years. The debate which followed focused again on health and safety at work, and for a while on pensions. There was a brief and serious discussion of women's rights, particularly in the trade union movement itself, but without any reference to the social security system in which some of the most fundamental problems of sex discrimination are to be found. Child benefits and other issues to which we had devoted so much of our attention passed unmentioned. Jim Callaghan, speaking as Prime Minister, might have confronted the Congress with the realities all these men had seen in Britain's declining industries. Instead he asked them to be patient and vote for him; better times would come. He made shameless use of the threat of an early election to keep the Congress united and docile; then announced a few days later that he was going to soldier on into next year. It was a shoddy manoeuvre, for which the movement repaid him when the election came.

But in Blackpool again in 1979, under a Tory Government, a few fresh notes were struck. Ken Thomas of the CPSA, representing civil service clerical staff, spoke in a reasonably friendly way about the supplementary benefits review, and called successfully for a major reappraisal of the whole social security system to be made by the TUC itself. That may eventually lead to wider-ranging debate about social security questions within the movement. But it will be years before anything emerges from the exercise. Meanwhile a lot of irrevocable decisions will have been taken.

In the evening the Child Poverty Action Group and Shelter – poverty and housing pressure groups – held a joint meeting for delegates: the first of its kind. Only about half a dozen came, along with visitors like me: but Ken Thomas spoke again, calling upon unions to subscribe to CPAG. His was the first to do so. Others have followed. It was a new and hopeful development that civil servants and their critics in the poverty lobby had come to recognise that they had a common interest in making the public services better.

The youngsters on the Right to Work March seemed to have become part of the cheerfully tolerated street theatre of the Congress, but their slogans were as tawdry as ever: "Len Murray – out!" "Axe Thatcher!" The slight frisson of foreboding they once created had faded. The minority of purple-haired punk rockers among them reinforced the theatrical impression, but they at least were mainly working class: most of the others were better fed, better clad and better spoken than our typical unemployed claimants.

My main and deeply depressing feeling at this Congress was that the whole ponderous ritual was performed to an increasingly irrelevant script, written a long time ago. The main actors no longer believed their lines, yet lacked the courage to write new ones.

It was not surprising, under Thatcherite government, that no-one could talk about policies for deciding the level and distribution of incomes, or about the 'social wage' of public services which Barbara Castle had tried so hard to bring into the debate about incomes policies. For there were to be no incomes policies and the social services were all to be cut. Trade unionists had been driven back into mere money militancy: morally squalid. Many knew well that the only way of making some sense of free collective bargaining was to close ranks and reorganise the structure of the movement. If there were fewer unions in each plant, negotiators could fight for the longer-term development of their industries and a fairer division of their spoils, instead of the mutually destructive, short-term sectional interests which are all that many of them can now represent. But no one mentioned such possibilities.

These men knew – none better – that British industries were closing down all around them at a terrifying rate. Unless their members' productivity improves steadily, they will have declining incomes, and many will never work again. Unions too are declining as a result. Yet apart from a debate about micro-electronics, no-one talked about productivity or how to improve it. Better productivity will call for better training. Many knew that the British system of apprenticeship is one of the biggest obstacles to improvements in productivity. The unions are deeply involved in the Manpower Services Commission whose studies have shown that Britain's system of industrial training is worse than that of any other major industrial country. These problems were never discussed in debates on education and the economy.

Delegates knew that Britain invests too little and too inefficiently in re-equipping her industries. We get a lower rate of return on these investments than our competitors. Much of this is their own money: the largest flow of investment in British industry now comes from workers' pension funds. There was a motion seeking greater power for unions in the management of these funds. That very morning the financial columns of the newspapers reported that £6 millions more of the postal workers' pension fund – one instalment only in a continuing flow – were going into a shopping centre in Pennsylvania, USA. Since then the National Coal Board's pension fund has spent £66 millions on American property, giving it the ownership of the Watergate building in Washington among other things. No-one mentioned such issues, or said anything about the obligation of pension fund managers to ensure that their members' children still have jobs in future. Marks and Spencer buy 90 per cent of their goods from British producers, reckoning that prosperous workers will be good customers. The trade unions, along with the business élite in the City of London, have less imagination. Delegates focused instead on the danger that pension funds might invest in ideologically unsound parts of the world such as Chile and South Africa.

Most trade unionists know well that systematic reductions in working hours are almost impossible to achieve. The people who work the longest hours generally have the lowest hourly rates of pay, and the largest numbers of children to support. Anyone who tries to impose upon them leisure which they do not think they can afford is simply asking for more overtime and moonlighting. Restrictions on working hours do not generate extra jobs. Unless they are coupled with reductions in workers' incomes they could not possibly do so. Early retirement is equally ineffective as a general solution to unemployment. Many of the TUC's leading members serve on the Manpower Services Commission and its committees whose research has demonstrated these things. Yet early retirement and shorter working hours – with increased, not reduced, pay – were repeatedly presented to Congress as the only remedies for unemployment.

Meanwhile, everyone knew that the resolutions passed with most applause, like the decision to stay out of private health insurance and refuse to negotiate contracts for private medical treatment, would be disregarded in practice – as they have been. BUPA, the agency which organises private treatment, is now booming as a result. Congress is a forum, not a planning and decision-making body. It is dominated by some very able men whose life's work has equipped them to respond to initiatives taken by others. Their power to veto these initiatives is immense, but in fundamental matters they are not equipped to give a lead themselves. And when they speak, the dominant voices are those of the better organized manual workers and the lower middle class – the miners, the engineers, the electricians, the local government officers and so on – not the voices of people on the fringes of the labour market – the low paid, the unskilled, the unemployed, the one-parent families, the disabled and the handicapped. Meanwhile we have acquired a government which has turned its back on collective responsibilities for the poor and the unemployed, making instead a virtue of the beggar-my-neighbour morality of small-time capitalism. Its philosophy strengthens the hands of the money-militants, helping to create the kind of trade union movement which such a government deserves.

It's no wonder that some people have come together to set up the new Social Democratic Party. The pronouncements emerging from the Labour and Conservative Parties often seem so irrelevant to Britain's most urgent needs. But whoever gains power will have to deal with the same fundamental problems: the revival of investment, the reorganisation of industry, the redeployment and retraining of labour, the protection and representation of the workers involved, questions of productivity, management and training, the distribution of incomes and the levels of prices, and the provision of adequate social security and welfare services for those who cannot get jobs. Trade unions, working people and the rank and file of the Labour movement have to be deeply involved in any serious attempt to tackle these problems. So do managers and their spokesmen. Reorganising a whole society and creating a better world cannot be done by decree from the top or by clever people in the corridors of power. Trade unions, along with other traditional movements, have to play a major part in that task. The SDP offers no escape from that.

CHAPTER 5

Issues and Interests

As the attempt to reform the supplementary benefit scheme moved into its second act we began to look for solutions to the problems being debated and to identify the groups which would play a part in formulating those solutions. New issues emerged as we went on, and some of those we had already identified were reformulated. This chapter deals with a few of these issues – there were many others – and some of the interests which contributed to the discussion. In each case I present the conclusions we reached rather than the course of the argument which led to them.

Discretion, Rights and Welfare

The Commission's main job was not to philosophise about policies and politics but to help in running the supplementary benefit scheme. The work of paying benefits was done by civil servants accountable not to us but to the Government. We could advise them, but we could only give orders about the small parts of the scheme which the law left to our discretion. So discretion and its place in the system were our constant concern.

Public servants responsible for meeting need and preventing hardship encounter an infinite variety of human circumstances. They must have rules to guide them in dealing with the more common cases. Otherwise they would never get through their work, there would be no consistency about their decisions, and their customers (who should also be able to see the rules) would have no idea what they were entitled to. But no book of rules – not even the enormous volumes of instructions which the SBC and its predecessors assembled over the years –

could tell them what to do in every single case. So, if the service is not to become intolerably rigid, leaving urgent needs unmet, its officials have to be given some scope for dealing more flexibly with some cases. That's why we and our predecessors were given discretionary powers. But, once planted in the system, the humane little flower of discretion tends constantly to spread until it becomes a rank weed, threatening to submerge the whole service. Ministers, the SBC and their senior officials – benign people all, wanting to do good but unable to get the big increases in public expenditure which would raise benefits to more tolerable levels – are constantly tempted to use discretionary powers to get a little more help to the poorest people, and a little public credit for themselves. Barbara Castle, asking me in a cold winter whether we could buy woolly blankets for pensioners, was only doing what others in her position had so often done before.

The pressure groups constantly campaign locally and nationally for more 'flexibility' in the system, and bring some of the sharpest minds in the welfare business to bear on individual cases, taking them to the tribunals and the courts with the aim of establishing new discretionary benefits. The law says, for example, that the social security services cannot pay for medical treatment or education; that is the job of the national health service, and the education and training authorities. But how about osteopathy, which is not provided by the NHS? Is it medical treatment; and if not, should the SBC pay for it? And how about private training courses for heavy goods vehicle drivers? Should an unemployed claimant be prevented from taking one of these courses just because he is living on supplementary benefit and unable to pay the fees for it? Or should we leave it to the government's training services, which say that they are already training more drivers than the haulage industry can use, to decide who goes on the free courses they provide? Such cases were taken up every year, and sometimes led to increases in discretionary benefits.

The road to hell is paved with good intentions. The Commission, the staff, the pressure groups and the claimants, were all working in unspoken collusion with each other to spread the weed. You do not see the dangers of discretion unless you get into the social security offices and meet their customers. There

– on Clydeside, for example – you find mothers already queueing up in June to claim discretionary grants for the new shoes and clothes they'll be buying for their children before they go back to school in September. This is a degrading and very inefficient way of distributing small sums of money. If we are to make such payments on a large scale it would be much better to give all claimants with children a bonus every summer – as we already do for all pensioners every winter. It would be fairer too. Some Glasgow offices, for example, have for a long while been giving out ten or even twenty times more discretionary grants per head than offices not far away in the Highlands. Unemployed claimants are less likely to get these grants than other claimants, although their needs are usually greater, because they never get the higher long-term rates of weekly benefits. People ask for these extra payments because that is the only way in which they can increase their meagre incomes; but that does not mean they like the system.

Discretionary benefits are the most unpopular part of the service. Lone mothers cannot have enjoyed being urged by a pressure group to seek exceptional needs payments for sanitary towels. Discretion, once it runs wild, leaves claimants uncertain about what they're really entitled to. And even those who get some extra help are convinced that others – luckier, better informed or less honest than themselves – are getting far more. Nearly half the appeals which go to tribunals deal with claims for discretionary benefits. These benefits are unpopular with the public too. They provoked many of the angrier complaints people sent to me and to their MPs. The unlayable ghost of the non-existent man said to have got a furniture grant for a colour TV set was only one of the more bizarre examples of the folklore about discretion.

What the pressure groups, the social workers, the MPs and the welfare rights workers rarely recognised was that the cases which they took up tended to be the flowers of a system which had a darker underside. If a case was taken up by a powerful or well informed advocate, the system had enough flexibility to meet almost every need. But most claimants never see an MP or a social worker; and discretion to say "yes" can also be used to say "no". In hard pressed offices where the service would break down altogether if every claimant asked for every single thing he might get, the bombardment of demands was only kept precariously under control by local rules never to be found in the code books. We found some offices saying "no grants for clothing for children under school age" or "for men without a fixed address", for example. Pressures were also contained by the claimants' ignorance of their rights, by queues and squalor in the waiting rooms, jammed switchboards, lost files and the discourtesy of harassed and inexperienced staff. These deterrents were not deliberately organised. Fundamentally they were not even the fault of the staff. They were the fault of the SBC and the government which had promised more than the system could really deliver. We could not put these things right until we had a system which the staff could cope with in every properly organised office. Meanwhile, things were getting worse. The weeds were spreading.

But there was no lobby for change. To MPs, social workers and the pressure groups the system at least offered a chance of achieving small gains – a pair of shoes for an anxious or angry mother: something to justify another day's work. To the government, discretion offered a salve for tender consciences. Although it provoked a good deal of conflict, it cost very little and served to distract political attention from more fundamental problems: problems such as the inadequacy of scale rates – particularly for claimants with children – and, beyond that, the inadequacy of child benefits for low-paid workers with children. Even to the staff, who bore the brunt of the stresses created by this system, work on discretionary benefits offered a chance of retaining or increasing jobs; and that could not be disregarded at a time when cuts in the civil service were repeatedly threatened.

Thus to arrest the continuing spread of discretionary benefits and compel everyone to think again, we had to take rather belligerent initiatives: no-one else was going to do it. For a couple of years, with the full support of the Commission and our senior officials, I wrote articles 'Against Discretion', made speeches about it at every professional conference, and posed these problems pretty starkly in our Annual Reports. The angry response of some of the welfare rights people and social workers and my own ripostes to them threatened for a while to focus the whole debate about supplementary benefit upon a central dilemma. Do you want administrative flexibility, policies shaped by the Commission and its civil servants, and 'creative justice' attuned to the infinite variety of human needs? Or do you want legal precision, policies shaped by Parliament and the lawyers in tribunals and courts, and 'proportional justice' treating broad categories of people in predictable and reasonably consistent ways? Do you want discretion or rights? These were symbols, slogans and over-simplifications. Amidst the dust of a battle to change the whole culture of the social security system it was not easy to sort out the subtleties of some very complicated issues.

Why exactly does a social assistance scheme need flexibility? Why not make simple rules and stick to them? The law which obliged us to treat every couple living together as husband and wife in the same way, whether they were actually married or not, could not be interpreted in exactly the same fashion in anonymous, polyglot Paddington, and in Stornaway where everyone knows everyone and a fearsome morality rules. (I met a young man there whose minister was demanding that he and his wife kneel before the whole congregation on penitents' stools for public condemnation before their infant daughter could be baptised, because she had been born less than nine months after their marriage.) The flexibility which such differences in culture demand is not strictly a matter of discretion. It is a matter of judgment. The rules remain the same in all parts of the country. But what 'living together as husband and wife' and other provisions of the scheme actually mean has to be interpreted in different ways by social security officials in different places – and will be interpreted differently by independent local tribunals which deal with appeals against their decisions.

The difference between judgment and discretion may seem a bit of a mystery, but it's really quite familiar. A policeman has to use his judgment in deciding whether a driver committed an offence. University examiners use their judgment in grading the candidates' work. But each then has some discretion about what to do in particular cases. The policeman may decide not to prosecute an offender (he's unlikely to do it again), and the examiners may decide to pass someone who, strictly speaking, failed (he was off sick just before the exam).

So how about discretion? The job of a social assistance scheme is to prevent hardship. It needs discretionary powers, first, to deal with the unforeseeable emergencies which any of us may encounter. If your house is burnt down tonight with everything in it and you have no-one to turn to for help you may yourself need a discretionary payment – made, if that seems sensible, on a loan basis. Refugees arriving destitute from other countries have all been helped under these powers. The more promptly they can be helped, the more quickly they get on their feet and become self-supporting. The 'prevention of *hardship* in face of *urgent* and *unforeseeable* needs' – these are the key words for defining and limiting the uses of discretion in such cases. This kind of discretion is the least contentious and least difficult to handle. Yet even this is not entirely trouble-free. When a man with a car-load of children and no money on him broke down on the motorway one night and one of our officials sensibly made him a grant, later repaid in full, for the new tyre which enabled them to get home, headlines and angry letters reverberated for months afterwards.

Secondly, discretionary payments will always be needed to enable claimants to buy things which they cannot pay for out of their weekly benefit: travel to an interview for a job; the basic (usually second-hand) furniture and equipment for an unfurnished house or flat; and the replacement of major items such as a bed or blankets. These are examples of such needs. But – the Commission argued – we could in future give much clearer, simpler and more widely published explanations of these benefits and the kinds of claimant who are entitled to them. Many people still did not know that they could ask for this kind of help.

Discretion is needed, thirdly, to adapt the service promptly to new and unforeseeable developments. Anything important which happens in Britain hits the poor sooner or later. When Dutch elm disease swept the country many trees had to be felled, often at great expense. Some, already dangerous, stood in the gardens of the SBC's customers. Should the cost of felling them be met by the SBC, or by the local planning authorities which were responsible for deciding whether the trees had to go and had powers to pay the bill? (We decided that if the tree was an obvious danger to the claimant or the public – in the front garden, say – we would pay. But if not – if it stood in a neighbouring field, for example – then we would expect the planning authority to pay).

This is discretion used as the flexible leading edge of a public service voyaging through an unpredictable and constantly changing environment. There were many other examples of it. We had to cope with the new forms of fee-earning health care now being invented (osteopathy was only one of many). Our decision to take a tough line on these was designed to compel the health services – which are much better equipped than social security offices for the task – to decide what is or is not acceptable treatment for particular ailments. That will also ensure, when treatments are accepted by the NHS, that all poor people can get them, not only those living on supplementary benefit. Local authorities might not now be providing free chiropody for many old people if we had rushed in from the start to pay our claimants' fees for this service. We took a more generous line with the new forms of housing tenure (rental purchase, co-ownership, equity sharing and so on) which are constantly being invented. Each falls somewhere between owner occupation and tenancy, but is not quite suited by the reasonably effected arrangements we have made to meet housing costs in each of these more familiar tenures.

The fundamental questions to ask about this sort of discretion are, not how flexible or generous the service is, but: Is clear guidance promptly given to staff when the ship of state first bumps into new developments of this kind? Is that guidance published for all to see? Can people who are aggrieved by the decisions made get good independent advice and appeal to independent tribunals – and on to the courts if they wish to go that far? Do the tribunals and courts give clearly reasoned decisions which the bureaucracy, the customers and the lawyers can follow, or dispute? Is an independent body (such as the SBC) watching and reporting publicly how things unfold, and calling for amendments in the law when necessary? Will Parliament promptly incorporate the amendments it sees fit to accept, with the help of some MPs who specialise in social security matters – MPs who are therefore exposed to communications from the pressure groups and others who are expert in this field? If every link in this chain works well, then discretion becomes not an alternative to rights but the route to a constantly developing pattern of more clearly understood rights. It is only when some links in the chain are weak that the service becomes trapped in the dilemma of choosing between discretion and rights. To make discretion work properly we therefore needed to strengthen every link in the chain: to publish the rules in comprehensible English, to encourage the development of independent advisory services, to ensure that tribunals give clearly reasoned decisions, to report publicly on the evolution of the whole service, to explain its problems to MPs – and so on. Liberal-minded officials grasped that, but their more conservative colleagues opposed every one of these steps.

Finally, there is the discretion which every social assistance scheme needs from time to time to deal with specially difficult cases. I was out with a visiting officer on a wintry day in the centre of one of Britain's most prosperous cities. Without any premonition of trouble we knocked on a battered front door in a nest of rickety streets completely surrounded by cleared sites and new council flats. For years the demolition men had been circling this neighbourhood – closing in on it like some massive combine-harvester cutting the corn, marooning the poorest tenants and the more incompetent or unscrupulous landlords in the middle. Behind the door on which we knocked we found a married couple and four of their children, including one young daughter with a wan little baby of her own. A teenage boy, recently returned from an institution of some sort, had some reasonable clothes and bedding. His father had some worn though wearable clothes, but no bedding. No-one else had any proper bedding or any clothes in which they could decently be seen on the street. They were sleeping under old coats and rags. The mother of the family, with a broken leg encased in plaster to the hip, was sleeping on a battered settee. There was no cot and no clothes for the baby, and no food in the larder. A fire was burning in the grate, but gas and electricity had been cut off, and both meters had been broken into. The back door swung lop-sidedly on one hinge. The place stank. Indoors and outdoors it was frosty cold. This was an extreme case. But every visiting social security officer meets one like it from time to time. Isolated and neglected old people are often the victims. As you walk in through the door there's no point in asking how people got into this mess, whether their needs were 'forseeable', whether their weekly benefit is supposed to cover fuel, food and ordinary replacements of clothing (it is), whether they have recently had exceptional needs payments for furniture, clothing and bedding (as this family had), or whether social workers or some other service more expert in helping the most vulnerable and disorganised people should have been on the scene earlier. Nor is there any point in saying that the children involved should be removed from home. That will occasionally be the only thing to do, but harsh experience has taught us that the State may not do a better job of caring for them – and anyway no-one can prohibit their parents from having more. All of these questions may be important in the longer term. But you have to decide what to do there and then.

Money had to be found promptly to meet this family's more urgent needs. Social workers had to be informed (and very glad they were to hear of the young mother and her baby whom they had lost track of when she moved out of the city months before, escaping from the wreckage of a violent marriage). Later, advice had to be offered about the management of money and debts. The electricity and gas boards and the housing department had to be contacted, and direct payments to be deducted from benefit had to be arranged for fuel and rent. And it all took hours of skilled and patient work, in close collaboration with other services.

The fundamental questions to be asked about this kind of case are, not how flexible or generous the service should be, but: Do the social security staff have the time and training to handle it? Do they and the other services involved understand the scope and limits of their welfare responsibilities? Do all of them collaborate closely in helping the claimants? And do we have the legal powers, the administrative capacity and the public understanding necessary to draw a line between the few cases in which a lot of discretionary help may have to be given, and thousands of others in which the claimants should meet less urgent needs, less threatening to health and welfare, out of their weekly benefits, without extra discretionary help? Only if the service can reduce the mass of exceptional needs payments made in relatively straightforward cases can social security staff give proper attention to the small minority of really difficult cases which will always call for lots of discretion.

To sum up. Although discretionary benefits accounted for only one-twentieth of the supplementary benefit distributed each year, they presented problems which reached into every corner of the service. Any social assistance scheme needs discretion to meet emergencies of the fire, flood and refugee type; to meet needs which its weekly payments cannot be expected to cover (furnishing an empty house, for example); and to formulate rules for dealing with developments which could not be foreseen when the scheme began (Dutch elm disease, for example). With good administration and open government, all these three kinds of discretion can be made to work well and kept within clearly understood limits. The flowers bloom where they should: in the flower beds. It's the fourth kind of discretion, for dealing with cases of special difficulty, which threatens to go wrong, either because it is used far too sparingly, or because it runs riot all over the garden. It usually does both – in different offices – destroying consistency and confidence in the fairness of the system. To get this right, several things are needed.

First, there must be published rules which tell the staff and the tribunals how to make judgments about things which should, so far as possible, be matters of fact. For example: Is the family's home, health or safety threatened? Is the household likely or unlikely soon to become self-supporting? Are there children or other particularly vulnerable members among them?

Second, there must be a clear understanding of the service's welfare responsibilities. We spent many months trying to formulate that in consultation with other services and the trade unions involved. Our first responsibility, we said, for every customer's welfare, is to provide a prompt, courteous and efficient service. For the minority of customers who face special difficulties, we should offer advice about budgeting, debts and other money problems; we should arrange direct payments (usually for fuel or rent) when that would be helpful; and we should put them in touch with other services willing and able to help them (but only with the customers' consent – unless he is too ill to give a decision or the safety of children is involved).

Every social service, whether it is concerned with housing, education, prisons or employment, owes the public a similar explanation of the extent of its responsibilities for people's welfare, and the steps it intends to take to fulfil these obligations. Otherwise it tends to fall back on cruder ways of measuring its success, such as counting the output of dwellings, or the numbers of vacancies filled by job centres. Under pressure from the Commission and our sub-group on the quality of service, the DHSS made a start on this task in the supplementary benefit field – led by Geoffrey Beltram, an under secretary working with us who cared deeply about these problems. We also worked hard in conjunction with the Islington Social Services Department (with whose social workers our relations had been particularly bad) to organise better collaboration between such services and our own.

To attain these higher standards of service, even in offices where the work was most difficult, we needed more staff to specialise in helping customers in the worst difficulties. They should be better trained to give this kind of service, to collaborate more closely with other public services, and to make more consistent decisions about claims for discretionary benefits which did not fall within the first three forms of discretion – claims, that is to say, from people repeatedly seeking payments for things which their weekly benefits were supposed to cover.

In some offices, handing out masses of exceptional needs payments, these policies would bring about a sharp reduction in small grants for shoes and clothing. Meanwhile – in some of the same offices and in many others – there would be more grants for things which the weekly benefits were clearly not intended to cover: things such as furniture and bedding. To achieve these changes fairly we urged that all claimants – or at least all those with children who had lived on supplementary benefit for six months or more – should automatically get a lump sum payment twice a year. That we never got. But we made some headway with all our other proposals before we were through. We lost ground too. By withdrawing all powers – very rarely used though they were – to give help to single strikers in urgent need, the Conservative Government was to break with a centuries-old tradition that those who administer the poor laws must in the last resort prevent people from starving, no matter what the cause of their plight. But that comes later in the story.

Saints and Sinners

The Commission were always reluctant to intrude on people's private lives: "Give them the money and let them manage their own affairs" was our general rule. But if people became incapable of looking after themselves and there was no-one else to care for them, then the State had a duty to shelter them in 'Part III accommodation' (so named because it was originally provided under Part III of the National Assistance Act of 1948) or by paying someone to care for them privately. If they were living on supplementary benefit we would then give them an allowance to cover pocket money and the charge for their accommodation. The total would be equivalent to the standard retirement pension. If they could no longer manage their own affairs, we could make someone else – a close relative, a welfare worker or the warden of an old people's home, for example – an 'appointee' to collect and use their money for them. It was all logical enough if you were either completely independent or completely dependent: either way the State had made arrangements for you. But some people don't fit into either category.

'Patchwork' is the name of one of the best organised communes we dealt with. They had about 600 members living in about a hundred houses (more now) – mostly rather rickety 'short-life' property which was due to be demolished before long. Every resident has his own bedroom; but kitchens, bathrooms and sitting rooms are shared. About three-fifths of their people have special needs of some sort, but in each house these needs are deliberately mixed. The frail old man, the ex-prisoner, the unmarried mother, the addict on the way to recovery can each make a contribution and live with self respect, provided they are not shut up with people who all suffer from the same handicaps. The other two-fifths of the residents have no special needs. They go out to work in the ordinary way. Anyone who works for Patchwork itself – whether as builder's labourer or accountant – lives in one of the Patchwork houses and gets a standard rate of pay which depends only on the number of people he has to support: he earns more if he has a wife or child than if he is on his own. The only rules are that everyone must pay the rent, and refrain from doing anything which the other people in his house regard as intolerable. Standards vary a lot. But there is no shortage of candidates for any vacancies available. Patchwork was founded by young people who believed that it is inhuman to shut yourself away, alone or with your immediate family, in a semi-detached box, or to pass by on the other side of the road when you meet people who need a bit of help. They believed they had found a better way of living.

We encountered many other collective living arrangements of this kind. Most of them were devised by and for people who had special difficulties to contend with: offenders on probation, homeless people, alcoholics, battered wives, the mentally handicapped and so on. The leading spirits in these groups included saints and sinners of every kind. Sometimes themselves damaged in some obscure way, they often made creative use of their capacity to share in the pain of the outcast.

These groups presented all sorts of administrative problems. For example, should those of their members who live on supplementary benefit be treated as separate householders, or as members of a jointly shared household, or as dependent members of someone else's household – each of which would get a slightly different rate of benefit? With the help of officials, we did our best to sort out these problems, recognising that we were dealing not just with deviants but with life styles which were different from the conventional ones, and often more humane.

To be born again you must first die. People who are trying to rebuild a shattered personality or a shattered life can rarely do that all by themselves. They need, if only for a while, the close support of friends – the collective conscience of a sort of family. They must also have money, paid on terms which enable them to sustain whatever living arrangements they need or can tolerate. A good social security service makes a lot of other things possible: there are no battered wives' hostels in countries such as Italy or Russia where the state provides no income for a woman who takes her children and walks out of her home. Meanwhile other services too, concerned with housing, health, employment and so on, have to be equally supportive if such enterprises are to survive.

People are prepared to extend more tolerance to alcoholics than to many other deviant groups: probably because so many know someone – an uncle, an old friend, a colleague – who has become entangled in this affliction. While visiting social security offices in Leeds in June 1978, I went to the 'detoxification unit' funded by DHSS, which only took people so drunk that the police would otherwise have arrested and charged them. These men were then 'talked down' without using drugs. Those who could stick it for ten days were passed on to one of several houses in the inner city, also funded by the DHSS. In each of these lived a small group trying, with a bit of help from a visiting social worker, to sustain each other in their attempts to escape from addiction. They were able to use a day centre with a canteen and workshops which served people without a settled way of living. Other residents were recruited from this centre. From these houses men moved on to ordinary council flats which they shared without any supervision – but only when the group in their second-stage house thought that they were ready to try it. Even then, a bed was kept ready for them for some weeks so that they could move back into a closer and more supportive community any time they wanted to. At each stage the local social security office paid benefit to cover the costs of their shelter and care.

The main principles of the enterprise were clear, and often successful: to 'decriminalise' and 'demedicalise' alcoholism which otherwise puts people into prisons or hospitals; to create and sustain groups with similar experience who could help each other to cope with alcohol or escape from it; and to create for that purpose a network of small communities in clean, friendly, homelike settings. The little houses with their small rooms, colourfully furnished with second-hand carpets, pictures, mirrors and clocks, were such a relief to the spirit after the long dormitories and chill brickwork of our own new and far more expensive reception centre in the same city. It is too early to be sure how successful this project will be, or whether the local authorities will take it over. It was developed for, and by, alcoholics. But there is no reason why the idea should stop there. There are many other conditions which could be usefully decriminalised or demedicalised.

Visiting Portsmouth in March 1977, I saw a rather similar strategy devised for homeless and rootless people. It all began when the SBC closed the awful old reception centre we had inherited long ago from the poor law. We promised to take homeless men by minibus each night to a new centre built in Southampton. But local people protested at this neglect of the homeless in Portsmouth, and made a survey which revealed lots of men sleeping rough who had never used our centre at all. Seaports and military bases always attract, and create, homeless people. Before long, by dint of a lot of hard work, the city set up a whole network of local services for people without a settled way of living. There was a soup kitchen run by a retired man who seemed to spot every newcomer among his customers and tell him where he could find refuge; a shelter run by a voluntary group in buildings jointly provided and supported by the hospital service and the local authority; a voluntary home looking after homeless girls; and a row of old houses in the centre of town sheltering small groups of men extricating themselves from alcohol and isolation. The last of these enterprises was run by Sister Anna from Sicily and Sister Annunciata from Kerry — two women filled with a fiercely caring passion for their men, and famous throughout the town as 'the nuns' Mafia'. The whole network has since developed a good deal further. It was backed by the social security services, the health services, and a Housing Department which was beginning to allocate tenancies to some of the people whom they had previously neglected. Good places such as Portsmouth – there are also encouraging projects of this sort in Glasgow, Worcester, Coventry and Birmingham – convinced us that we ought to pull out of the reception centre business and leave local government and the voluntary organisations to take care of people who might otherwise be homeless.

But things do not go so well everywhere. It all depends on humane, courageous and effective people. And they in turn depend on a good local supplementary benefit team — prepared, for example, to find ways of covering hostel rents due from birds of passage who may be reluctant to claim benefits, to pay their rent or to stay in one place for long. In Oxford, where such birds have congregated since the Middle Ages, they were harassed by the police, and the local authority gave only derisory support to the marvellous work done for homeless people by Mike Hall and his helpers at Simon House. The council refused for years to let them build a new hostel on an ideal site – central, but well away from ordinary housing – with money offered by the Housing Corporation. (The new hostel is now open at last, thanks to tireless local campaigners.)

In South Wales, London and elsewhere local councils made shameless use of town planning powers to keep out even the smallest and best managed hostels which local housing associations offered to build for people with special needs of various kinds. Spokesmen for the tidy, conventional, semi-detached ratepayers did not recognise such people as human beings with equal rights to living space and the help of local public services. I was grateful to the Borough of Brent which enabled us to build a centre for the homeless, and their councillors who came with Reg Freeson, the local MP, to our opening ceremony. But in Poplar, with homeless men plainly to be seen on the streets in bitter cold weather, our attempt to build a similar unit was defeated at a long public inquiry by an unholy alliance of the local authority, neighbourhood associations, a law centre, a priest and the local MP. As they passed by on the other side of the road, all were anxious to assure us of their deep concern that shelter be found for the homeless – somewhere else.

Faced with demands that they cut their own expenditure, many local authorities are now treating support for voluntary groups as the expendable margin of their activities – first candidates for the axe. Voluntary work is bound to suffer. Far from being a replacement for the state's services it tends to grow in collaboration with them and in response to encouragement from government. If statutory and voluntary services both dwindle, we shall all have to rely increasingly on private profit-making enterprise. In counties such as Kent, where the local authority is closing its own homes and paying commercial operators to care for some of their vulnerable residents, local solicitors have told clients with money to invest that private homes for the old and the handicapped can now be a highly profitable business.

Private homes have been growing fast in recent years, particularly in what were once the boarding houses and private hotels of the cheaper resorts such as Margate and Rhyl. There were already about 150 private homes in Thanet when I was there in May 1979. Some were excellent. I visited Mr and Mrs Pargeter, a couple aged about sixty, who were looking after some sixty-five men in two converted hotels. Most of these men came out of big institutions for the subnormal where they had been shut away for years. "These are miracle boys" said Doris Pargeter, with vivid, proud affection. (Most of the 'boys' are in their forties and fifties.) "Many of them couldn't even talk when they came to us. We start with nursery rhymes. Then we sing. We've got a choir, and they go in their best suits to sing in all the churches round here: win prizes, too, when we go on holiday to Butlins."

The Pargeters bought an empty café across the road where their 'boys' serve tea to each other, play games and welcome handicapped people from all over the town. "They were being charged 17p on the sea front, so we said we could do it for 5." One day the parson called. "And about bloody well time, too" Mrs Pargeter told him. "Now he gives us lots of help." If one of her men falls ill, she sits up with him – sleeps in his room all night if necessary. "And if he dies I lay him out with two of the boys to help. We shed our tears over him, and I tell them 'He's gone to Jesus and we'll all meet again in heaven. We won't be living on social security then – but we'll have a good laugh about the times we've had together.' Then we all go to the funeral next day." The Pargeters give these men all the pocket money due to them – daily if they cannot cope with it weekly. They lay in good second-hand clothes for them from all the jumble sales in the district. And they insist that they can feed, clothe and care for their residents – paying for their haircuts, shoe repairs and so on too – with the money they get from social security. These are feet-on-the-ground, head-in-the-stars people – good shepherds of the private homes industry.

But there are other homes which ship busloads of handicapped people in on the day they open. (Once you've got eighty or more, the local authority won't dare to close you down because they couldn't afford to shelter all these people themselves.) Some will *only* take people living on social security payments and insist that the proprietor of the home be made the 'appointee' to draw their benefits for them. Pocket money may seldom be handed over: it's quite legal to provide services 'in kind' instead. It is often proprietors of this sort who demand extra grants from the local authorities, and constantly nag the DHSS for higher weekly payments. If people like the Pargeters are the good shepherds, these are the hirelings of the industry – in it for the money.

On the Commission we worried a good deal about these things. It's not at all surprising that there have been scandals about the treatment of elderly and mentally handicapped people in private homes. We pressed for half a dozen developments which would help to protect them.

First, there should be more coherent government policies about the development of residential care, the parts to be played in it by public and private enterprise, the standards to be aimed for, and the distribution of homes required in different parts of the country. Many other industries police their own members. Years ago the builders set up their own National House Builders' Registration Council which guarantees house buyers against defective work, keeps a constant watch on the standards of registered builders, and strikes them off the register if they let the side down. The old and the handicapped are entitled to as much protection as house buyers. If only to protect themselves against their shoddier competitors, the good private homes should set up and police a register of their own. But they won't do that unless the DHSS and its Ministers make it clear that they will step in themselves if nothing is done. We found the civil servants dealing with health and personal social services much less prepared to give a lead in such matters than their colleagues on the social security side of the Department. But before we were through, things seemed to be moving – thanks largely to the help of David Hobman, Director of Age Concern, who joined forces with us on this.

There should be more and better training for the staff of private and public homes alike. This most difficult kind of caring attracts fewer trained people than many less demanding forms of social work. That has often been said before, but to little purpose. The problem is a fundamental one. Those who are supposed to care for the poorest and the most completely outcast members of society have generally been less well trained and less highly paid than people dealing with more respected customers: they share some of the social stigmas which afflict those whom they look after.

Local authorities or local social security offices should have powers, when necessary, to compel the proprietors of homes to keep accounts which show how money for their residents is spent and how much pocket money the residents get. Voluntary groups such as Mind, Age Concern and the Transport and General Workers Union Retired Members' Association, which have local branches of volunteers who are concerned about these questions should be encouraged to keep in touch with people living in homes and to watch over their welfare. (One of the nastier cases of exploitation which we discovered only came to light because members of a local Mind group found out what was happening in a home for the mentally handicapped.)

Finally, and for the longer term, we should reflect on the fact that the great majority of those in homes for the mentally handicapped are men. Why do women seem to manage better? The same goes for alcoholics, ex-prisoners, homeless and rootless people, and other vulnerable groups. There may be basic genetic differences at work. But perhaps their families and the neighbours feel more willing to care for women at home? Perhaps a girl pottering about doing a few domestic chores is more acceptable than a boy doing likewise? (For many families with two working parents supplementary benefit, at present levels of unemployment, now pays in effect for a domestic servant – the daughter who cannot find a job. No-one complains, or dubs her a 'scrounger'.) Or perhaps handicapped and deviant men are more threateningly powerful and sexual, and evoke less protective feelings than their sisters? We must ask how in future the community could extend greater tolerance, and give better care and more acceptable roles to men as well as women.

As Husband and Wife

These were some of the new issues on which we focused

attention and sought help from people outside our own service. We also had to deal with the old issues too. 'Cohabitation' was one of them. Even to explain exactly what it meant was difficult.

In a working-class suburb of Birmingham a woman, separated long ago from her husband, lived with her mentally handicapped son. They had nothing but the meagre income provided by supplementary benefit. Down the road a man in his fifties – a window cleaner – lost his wife who died after a long and harrowing illness. Stricken by grief, he was unable to look after himself properly. So the woman took him in and cared for him. He managed to keep working, paid for his board and lodging, helped her to look after the handicapped boy and did a few jobs around the house. But a neighbour wrote an anonymous letter about them to the DHSS and before long an official was knocking at their door. He asked a lot of questions. What rent did the man pay? Who did the shopping? How much help did he give in the house? Where did they sleep? What did they call each other? Did he take the boy fishing with him? Later the woman's benefit was cut off on the grounds that she and her lodger were living together as husband and wife, and he must therefore maintain her. Since he could not afford to keep her and the boy out of his meagre earnings he drifted away, leaving her to claim supplementary benefit again a few weeks later. Both insisted that they had never thought of themselves as husband and wife, and there was no reason why anyone else should do so.

A graduate student in Oxford claimed supplementary benefit. His grant had run out before his thesis was completed. The visiting officer found him living in one room which was almost entirely filled by a double bed. The garments and cosmetics scattered about made it clear that the room was shared – by a girl working as a secretary, he explained. But they were not living as husband and wife. They were only together for this term: after that – who knows? The DHSS did not cut off his benefit, deciding that this was not what most people meant by a husband-and-wife relationship. Not in Oxford, any way. "And besides", said the visiting officer, "how do you argue with a man who's studying to be a doctor of philosophy?"

When I first came to the Commission, cases like these caused more anxiety and provoked more anger and complaint than any others we dealt with. Benefit was refused or withdrawn on grounds of 'cohabitation' (as it was then called) in about 8,000 cases a year. The claimants were nearly always women, and three out of four of them had dependent children. These cases brought the State into the most private areas of people's lives. They compelled officials to investigate matters they would much prefer to keep out of: all for the administration of a basically unworkable rule.

Decisions about people's claims for benefits should be based on clearly defined principles and ascertainable facts. But what does 'living together as husband and wife' mean? Could *any* definition of this relationship be devised which would fit equally well the circumstances of middle-aged working-class mothers and young male students, remote Highland villages and the anonymous, teeming metropolis? Parliament, which compelled us to apply the rule, had never tried to define it. And when in 1973 the Lord Chief Justice was asked to "give some guidance upon the phrase 'cohabiting as man and wife' " he swiftly handed back the poisoned cup, saying that the phrase was "so well known that nothing I could say about it could possibly assist in its interpretation hereafter". How on earth did the State get into all this?

In most countries people compelled by poverty to ask for social assistance have to show that their families, wherever they may be living, cannot support them. In Germany they have to pass a three-generation means test, calling for information about the incomes of the claimant, his parents and his children. But in Britain, even in the days of the local poor law, questions were only asked about relatives of the claimant who were living with him. It was a household means test, not a family means test. And it was hated. That's why it was abolished at the insistence of Labour Ministers who served in the coalition government during the war. Henceforth the 'unit of assessment' became the individual or a married couple, and any dependent children living with them. No special arrangements were made in the law for people 'cohabiting', but the Assistance Board and their successors were expected to use their discretionary powers to ensure that such people were treated just the same as married couples. That meant that a

man living with a woman could claim money for her and her children whether they were married or not. But it also prevented her from claiming in her own right. And if he had a full-time job he was expected to support her and her children. There were very few lone parents on the books at that time: so few that no separate statistics were kept of their numbers. Since then the numbers of divorced, separated and unmarried parents have grown steadily all across Europe. And in Britain the proportions of them who depend on social assistance seem to be higher than anywhere else. That is due partly to quite creditable reasons: mothers on their own have more assured rights to benefits and to housing than they have in many other countries; they are not compelled to go to work; and their benefits are more generous in comparison with wages. But it is also due partly to less creditable reasons: women's wages and the benefits they can draw for their children when they are at work are generally lower here; and day care for children is scarcer and poorer than in many other countries.

Whatever the reasons, constantly growing numbers of lone parents live on supplementary benefit. There were 320,000 of them in 1979 – 11 per cent of all our claimants, caring for nearly 600,000 children between them. A count made in 1971 showed that one-parent families on supplementary benefit amounted to two-thirds of all the unmarried mothers, more than half the separated mothers, one-third of the divorced and one-fifth of the widows in this country. Meanwhile sexual relationships and other patterns of behaviour have been changing. In the early 'seventies more and more allegations of cohabitation were being investigated, and more women were being deprived of benefit on these grounds. But they were less inclined to tolerate this kind of thing than they used to be. More and more of them were appealing to the tribunals and to their MPs. What should be done?

There are similar cohabitation rules all over the place. They are supposed to apply to widows' pensions, war pensions, civil service pensions, family income supplement, child benefit – indeed, to every scheme which makes any special provision for widows and other people left on their own, or for people caring for children single-handed. But other schemes are less contentious: partly because the extra money gained from child benefits and other payments which favour lone parents is less than the extra money lone parents gain when the whole household is living on supplementary benefit; and partly because the public tolerates laxer or more generous administration in other schemes than it is prepared to tolerate when it comes to means-tested benefits for the poor. They are less likely to write anonymous letters to the DHSS about widows and war pensioners: "After all", they say, "how she lives is her own business: she (or her husband) *earned* her benefit."

Over the years the SBC, perturbed about this part of their work, made successive studies of the question. The latest and most thorough had been completed just before I took over the chairmanship. We found that although most cases were well handled, things went wrong much too often. A lot of the women whose benefit was cut off were back on our books again a few weeks later – which suggested either that their relationships had not really been like that of husband and wife, or that our intrusion had broken up what might have become a more lasting union. So we went back to the basics to see whether we could ask the Government to abolish the 'cohab rule' altogether. But nothing we could do would reverse fundamental social trends which were producing more and more lone parents. Like other fair-minded people, we wanted to see more help given to these parents and their children; and it was plain that over the next ten years or so Parliament would be doing that, and our scheme would be one of the instruments used for that purpose. But you cannot expect the taxpayers to provide extra help for one-parent families unless someone tries to ensure that the money only goes to families which really do have only one parent in them. Whatever the pressure groups might say, Parliament was not interested in abolishing the rule and neither was the electorate.

Since we could not get rid of the rule, there was nothing we could do but try to operate it more sensibly. So we resolved to lay out much more clearly what we meant by 'living together', and to give every claimant involved in the procedure a printed explanation of the rule and our principles for administering it. Henceforth *no* questions should be asked about sleeping arrangements or sexual behaviour. We resolved to give claimants more time, if they seemed to need it, before deciding whether or not they were 'living together'. And when benefit had to be cut off we resolved to be more generous in tapering off payments in cases where hardship would otherwise result. Indeed, we would go on paying indefinitely if low wages and the presence of children from an earlier partnership would otherwise have driven the family's income below the supplementary benefit level. We called for better-trained staff who would specialise in dealing with these cases. They should consult their supervisors more carefully before taking drastic decisions, and collaborate more closely with other services whose help might be needed. Finally we asked for a change in the wording of supplementary benefit law which would abolish the term 'cohabitation', with its sexual connotations, and substitute what seemed the more decent and objective phrase, 'living together as husband and wife'. We published our report *Living Together as Husband and Wife*, on 4 March 1976. The press conference was a shambles. The BMA called a press conference on the emigration of doctors an hour beforehand, half the journalists went off to that, and the fierce women sent along by the pressure groups whom I had invited to liven up the occasion terrorised the few press men who remained into almost complete silence.

But of all the leader writers, only one – in *The Morning Star* – failed to approve our main conclusions. An MP wrote to me, saying it was high time the Commission dropped all this 'Victorian nonsense' and abandoned such rules. An emollient reply was drafted for me to send back. But I threw it away and wrote instead to tell him that the Victorian nonsense was his, not ours, since the rule was imposed on us by Parliament. Any time he could get a majority of his colleagues in the House to repeal it I would be delighted. Till then, we had to administer the present law. (He saw the joke and wrote a friendly reply.)

Our proposals were the best choice of evils. But the whole experience left me ruefully feeling that it had perhaps been a mistake to publish a report about them. (An unavoidable mistake, for the public were entitled to know where we stood.) I tried repeatedly to explain at public meetings that we were not sex police and not in the least concerned with people's morals. "You don't have to do a lot of snooping to find out who my wife is. We use the same name. We live together in the same house and have no other home. We have children, eat together, go shopping together, go on holiday together, share the same overdraft, quarrel about who uses the car. . . . Unless *some* of these things are to be found in it, the relationship is unlikely to be that of husband and wife." But it was no good. Whatever I said, any public discussion left people (including, I feared, our own staff) with a confused idea that it was really all a matter of who slept with whom. Meanwhile, we still had to get something done about our new procedures. This would call for fresh instructions to staff, training, and endless negotiations with the civil service trade unions who opposed the creation of new specialists. These, they argued, tended to make other people's work less interesting and responsible (which also weakened their case for higher pay).

What, in the longer run, should be done about this rule, in a world where there are going to be more separated and divorced couples, and more lone parents? (A world, too, in which the Finer Committee's expensive proposal for a guaranteed maintenance allowance, paid by the state to all lone parents, is dead.) For lone parents who want to earn their own living there should be more opportunities to work, full time or part time; better wages for women; and better child care arrangements. Until we can organise our economy properly and bring the general level of unemployment down, progress in those directions is bound to be slow. Mothers or fathers on their own who cannot earn their own living, or who decide (as they are fully entitled to) that they would prefer to care for their children instead, must get paid for the important work they do. If the Social Services had to do the job instead it would cost far more. The payment can be based on any one of three different principles.

(1) We can treat lone parents as poor people, needing means-tested social assistance of some sort – as we do now. That is the cheapest solution. It gets help to those who need it most. But it fastens some sort of cohabitation rule upon them.

(2) Or we can treat them as victims of an insurable risk. We already do that for widows, most of whom get enough in benefits – paid regardless of their incomes – to lift them

well above supplementary benefit levels. They are a popular group, and the fiercest lobby in the business: no-one asks of widows – as they do of unmarried mothers or the divorced – whether they were responsible for their own plight. In future we could extend their kind of insurance benefit to people who are divorced, separated or unmarried and looking after children. Insurance benefits, being linked through contributions to the level of wages, have until recently kept pace with inflation better than other benefits. A new contributory scheme of this kind would be expensive because it must be generous enough to lift people off means-tested supplementary benefit; and it would still leave them entangled in a cohabitation rule of some sort. If the extension of such benefits to new groups of lone parents took shape piecemeal, it might divide the 'family lobby' rather than unite them. Moreover this device would not really be aimed at the crucial needs involved.

(3) The crucial needs arise from an unavoidable responsibility for caring for someone who depends on you. That could be recognised in a scheme for supporting lone parents, along with many others who care single-handed for particularly frail or handicapped people. The scheme for parents would have to start with a really adequate level of child benefits. Likewise, for those caring for an adult the scheme would have to be built on an adequate system of disability benefits. Then, as with child benefits today, a premium could be added to both schemes for those who have to do the job single-handed. That premium should not grow too large lest it bring increasingly intolerable cohabitation rules with it – which is why the basic level of child benefit should be raised first. Being addressed to family responsibilities, this proposal should help to unify rather than divide the pressure groups which together constitute the family lobby. But such benefits have not in the past kept pace with inflation. And, even if in future they were taxed, they would be expensive. Yet they would be a much better way of spending money than the present married man's tax allowance which reduces income tax for all married men, rich or poor, whether or not they have dependents in their households.

None of these solutions would altogether solve the problem. But the third would be best because it deals with the essential needs involved. These arise from a household's obligation to devote many unpaid hours of work to caring for its dependent members, and from the fact that some households have only one fit person of working age who has to choose between doing this, or going out to earn a living, or driving themselves to exhaustion trying to do both.

With the help of a good deal of hindsight I have tried in this chapter to summarise our main conclusions about three major clusters of issues, without explaining how our ideas evolved or who played a part in shaping them up. But we never tackled these questions all by ourselves. It is time to turn to the people who were contributing to the debate, inside and outside the civil service. Since they were much concerned about the 'living together' issue it seems fitting to start with the women's movements.

Women's Rights

Late one night in October 1977 I was sitting in one of Capital Radio's studios opposite Adrian Love – a lean, denim-clad young trendy with an incisive wit. After a few hurried words of greeting, we set out together on an hour-long phone-in programme. I did my best to respond to whoever rang up, while he very effectively chaired the proceedings and played the taped advertisements interspersed among the questions. Three of our first five calls came from women in Gingerbread – the one-parent families' group. "They're always first off the mark" muttered Adrian; "I think they keep a round-the-clock radio watch." But their questions were good sharp-edged ones.

It was the same when delegates came to my office from the Federation of Claimants' Unions, and at the public meetings we were beginning to hold to discuss the ideas coming up in the review of the supplementary benefits scheme. Women were often our most challenging critics. They not only made complaints, proposed reforms and sought information; they also conveyed a sense of outrage about the assumptions and practices of the man's world in which we live. So much of poverty consists of the plight of women – widows, lone parents and the wives and mothers of the unemployed and the handicapped. We had to understand the movements which expressed their feelings.

The soap operas, the advertisements on the back of the cornflakes packets, and the stories in the women's magazines still convey the picture of the family which William Beveridge had in mind when the social security system was taking shape after the second world war – a family in which marriage is for keeps, fathers go to work, mothers stay at home, children go to school and all of them do these things full-time. "On marriage," said Beveridge, "a woman gains a legal right by her husband as a first line of defence against risks which fall directly on the solitary woman. The attitude of the housewife to gainful employment outside the home is not and should not be the same as that of the single woman. She has other duties."

The supplementary benefit scheme still treats the couple, together with any dependent children living with them, as the basic unit to be provided for. And it is the man who is expected to support them. If he cannot do so, and is neither sick nor retired, then he must register for a job before he can claim benefit; and as soon as he gets a full-time job he must stop drawing benefit, no matter how low his pay may be. If he leaves his job voluntarily or is sacked for misconduct, he suffers punitive reductions in benefit for up to six weeks when he comes back on the books. If he appears to be making no effort to find work, various sanctions can be brought to bear to encourage him to try harder. In the last resort he may be prosecuted – and about half a dozen men are each year. But his wife is not required to register for work while she lives with him, and will never be pressed to find a job. If she does, that does not disqualify the family from benefit (although she will only be allowed to earn £4, plus travelling and other work expenses, before their benefit is reduced by her wages, pound for pound).

These arrangements must always have posed problems for the large number of working-class families – far more than Beveridge recognised – who depended partly or wholly on a wife's earnings. In the past these earnings were often intermittent or concealed. But women have now, on a much larger scale, entered the 'formal' economy in which workers are

statistically recorded, taxed and insured. They were drafted
into what had hitherto been men's jobs during the two world
wars, but most went meekly home again as soon as men
returned from the forces. Their new hold on the labour market
has built up more slowly, not so much by taking over men's
jobs, but because industries and occupations generally filled by
men have declined, while others generally filled by women
have increased. Agriculture, mining and manufacturing have
lost huge numbers of men. Meanwhile, service industries have
gained even more jobs, mainly filled by married women doing
white collar work, often part-time. The men's losses were
concentrated particularly heavily in Scotland, the north of
England and parts of Wales where so many of the declining
industries were. The women's gains were concentrated
particularly in the growing towns of the midlands and the
south – towns depending on government work, new light
industries and commercial offices.

By 1971 only 46 per cent – less than half – of all married
couples conformed to the assumptions of Beveridge and the
story writers in the women's magazines, with men going out to
work and women staying at home to look after the house and
the children. Both men and women were in work or seeking
jobs in about 40 per cent of cases. In about 12 per cent both
were retired. And in the remaining 2 per cent, the wife was at
work or seeking a job and the husband was not. These trends
have probably gone further since then as more and more
couples share or exchange the role of breadwinner and that of
caring for dependent members of the family, and as more and
more men have lost their jobs.

A social security system founded on Beveridge's assumptions repeatedly makes difficulties for families which adopt the
new patterns. The man in the household may take over the
domestic duties, or go back to college to take further training,
while his wife goes out to work and earns their living. Or each
may do these things part-time. But if she then loses her job, or
becomes sick, or has a baby neither of them can claim supplementary benefit. For she is not entitled to claim, and he can
only do so if he first registers for work and shows he is prepared
to take a job. Worse still, if she does stay at work, perhaps at a
very low rate of pay, she cannot claim family income supple-

ment, because FIS has to be claimed by the man in the household if there is one. If he leaves her, she can claim FIS as a working lone parent, or stop work and live on supplementary benefit instead. But if they stay together and don't want to starve, he may be compelled to resume what the law regards as his proper role, working or claiming, while she has to give up her job and look after the children. Such cases and the problems they provoked were among the most harrowing of those which crossed my desk each year.

Our scheme was unfair to women in other ways too. During the 'fifties and 'sixties the huge influx of women into work had gone to a large extent into part-time jobs. But the supplementary benefit scheme assumed that people either worked full-time or not at all. That's why claimants were only allowed to earn £2 a week, their wives only £4, and lone parents £6 before we had to deduct earnings from benefit, pound for pound. When visiting claimants, I met women who had felt compelled to abandon work when their husbands lost their jobs. I met lone parents, too, who would willingly have made arrangements for their children so that they could go to work part-time. But why bother? They would miss their children and end up working for the State. The few pounds of their earnings they could keep would quickly be swallowed up in paying for the services – the frozen food, the launderette, the hair-dos – which a working woman particularly needs. Too often one sensed that these women would soon lose the confidence to return to work.

Who would help us get these things put right? Feminist groups were already protesting about them. But they represented different and partly conflicting movements. First there were trade unionists and political activists concerned with social justice – and therefore with the rights of women who are so often confined to the lowest paid and least secure jobs. Many of these people were not campaigning feminists. But they took up women's causes because, as women gained a firmer foothold in the labour market, there were more and more of them in the groups they represented.

This branch of the movement was strongest in the growing, prosperous towns of the south and the midlands where women were gaining jobs fastest. It was much weaker in the coal fields and the centres of heavy industry in Scotland and the North East. Campaigners of this sort had helped to make real gains for women over the years. In the Civil Service, as in other professions, they had got rid of the rules which before the war compelled women to retire when they married, and they had in the early 'sixties secured equal pay for men and women doing the same work. But they were less concerned about mothers, housewives, pensioners and women in general than they were about organised workers. Trade unions were only beginning to press for better child benefits. They were often the first to object to arrangements which would have made it easier for women to work part-time or to resume work after a few years spent at home caring for children. And they were scarcely concerned at all with supplementary benefit claimants.

A second loosely linked set of women's groups were centrally concerned with the rights of women in competition with men. These were mainly led by middle-class graduates, many of whom were more determined to gain equal rights for women in an unequal world than to create a more equal society. They were strongest in London and the southern university towns where such women were most heavily concentrated. They focused upon jobs, pay, training and promotion – the central concerns of the Equal Opportunities Commission – and they relied on Parliament and the courts to make and enforce new rules, as middle-class people have always done. Sometimes these tactics worked. From 1975, as the Equal Opportunities Act began to bite, women's wages started, slowly but significantly, to catch up with men's. But women in industrial areas and in the less skilled manual jobs gained much less from this branch of the movement. Indeed, in manufacturing industries the decline in jobs for women was proceeding proportionately faster than the decline in jobs for men. However we got some help from this sort of feminist because they were concerned with the woman bread-winner's right to claim FIS, and with her right to claim supplementary benefit on equal terms with men when she needed it.

A third branch of the movement was concerned mainly with the integrity, self-confidence and inner consciousness of women as persons. Excluding men, they worked in sisterhoods of various kinds for personal growth and heightened awareness of women's identity, focusing particularly on sexual behaviour, new forms of family, new forms of health care, abortion, childbirth at home, the protection of battered wives, the right of lesbians to adopt children and other questions which deal with women's rights to claim their own lives and bodies. They operated on a smaller and more local scale than the previous groups. They rejected the tendency – a typically male one – to rely on big organisations, negotiated deals and legislation. And they often relied for leadership on women whose experience in childhood or in their own marriage had led them to reject conventional styles of family life.

This third kind of feminist spoke for many people living on supplementary benefit. Some of their 'spokespersons' were so belligerent towards men and bureaucracy that they alienated the staff in social security offices and achieved little. But others did very effective work for battered wives, lone parents, homeless families, women who may have been unfairly alleged to be living with someone as his wife, and others who needed companionship, moral support or a tough advocate.

These groups, too, were stronger in the big cities of the south than elsewhere. Women's self-confidence varies, and rules about such things as 'living together as husband and wife' have different meanings in different parts of the country. That became clear when instructors in the DHSS's national training schools wrote, acted and video-taped a convincing little drama to illustrate for their students the new rules which eventually followed from our proposals. It was prepared by instructors at the Preston school who thought the imaginary claimant interviewed in their drama *was* 'living together' with her lodger. Their colleagues at the Billingham school in the north-east of England generally agreed. So did staff going as students to both schools. But instructors and students at Hinchley Wood, serving southern Britain, were generally convinced the couple were *not* 'living together'. (So was I.) Confronting and discussing that typical dilemma of a nationwide social assistance scheme could have been good education for all concerned. Disappointingly, the instructors re-wrote their script to make the case clearer and avoid inconsistencies. Bureaucracies are troubled by ambiguity.

Sometimes united, sometimes in conflict, the three branches

of the women's movement might be said to be working, respectively, to achieve a liberated society, a liberated sex, and the liberated woman. But that rather glib summary is an oversimplification which conceals the diverse motives and traditions within each group.

Some of the young women working in Alan Palmer's review team took up the question of equal treatment for the woman breadwinner claiming supplementary benefit or FIS. The Commission were determined to get these obvious injustices put right, and spent hours discussing the exceedingly complex problems posed by any reform of this kind. We produced a long chapter, spelling out the options, in our annual report in 1977. But officials did the hard work involved. Many of the old hands resisted these proposals, fearing they would introduce needless complications into the scheme. We were confident, however, that we would surmount their opposition if we could formulate workable proposals for reform. Extending FIS to the woman breadwinner would not cost much; and giving married women equal rights with their husbands to claim supplementary benefit if they were their families' breadwinners would cost nothing at all in benefit, although it would probably call for some more staff. Meanwhile the EEC Commission in Brussels had in December 1976 produced a draft directive for their Council of Ministers which called upon all members of the Community to give equal treatment to men and women in social security schemes – a proposal which our Ministers would find very difficult to disregard. The EEC's directive was not just a coincidence. Officials in DHSS, including members of the team reviewing the supplementary benefit scheme, had battled hard (against others in their own Department and in the Treasury) to get this directive prepared and approved.

We discussed these problems with the TUC, the pressure groups, and the Equal Opportunities Commision – from whom we got the warmest response. Ladies Lockwood and Howe, their Chairman and Deputy Chairman, were both very helpful. But it was not enough to look only at the customers of our service. We turned next to the other side of the counter and considered our own staff. Did women get equal treatment there? We first explored this issue in the Fawcett Lecture (one of a series honouring a great pioneer of the feminist movement) which I gave at Bedford College in February 1978. We took the argument further in a chapter of the Annual Report we published in 1979.

Although the answer to this question proved to be a good deal less discreditable to the service than the answers to the previous questions, the Commission's determination to take up the issue provoked a lot more resistance within the bureaucracy. Many officials plainly felt that this was a question of management, well outside the Commission's powers. Moreover, if taken too far, it would provoke trouble with the trade unions representing the staff. With cuts in staff already being demanded by the Labour Government, management's relations with the unions were precarious enough without introducing unnecessary contentions. Our concern was about the quality of the service offered to the public. Thanks largely to the persistent support of officials working closer to the Commission, the reluctance of the Establishment branch of DHSS to let us have the data we needed to explore this issue was surmounted.

We concluded that the Kemp-Jones Committee which had reported in 1971 on 'The Employment of Women in the Civil Service' (under the chairmanship of a woman from the DHSS) was probably right in saying that: "men and women with similar qualifications now generally compete equally for entry into the service", and "departments are, on the whole, fair in their treatment of women in relation to promotion and probably better than most outside employers". But the results achieved were much less reassuring.

The proportion of women among established civil servants in the administrative and clerical grades of DHSS, starting from the larger grades at the bottom of the hierarchy were: clerical assistants, 83 per cent; clerical officers and the similar grade of local officer II, 71 per cent; executive officers and local officers I, 43 per cent; higher and senior executive officers, 16 per cent; principals and above, 7 per cent. More than two-thirds of these officials were working on social security. In the social security services themselves the core of senior managers was even more completely male. Of the 552 local office managers, only 5 per cent were women, and of the twelve Regional Controllers (the big barons of the provinces) none were women. Thus we had a service largely staffed by women and managed by men. Yet most of our customers – taking supplementary benefit claimants and their dependents together – were women.

The imbalance was due partly to the fact that the senior managers were mostly men in their fifties who had been recruited to the civil service just before and after the war, before the massive influx of women into administrative and clerical jobs had got under way. But it owed even more to two other features of the service. Women did pretty well until the age when they started having children. Then, because the DHSS offers very few (and declining) opportunities for part-time work, and makes it difficult for people to return to full-time work after a period of several years out of the service, most of them disappeared. Thus a service dealing with poverty and family problems of every kind was operating as though experience of raising a family and managing its affairs was a disqualification for this kind of work. Teaching, nursing and social work, all of which also rely heavily on women, are more successful than the civil service at retaining experienced people and enabling them to return to work after a break.

The reluctance of the trade unions to change things is understandable. Their pensions (for the long years from age sixty) depend on the salary attained in the last year of service. The unions are accountable to members – the women as much as the men – who do not want a lot of married women returning to compete for the few senior posts available. But that should not be allowed to deprive the service of experienced staff, now compelled to resign, who could do a better job, with lower turnover, at lower cost in training than the new recruits who replace them.

We made no progress on this issue. But all these questions were worth raising, for they will not go away. Although the economic disaster into which Britain is now being driven will set back many of the developments on which women have pinned their hopes, it appears to be destroying jobs for men about as fast as jobs for women. Thus more and more families will probably depend upon a woman's earnings. Men and women alike, and their children too, will more often be working part-time or short-time. They may also go back to school temporarily or part-time – and that poses more problems for a service which insists that it is the job of the education authorities, not the DHSS, to support students.

The Supplementary Benefits Commission was not a platform from which to conduct campaigns for women's liberation and every other kind of social reform. But new life-styles, new family relationships and new work roles were taking root, and it was our duty to adapt our service to these social changes. Failure to do that inflicted hardships which were seen – often justifiably – as discrimination against women. But these injustices arose, more fundamentally, from discrimination against men and women who had chosen, or been compelled, to organise their lives in ways which the bureaucracy was not yet equipped to recognise. When I asked social security staff in our local offices whether they would welcome arrangements which made it easier for experienced people to go part-time for a few years and come back later to full-time work, those who nodded their heads in approval were usually the young married staff, men as well as women. Those who rejected the idea were usually older, women as well as men.

The missing movement among all these campaigns for liberation is a consciousness-raising group for men which would help to liberate them from inhibitions about tenderness, from a sense of inadequacy with children, and from all sorts of pressures to live up to other people's preconceptions about what a man should be. For lack of such a group, present campaigns for women have led many people to reject the care of children, family and home as humiliating or worse, because women have for too long been unwillingly confined to these tasks. Yet, performed well, by men or by women, they are more demanding and creative than many of the jobs done in a social security office or any other place of work. This was yet another reason why our plea for easier interchange between part-time and full-time work for civil servants was so fiercely resisted by managers of the system. If women could devote themselves half-time, or temporarily full-time, to looking after their families without losing their place in the service, men would soon be asking for the same rights. And a good thing that would be.

The Poverty Lobby

The pressure groups which together form the 'poverty lobby' came into their own as people recognised that more traditional political movements were never going to do justice by all those who were excluded from an increasingly affluent society. Other factors were at work too: it was during the 1960s that people who had gained their first, formative political experiences since the second world war came to form a majority of the electorate. For them, inflation, full employment, rising living standards and growing public services were part of the natural order of things. The State played a dominant part in their lives as the provider of education, medical care, subsidised housing, legal aid and much else. Faced with an unresolved social problem, earlier generations turned first to collective action – forming trade unions, co-operatives and friendly societies – or to philanthropy – raising money and recruiting volunteers for charitable work. The new generation turned first to the State and the media – circulating petitions, ringing up journalists and organising 'demos' to support their demands for action by government.

But while they looked to the State to solve a growing range of problems, this new generation of reformers had learnt that governments and the movements on which they rested were also among the causes of these problems. Philosophies and strategies first learned in the Campaign for Nuclear Disarmament, which took up an issue neglected by all the main political parties, were later brought to bear on problems of race relations, housing, women's rights and poverty in general.

The people on whose behalf these campaigns were mounted were often impoverished not so much by basic scarcities of resources as by their exclusion from the services which central and local government provided for the mass of the population. They were the newcomers to the city, the furnished tenants who did not get rehoused in slum clearance schemes, the blacks who did not get their fair share of the jobs filled by the employment services, the lone parents who were given low priority for council housing, gypsy families excluded from their accustomed sites by planners and the police, and so on. Some of the campaigners dramatised their causes in old fashioned radical terms, presenting the excluded minorities as victims of capitalist oppression. But cooler study of what was actually going on often showed that the poor were in fact victims of government and the majorities which gave governments their power – often Labour majorities, since the poor tended to live in the more impoverished working class towns. Government was often their employer too – paying low wages in the hospitals, on the buses and elsewhere. In or out of work, the poor also felt that they were the victims of the practices of staff in the public services – police, social security, housing and job centre staff, for example, all increasingly strongly represented by trade unions. Thus the groups which assembled around the causes of the poor during the 'sixties and 'seventies constituted a poverty lobby called into being by conflicts of interest between the impoverished and the people of middle England. By 'middle England' I mean the established local citizens with secure jobs and average incomes who had been waiting for years on the housing lists and resented 'queue jumpers' who were rehoused because they were homeless, the people who did not want gypsies, alcoholics, ex-prisoners or mental patients living down the road, the people who welcomed immigrants to man the buses and staff the hospitals, but did not want them living next door or competing for their own jobs and housing.

To call the campaigners the 'poverty lobby' is a journalistic over-simplification which stresses the common causes of the pressure groups, not their differences which are also important. Working in the SBC's field there is the Child Poverty Action Group, its low pay research unit and citizens rights office. Best informed and most professionally organised of the lot, the CPAG is redolent still of the London intellectuals who originally set it up. Tony Lynes, Frank Field and Ruth Lister, its three successive directors, are outstandingly able people. It has a few local groups which sprang up spontaneously in university towns, and it is beginning to seek contacts with trade unions. But it has never aspired to become a national movement or had the staff to create one. Poor people who seek its help get an excellent service, but rarely become involved in its work. Operating on its more limited front, the National Coucil for One Parent Families is a similar pressure group which does an excellent job of case-work, while keeping an eye on the government and agitating for reforms which will help the families for whom it speaks.

To form an effective national movement with local branches up and down the country you need a common interest capable of uniting people in different social classes. Age Concern, Shelter (the housing pressure group), Mind (concerned with the needs of the mentally ill and handicapped), and the groups representing the physically disabled, mentally handicapped children and 'gay' people have all achieved this to varying degrees. We were challenged by all of them from time to time, both about individual cases and about general policies. Genteel and most unstrident of them all is the National Council for the Single Woman and Her Dependents; and very effective too. Speaking for women who sacrificed careers and marriage to stay at home and care for elderly or handicapped relatives, they played a crucial part in pressing for the introduction of new benefits for the disabled and those who look after them. These groups are all middle-class led and mostly London based. Although all are concerned to some extent with people who are out of work, the most glaring omission from the list of interests they represent is – as ever – the unemployed.

Other groups have been set up by the customers of the public services themselves. Built up from the grass roots, they are usually a loose federation of local activists whose capacity to stay united, to gain a hearing at the centres of power – or even to pay their fares to London – is precarious. Gingerbread, speaking for lone parents, came to meet me several times and took up individual cases and policy questions effectively. The Federation of Claimants' Unions (which does speak for unemployed people, along with other claimants) operates most convincingly in parts of east London and in Strathclyde. We met them first in October 1977. One of our officials said afterwards "How ill most of them looked" – a piece of education which was one of the purposes of these meetings. Grass roots democracy, coupled with the constant turnover of claimants, means that CU delegates are a changing group with whom the bureaucracy has difficulty in establishing continuing and trustful relationships. But they learnt to be tough yet good tempered, and to focus on policy questions rather than wasting time with individual complaints which can be better dealt with in other ways. Standing liaison groups, representing the users of social security services at each social security office, could provide a firmer basis for developing this kind of relationship where it is most needed – at the local level.

Things did not always go so constructively. CHAR, the Campaign for the Homeless and Rootless, tried to operate both as an indigenous group of the State's customers speaking for themselves, and as an intellectual pressure group. Those for whom they spoke were the most desperately deprived of all our claimants. To act in both roles called for particularly robust leadership, which CHAR lacked. They spoke with different and uncoordinated voices, sometimes seeking meetings with us or our officials, and then without warning raucously vilifying us all through press releases. Eventually they got themselves (and me, trying to keep communications open in the midst of the uproar) publicly attacked by the Civil Service Union which represents staff in the reception centres for homeless men and women. Later, when the Commission was at last on the brink of getting a thorough, and overdue, official inquiry launched into serious allegations which CHAR had made about violence by staff of the Camberwell reception centre, they blocked it for many months by setting on foot a prosecution in the courts which eventually failed ignominiously. Things would have become worse still if Robin Cook (MP for Edinburgh Central where there are many homeless men) had not acted as CHAR's adviser and intermediary: a shrewd, humane man, with no wish to gain any advantage for himself from these conflicts.

How much did the poverty lobby achieve in our field? They took up thousands of individual cases, got mistakes put right and thereby helped to improve standards of service. They also used their experience to press for larger changes. As I and our officials came to understand each other better, I could sign most of my letters to MPs without doing more than skim the replies drafted for me. But letters from the pressure groups I always studied with care: the better organised of them wrote to me rather than to our local offices only when a point of principle was involved and they had thoroughly researched the case.

Specific changes in policy or practice brought about by the

lobby were usually small. But they were not trivial. Mind stumbled accidentally upon some ancient guidance, prepared back in the days of the National Assistance Board, about the selection of people to attend re-establishment centres which take men who seem to have lost the capacity for regular work. These instructions would have excluded men who were flagrant homosexuals or likely for other reasons to disturb the neighbours. We had often been attacked over these centres for running what some people alleged to be a kind of prison camp. Now we were attacked for excluding deviant minorities from the opportunities the centres might offer. But Mind's point was a good one. Shortly afterwards, in October 1977, I met a spokesman of this group, together with others representing offenders and gay groups, to discuss the whole issue. I do not know whether they realised that they were in a small way making history: the paper we presented for discussion was in fact a draft of the revised 'A' Code instructions prepared in response to their original, justified protests.

More often we collaborated with pressure groups on projects in which we ourselves might take the first initiatives. We worked with David Hobman and his people at Age Concern to get higher standards of care laid down and more effectively enforced in the rapidly growing number of private homes for aged and mentally handicapped people. We got the help of Paul Lewis at the National Council for One Parent Families in presenting fair comparisons of the living standards of lone parents and other claimants in our Annual Report for 1978. We sought the housing pressure groups' support for a reorganisation of housing subsidies for the poor. We worked with the fuel pressure groups to formulate better policies for helping poor consumers meet the rising costs of energy. And I shall always be grateful to CHAR who were the only people who came forward to support us at the public inquiry into our plans for setting up a new resettlement unit for homeless men in East London.

These exchanges exerted a more pervasive influence which was perhaps more important than the few specific victories they won for the pressure groups. Regular meetings held with bodies like CPAG and the Claimants' Unions accustomed the Commission and its officials to the idea that any important change in policy or procedure would eventually have to be discussed face to face with the people who would be most directly affected by it. That knowledge affected the tone of our more private discussions. It certainly exerted an influence on the proposals emerging from the review of the supplementary benefit scheme, as I shall explain. No service dealing with impoverished and vulnerable people can afford to protect itself from this kind of influence.

In return, the pressure groups gained a clearer grasp of the directions in which public affairs and the government's thinking were moving. This enabled them to contribute later in a more cogent and timely way to public debate. That was to prove important when the Bill which reformed the whole supplementary benefit scheme was going through Parliament. The Opposition and Government back-benchers rely heavily on the pressure groups to help them prepare speeches and propose amendments to legislation. To do that public job effectively these groups must keep in very close touch with the more private debates going on in the corridors of power.

Once united, the pressure groups can exert an important reforming influence. But when divided they obstruct reform. I was invited to meetings at which all the relevant groups tried to work out policies for the support of one-parent families (starting on 3 April, 1976), and for fuel subsidies (on 8 December, 1978). They were interesting seminars, but on neither occasion did we reach any convincing agreement about policy. As a result, MPs have been equally reluctant to act. They are still waiting for a clear lead on either subject.

Thus if it is to be effective the poverty lobby must hammer out agreed policies about the main issues in its field. It is surprising that these groups have no regular gathering at which general policies can be thrashed out and the political networks required for effective campaigns kept in working order. Such a centre could also provide the Hansards, the lists of sympathetic MPs and journalists, the election manifestos, the indexed court cases, the summaries of research findings and Government reports and the other resources which they all need.

The housing lobby is better organised. In July 1978 I and our deputy chairman spoke at different sessions of Shelter's annual conference. This gathering of the housing clans takes place at the University of Nottingham. It brings three groups together: spokesmen of tenants' associations and local community activists (the customers of the housing services); civil servants, local councillors, housing association trustees and housing managers (the providers of these services); and the hairy, denim-and-anorak brigade (the reformers – mostly radical graduates of the late 'sixties and early 'seventies). Journalists, academics and others interested in housing come too. A ritual of conflict btween the lobby and the central and local bureaucracies is maintained but kept within bounds. For each side – the progressive officials and councillors, and their critics – depends on the other to make progress in the directions they want to go. The important Housing (Homeless Persons) Act, passed the year before, would never have been achieved or been put into practice effectively without that alliance.

A good deal of hot air is talked at such gatherings. Yet they are a forum in which the evolving moral standards of a civilised society and its governments are formulated and asserted. They have taken over the moral leadership of Britain from our emptying churches and our increasingly pragmatic political parties. This country would be a poorer place without them.

But the people who go to these gatherings must ultimately convince middle England – the general run of voters and taxpayers – if they are to get anything done. Now that the era of full employment, rising living standards and growing public services has come to an end, much of the willingness of middle England to listen to reformers has evaporated too. Already in the late 'seventies Labour Ministers were aware that, although they could never satisfy their critics in the poverty lobby, the government's aims were generally far more progressive than the electorate's. Their Conservative successors more brutally recognised that the lobby was electorally naked: it had no votes to deliver. "They are not leaders of a movement", said a Cabinet Minister at a meeting I attended in July 1979, soon after the election. "They're crickets in the field." Once that has been recognised, it becomes clear that the most effective way of dealing with the lobby is to tell it to go away. Ministers who meet the pressure groups and listen to them are half way to conceding them the moral authority which is their only remaining claim to be heard.

In this new climate the pressure groups must think again. Good casework on the problems of individual clients will be as important as ever. If they can organise and accurately present the evidence from that work they will gain a hearing in Whitehall. People who really know what is going on in the field and who are capable of communicating what they know cannot be indefinitely neglected. Government knows remarkably little about the latest impacts of its policies on people. As the new supplementary benefit scheme and other recent changes in policy come into force, the government will have to listen to people who can provide this information.

Meanwhile even a Conservative government with a large majority is not impervious to public opinion. But it will be moved by the opinions of its own back-benchers and the people they listen to, not by critics on the Left. Thus far it has given way before the rural lobby and the churches over sub-postmasters' anxieties about proposals for new ways of distributing benefits and over proposals to cut free school transport. Conservative women's groups have gained a hearing in pressing for better child benefits. Small businesses are treated with respect too. Pressure groups will be more effective if they can build a network of local supporters which extends into these and other areas of the nation's life, hitherto unfamiliar to them.

Meanwhile, on the Left, the lobby needs to make common cause whenever it can with the trade unions. Too often the pressure groups have neglected or attacked the staff of the public services on which poor people depend. That does no good to anyone. With public service unions in a mood to recognise that a better service for the customers may mean greater public support and fewer cuts in staff, the time is ripe for reconciliation and collaboration.

These are essentially questions of tactics. Strategies need re-thinking too. The lobby should recognise that the living standards of the *working* poor – the ordinary, low-paid family with a couple of children – are the fulcrum on which every other form of social provision has to be levered forward. These people cannot be expected to care for those who are even more impoverished unless they first feel that the community cares for them. The working poor are often members of the trade unions, political parties, churches and other groups with which the lobby should be making closer contact. To build an alliance with them the lobby may have to carry words like 'family' and 'children' on its banners – symbols to which ordinary people find it much easier to rally than 'poverty'.

The Academics

We were going to need the help of the academic community too. On 30 June 1976 Geoffrey Otton chaired his first meeting of the Social Security Research Policy Committee. This body, on which some outside advisers serve, considers plans for the DHSS's internal and externally sponsored research in the field of social security. It is a forum rather than a decision-making group, but it can be influential. Thus far its influence had been pretty baneful, provoking some cynics to call it the Social Security Research *Prevention* Committee. The outsiders did their best, but powerful under secretaries generally poured cold water on new initiatives. External research, they plainly felt, was a threatening intrusion to be kept at arm's length. They were not much more enthusiastic about the Department's internal researchers. Although these amounted to a potentially powerful team of economists, sociologists, statisticians and the SBC Inspectorate, much bigger and better equipped than any other group in Britain working in this field, they were divided into four separate sections and placed in different parts of London, as far distant from each other as possible. They rarely met. Although they produced some interesting work, very little of it was published.

Failing at this meeting to generate any enthusiasm for research among officials responsible for contributory benefits, Geoffrey pushed through an agreement that some work would be mounted, inside and outside the Department, in support of the forthcoming review of supplementary benefits, and on other important supplementary benefit issues – mainly problems of management and the 'take-up' of benefits.

In June a group of us went to the social security summer school which is mounted for a week each year by the DHSS in Cambridge. This is a training exercise for some eighty local office staff, among whom some social workers and officials from other branches of DHSS were mixed. But its real value lies in giving senior officials at headquarters an opportunity of swopping ideas and learning a great deal from intelligent local office staff who really know what's going on in the field.

I already knew most of the academics doing serious work on social security. Some came to our monthly seminars at the SBC, and I met many more at public debates I had been holding in universities and polytechnics up and down the country when visiting social security offices. In July, Geoffrey Otton, Alice Perkins and I went with about half a dozen other DHSS people to the annual conference of the Social Administration Association which assembled about 130 researchers and teachers, including most of the independent academics and many official researchers working in our field. We had good talks with them. There we chose the man we wanted as the next director of the summer school – Professor Roy Parker. He was on study leave in Canada, where we 'phoned him, and he agreed to take on the job for the next four years, making the school into quite a power house of ideas. The conference ended with a hilarious pantomine ('The Real Supplementary Benefits Revue'), written and produced by David Bull, active in the CPAG, with the help of his colleagues at the University of Bristol. In it the SBC and its chairman were cheerfully lampooned. We were beginning to build a network.

How should research be mounted and used? The Government has a doctrine about this, based on the first published report of the Central Policy Review Staff. Its author, Lord Rothschild, said later in response to some of his critics "I was only trying to explain how we did it in Shell", and the rules he laid down were in fact pretty sound for technological studies of the kind that the oil industry needs – studies in which the aims and principles of policy are not in question. (Research designed to produce a more economical internal combustion engine, for example.) But for policy studies, in which aims as well as methods are always in question, something more sophisticated is needed.

The Rothschild doctrine has encouraged government and the academic community to assume that the proper way to organise publicly funded research is to award a 'research contractor' a grant and send him off for two or three years to work on a 'project', designed to throw light on some limited, clearly defined, practical problem which his 'customers' in the bureaucracy want to solve. This teaches academics seeking government support for their work to steer clear of major policy questions and fundamental social issues. Governments don't like them. But they rarely have to say so. Instead, they set up Research Councils with specialist committees, or they consult highly qualified specialist advisers. Since really important problems can never be confined neatly within the confines of one specialism, senior academics themselves can usually be relied on to blackball the most challenging proposals. (If they get through the economics committee they're bound to fall foul of the sociologists, or the political scientists, or the statisticians – or someone.) Karl Marx and Sigmund Freud would never have got a grant from the Research Councils.

After labouring for two or three years on his project, the aspiring researcher has to write a report. It should be as 'scientific' as possible – meaning logically rigorous, accurate, and devoid of contentious passion. If it is a good piece of work its author will be rewarded with a grant for another project. Or he is made a professor and loaded with administrative duties by his university. Either way, he is unlikely to trouble anyone much. Thus scholars are tamed to work in a harmless and modestly useful industry in the service of the régime and the social order over which it presides.

Other scholars and their students, bored by this sort of work, wander off into 'purer' theory of the sort that calls for no research grants. Confined to the seminar and the library, they retain their intellectual independence and may say some quite fierce things. But, having been taught that reason must be divorced from passion, they too readily conclude that passion need not be disciplined by reason. And too often, without personal, immediate experience of the practical problems they are dealing with, or of the political realities of the day, their social criticism degenerates into an art form which has no cutting edge on events.

Things need not be so bad as this. A research project can be a useful way of organising a study, and ensuring that it is completed and its findings published and critically discussed. But the period from the day when a researcher starts planning such a project, through the phases when it is funded and he recruits a team to work on it, to the point when he completes and publishes his work and someone who could make practical use of his findings actually reads and ponders them is likely to be at least five years, and more often ten. By then the problems and priorities, the officials who originally sponsored the study and the Party in power will all have changed. Thus publications are at best only half the product of a research project. The other half, too often wasted, is the education of the people who work on it. If they do their job properly they become pretty expert about their field, and they get to know a lot of people working in it as researchers in various countries, and as politicians, administrators, journalists, local activists and so on. Properly developed, the research project can therefore become a vehicle on which other activities may in time be loaded and from which a variety of contributions may be expected. If the people proposing to do the work are good, and capable of getting better, and if the broad themes which interest them are sufficiently important to be worth discussing five or ten years hence, they are probably worth backing – not because they will provide technical solutions for predetermined problems, but as an investment in the education of people who will later make a contribution in ways which cannot be foreseen to the elucidation of problems which are equally unforeseeable.

Funding research should be an investment in the creation of productive social networks. As they learn enough to be effective, researchers and their students should be encouraged to contribute to policy analysis and public debate in ways of their own choosing: as teachers, as witnesses giving evidence to public inquiries, as political activists and journalists, as administrators, committee members and expert advisers, and more generally as members of a concerned and responsible intelligentsia sharing common interests in important problems. Nit-picking committees trying to manipulate the projects of research 'contractors' to match the supposed needs of official 'customers' lose sight of these basic realities. Too often they encourage researchers, hungry for money, to conceal what they really want to do, and encourage officials to pretend they know what their priorities will be five or ten years hence when in fact they do not even know what next year may bring.

At the SBC we tried to do better than this. We certainly got a lot of new research going, inside and outside the Department. We got a lot more of it published. We got our own people into a lot of seminars with outsiders where each learnt a good deal from the others. And if DHSS officials want a graduate student to review for them the literature on a particular aspect of social security, a professor to sit on a committee, or an expert to tell them about social security practice in other parts of the world, they now know whom to ring up.

More creative relationships were established for a while during the 1960s in the field of education. Some terrible mistakes were made during those years. Nevertheless, things happened: secondary education was largely reorganised, higher education was enormously expanded, and policies for primary education were recast. The academics made mistakes too: they were far too slow, for example, in exposing that crooked psychologist, Sir Cyril Burt whose bogus findings on inherited intelligence were quoted with respect for much too long. But they made important contributions to thinking in all these fields – not only by proposing solutions but by helping to establish among a wider public that policies for education were an important topic worth serious attention. Economists such as John Vaisey, sociologists such as David Glass, statisticians such as Claus Moser, doctors such as James Tanner, along with men who had outgrown any disciplinary label (Michael Young, James Douglas, Chelly Halsey, Basil Bernstein . . .) served on committees, contributed evidence to them, broadcast and wrote articles for the press, and engaged in lively public controversy about education. They sparked off each other and their colleagues in other countries. Ministers such as Edward Boyle and Anthony Crosland knew them personally. Their practical contributions to the debate, built on a good deal of earlier and more theoretical work, really began with the Robbins Committee on higher education. Soon a much wider public was involved: every national newspaper, posh or popular, had to have a correspondent specialising on education.

Policies for social security, taxation and the distribution of incomes merit, but do not get, equally serious attention. (Employment policies, however, are now beginning to attract the intelligentsia they urgently need.) The lack of an effective intelligentsia in the field of social security is one reason why British performance in this field lags so far behind many neighbouring countries, and why attempts to bring about reform are so easily blown off course by economic crises and passing shifts in the political wind. This is partly the fault of the Department in question. In the longer run a bureaucracy gets the kind of research it deserves.

For the present government, on many crucial issues, that means no research at all. As I write, violence engulfs poverty-stricken quarters of some of our biggest cities. In the past, under Labour and Conservative governments alike, some excellent research was done on these cities and their problems. Those who have read it are unlikely to be surprised by what has happened. They clearly include Peter Walker, the Conservative Secretary of State who sponsored much of this work and predicted this sort of trouble. Some of the research was initiated by the Social Science Research Council, some by the Department of the Environment, and some by the Centre for Environmental Studies which was originally set up by the government to do this kind of work. The man personally responsible for bringing much of this work to an end and for closing down the Centre for Environmental Studies altogether is Michael Heseltine, the present Secretary of State for the Environment. By a strange irony it is he who has now been chosen to go round the inner cities and 'see for himself' what is happening there. His time would have been better spent in reading, and acting upon, the findings of research launched by his predecessors.

CHAPTER 6

Reform

In the last chapter I discussed some of the issues we looked into as we reviewed the social assistance scheme and some of the groups which played a part in debating them. Many other issues and groups played a part in the story. In this chapter I return to the story of our attempt to reform the scheme. Act two of the drama, in which problems and solutions are freely debated, gradually gave way to act three, in which we attempted to reach agreement about a feasible set of proposals, followed by act four, in which some of these were brought to Parliament and incorporated in the law.

Reviewing the Scheme

Most of the Commission's work was devoted to keeping the system running: preparing for our monthly meetings; deciding how to cope with the firemen's strike; discussing difficult cases; redesigning forms and leaflets; getting briefed about the latest big fraud; getting a few words into the annual argument about the up-rating of benefits; meeting regularly with Ministers; receiving visitors and delegations (pressure groups, the staff trade unions, foreign scholars, journalists and research students); dealing with the weekly flow of letters from MPs; visiting social security offices; and so on. But our central concern was the review of the supplementary benefit scheme which our Ministers had launched in response to the questions posed in our first Annual Report.

Since September 1976 the review team, led by Alan Palmer, had been working away on the main problems with the help of others inside and outside the DHSS. Their analyses and proposals went to regular meetings of the steering group of under secretaries from this and other Departments of Government, chaired by Geoffrey Otton. Still the SBC's Chief Adviser, he had now taken on a much larger job, becoming the deputy secretary in the DHSS generally responsible for all social security matters. The review team's papers were also discussed by the Commission at their monthly meetings. But the team were independent of all these groups. Listening, explaining and amending their proposals, they had ultimately to present their own report to Ministers.

They were re-examining fundamental questions of social assistance which had not been publicly reconsidered since 1948. What should be the basic unit to be supported: an individual, a family or a household? Who should be entitled to claim? How should claimants' 'requirements' be defined and measured? Should particular groups be entitled to higher rates? (Long-term claimants, aged claimants and blind claimants were all payed at higher rates, for example). What resources of income and capital should be taken into account in calculating people's benefits, and what should be disregarded? Who should make the decisions? To whom should they be ultimately accountable? With what rights of appeal? How much discretion should they be given, and for what purposes? Questions like these called for expert knowledge of a labyrinthian system of laws, rules and procedures. The welfare – the survival even – of thousands of people depended on the answers given to each of them.

The Commission was determined to open up all these issues and to expose them to public debate. So was the review team. In doing that they were taking more risks than we were. This had hitherto been one of the more private branches of British government. Before we began, the SBC and its officials had done their best to avoid journalists, claimants' unions and staff unions. No-one could be sure how the public would respond to the opportunity of peering into this cupboard. If the Commission was publicly attacked, we would defend ourselves. But officials might well be uncertain whether to keep their heads down and see their proposals shot to bits undefended, or whether to do battle and risk embarrassing their Ministers with some unguarded or misquoted phrase. If they got involved in political disputes they might disqualify themselves

from advising future Ministers who could be the very people
with whom they had been disputing. We had to know why we
wanted open government before asking people to risk their
careers in this way. There were at least four reasons.

We had to know what we were talking about. The
supplementary benefit scheme was exceedingly complicated
and its operations varied from case to case and from place to
place. To understand how it really worked, we had to hear
from people who had experienced this service in every kind of
way – as claimants, welfare rights workers, social security
officials, researchers and so on. We would soon be submerged
in a flood of paper: expert memoranda, legal opinions and
statistics. If we constantly bore in mind that we would have to
discuss every proposal for reform with claimants and staff –
the people most directly affected by any changes to be made –
it would help us all to keep our feet firmly on the ground.

Many features of the scheme which mattered most to claimants depended not on the law but on the Commission's policies
and the constant stream of guidance we sent to local offices
about these policies. Yet no-one had elected us: we were eight
individuals appointed by the Secretary of State, representing
nobody. His authority depended ultimately on his Party's
majority in Parliament. But ours depended on retaining a
reputation for knowing a great deal about the scheme, and
frankly disclosing what we knew. We had to earn this credibility
publicly day by day.

Once it was known that the scheme was under review, a lot
of people would be sure to gain a hearing in the debate.
Taxpayers, tax gatherers and managers of the economy would
gain a hearing through the Treasury; managers and staff of the
civil service would gain a hearing through the DHSS, the Civil
Service Department and the civil service trade unions. The
more effective pressure groups representing some – but never
all – of those who depended on the scheme would also be
heard. Each had an axe of some sort to grind. Each would want
to suppress some proposals which might be worth exploring
before they could be given a proper airing. There would also be
leaks and hostile speculation in the press. (The editor of one of
the Sunday papers told us that he received about one leak a day
from civil servants or politicians in central government. "And

the Guardian gets more", he added.) Thus if powerful interests were in any case going to be heard, we had better give everyone a chance of getting into the act. And if hostile commentators would in any case do their best to make fools and knaves of us, we should at least focus their attention on relevant rather than trivial issues, and give more fair-minded people a chance of commenting too.

Major reforms of the social security system take longer than the life-time of a government. (The introduction of an earnings related pension scheme took fourteen years, and it will take many more before it makes much impact on our pensions.) Thus we did not want to get Ministers or their Party publicly committed to specific proposals yet, for that would encourage the opposition – who would probably form the next government – to take a contrary line. Ministers should not be committed until they were ready and able to act. Meanwhile we had to find ways of defining the issues to be tackled, raising public expectations that something would be done and keeping up a head of steam in favour of reform, so that proposals emerging from the review would not be shelved and forgotten. Although lots of people were dissatisfied with the scheme for various reasons, there was at the start no consistent pressure for change. Public controversy which gets too heated might defeat us by giving Ministers the idea that the whole question was too hot to handle. But we had to take that risk: unless we were prepared to generate a good deal of controversy, we would get nowhere. So every meeting we held with staff in local and regional offices, every conference speech, every seminar, and every encounter with pressure groups, journalists, social workers and others became an opportunity for talking about the problems and solutions being discussed in the review.

With the support of the Commission, the review team decided that they ought to have some well prepared choices to offer people before calling for general public discussion. But from the start they held private meetings up and down the country with staff, pressure groups and academics. We had a good one at the University of Bristol in September 1977. Officials argued freely with each other, and so did the pressure groups. I remember David Bull, active in the Child Poverty Action Group, indignantly challenging David Hobman, director of Age Concern, about the increasingly generous way in which pensioners' earnings were disregarded. "They're supposed to be 'retirement' pensions – and they bloody well *should* retire if they're drawing pensions and let younger people have the jobs!"

The review team got a research organisation to study public attitudes to social assistance. It was, amazingly, the first time such a thing had been done in any review of the social security system. Most people, it soon became clear, found the whole scheme bewildering, and many were convinced that it had been made deliberately incomprehensible to prevent people from claiming benefits. The team's report on the first set of major issues, prepared after long discussions with the Commission and the steering group, went to Ministers early in 1978. It was published under the title 'Social Assistance' in July. The decision to publish was taken by the Cabinet after discussion in a Cabinet committee. For a while all seemed to hang in the balance, and I was 'phoning members of the committee to explain why they should publish. Peter Shore agonised for a fortnight before we were allowed to include a chapter, already drastically shortened by his officials, proposing the reform of housing benefits – a topic to which I return in the next chapter.

David Ennals and Stan Orme kept the report at arm's length, as we had hoped they would. They said in a foreword that: "Neither the Government nor the SBC are committed in any way at this stage to any of the views expressed or possibilities for change discussed." They called only for "wider public discussion", and invited organisations and individuals to send comments on the report and their own ideas for reform to Alan Palmer at our headquarters. In order to provide copies of the report free, it had to be distributed by the DHSS. To use the Government Stationery Office, we would have to put a price on it. A short, clear summary was distributed at the same time (one going to every executive officer and their more senior colleagues working on the supplementary benefit scheme). All forty of the main background papers prepared in the course of the review team's work were offered free to anyone who wanted them. Officials had not been able to get approval for that bold step, but Stan Orme solved that problem by blandly announcing at the press conference that anyone could have the papers. (Universities and pressure groups ordered whole sets.) There was confusion here and there. July was a bad time to publish; then, when demand built up after the holidays, copies of these documents ran out and took too long to reprint. A poster advertising them went to all local offices, but many of them failed to display it. Nevertheless, about 20,000 copies of the full report and 40,000 of the summary were eventually distributed.

Supported by the two under secretaries and others at our headquarters, members of the review team then launched a series of meetings all over the country to discuss their proposals with social security staff, claimants, social workers, trade unions, academics and others – an entirely new experience for DHSS. I went to a lot of these meetings: wrongly perhaps, for my presence suggested that these were the SBC's proposals. Nevertheless, the public discussions educated me and, through me, the Commission. Other commissioners came too when they could. In all, the team held about 100 meetings in every part of Britain. They ranged from small private seminars to open meetings of several hundred people. The responses gained at each of them were summarised and reported back to headquarters. A few organisations, such as the Claimants' Union, the Child Poverty Action Group and the staff trade unions, had already submitted written evidence during the first stage of the review. But now a flood of comments came in – over 1,000 written statements, mainly from organisations, and a few from individuals. A research organisation was again commissioned to study public feeling about the proposals by holding intensive discussions in groups of various kinds. All these responses were laboriously summarised in a report to Ministers which was published in October 1979 – with a price on it this time (£3.70).

The team had been given a wide open invitation to review the whole scheme and its relationship with other services, but no authority to call for extra expenditure or staff. Indeed, the Treasury and the Civil Service Department were only prepared to agree to the review on condition that they would do no such thing. What they did therefore was to formulate more specific aims of their own. These were:

a. to examine the scope and purpose of the scheme and its method of operation, including its relationship with other central and local services;
b. to produce a simpler scheme which would be more readily comprehensible . . . ., with rules capable of being published . . .;
c. to deploy more effectively the financial resources likely to be available . . .;
d. to reduce the rising demands on staff . . .;
e. to devise arrangements which . . . would lead to a more effective appeals system;
f. to examine the role of the Supplementary Benefits Commission . . . .

In their Report they examined one major problem in each chapter, and proposed various solutions, showing the costs or savings of each in money and in staff. They ended by drawing up – for illustration only, they explained – a package of proposals in which costs and savings exactly balanced each other. They added another to show how a much more attractive package could be assembled if a fairly small increase in expenditure was allowed. Their original plan to conclude with a list of every proposal in their report, together with its costs or savings, was abandoned under pressure from the Treasury. Attentive readers could nevertheless assemble such a list for themselves if they wished, pick their own package of reforms, and fight for it.

As public discussion developed, the team's nil cost assumption and their refusal to propose a larger reorganisation of the whole social security system (back to Beveridge, or replace the lot with tax credits, for example) became the principal targets for criticism. Anyone who knew how hard it was for a family to live on supplementary benefit wanted higher benefits, and many were outraged that the team had not demanded that. Social workers feared that reductions in discretionary benefits would make life harder for many of the families they helped, or simply divert demands for exceptional needs payments from social security to social service offices. Many of the meetings and much of the evidence sent to Alan Palmer discussed the team's proposals point by point. But some people rejected the whole approach and alleged that the SBC and the DHSS were together trying to 'con' the public into accepting a plan already cut and dried which would impose 'rough justice' on the poor

– simplification not for the sake of claimants but to make life easier for administrators. A National Campaign Against the SB Review was launched.

Open Government

It looked for a while as if the whole attempt to get a serious public discussion of the problems of the supplementary benefit scheme might founder in the din of angry meetings. In a Parliament with no reliable majority, Ministers might then decide to leave this hot potato alone. The day was saved, partly because officials – led by Michael Partridge who enjoyed a bit of a barney – grew pretty good at coping cogently but coolly with opposition; partly because we kept talking to journalists, pressure groups, trade unions, and back-benchers on both sides of Parliament and convinced them that we were trying to do an honest job; partly because the National Campaign Against the Review was seen to be a crudely propagandist attempt to discredit the Department rather than debate the issues; but particularly because Ruth Lister and David Bull of the Child Poverty Action Group, along with effective welfare rights activists, insisted that the critics must not throw away the chance of contributing serious proposals for reform to the debate. Stan Orme met the pressure groups privately and reinforced this appeal at a crucial stage. In some of the circles where Ruth and David had to operate, theirs was a courageous line to take, and we were grateful to them. Open government was beginning to work.

The Commission held their fire, realising after some initial mistakes that we would only confuse things if we got into the debate prematurely. We would wait until public discussion had gone far enough to enable us to respond to it as well as commenting on the review team's proposals. This was to be our most important policy statement. We worked on it through the autumn of 1978. By January 1979 we were ready. Our statement began by explaining why more and more people were compelled to rely on the state for their incomes. There were more pensioners and one-parent families, and more people were out of work. Then we explained why more and more of them had to depend on means-tested benefits, showing how the social insurance schemes envisaged by Parliament immediately after the war had failed to develop, and arguing for policies which would reverse these trends.

"Unemployment is the great, and growing, unresolved problem in Britain today. For those without jobs, the main need is not better, or more, benefits but opportunities for work. . . . Within the field of social security benefits themselves, our top priority is for better child benefits" – and we explained why. "Our next priority is to give those who cannot get work State benefits as of right, without means tests. Failing that, they should at least have an income without investigations as detailed and elaborate as those required by the supplementary benefit scheme. . . . For one-parent families, a more complex mix of policies will be needed." We made proposals about them too. We also called for a simpler and fairer system of benefits to help the poorest people pay for their housing and fuel.

Then we examined the supplementary benefit scheme. Some of our proposals would cost little or nothing: full publication of the rules, which should all be approved by Parliament, and a simpler short-term claims scheme for the unemployed (once we had a more rational system of housing benefits in working order) came top of that list. Other proposals would call for more money or staff: giving long-term unemployed claimants the higher long-term rates of benefit on the same terms as everyone else, reducing for everyone the qualifying period for these rates, and various steps which would get more help to claimants with children came top of this list. Equal treatment for married women, and regular lump-sum payments replacing most of the discretionary grants were among the others. Thanks to the help of officials, we were able to show the cost of each proposal in money and staff, and as a percentage of total expenditure on supplementary benefit. We concluded that 'the total cost of all these measures will be much greater than the £200 million needed for reforms within the supplementary benefits scheme, but well within the sums often given away in tax reductions at budget time'. That was to be a prophetic statement.

Having prepared this response to 'Social Assistance', we showed sections of our draft, as usual, to other Departments of

Government concerned with them, and sent the whole thing to the Treasury. There the lady who dealt with SBC affairs replied in her characteristic style. Writing from 'H.M. Treasury' on 25 January to the DHSS official who had sent her the draft, she said:

1. I spoke to you yesterday about what I hope is a very early draft of the response of the Commission to the review of the supplementary benefits scheme. There is clearly room for improvement.

2. I am glad to see that on the first page it is made clear that the views expressed are those of the Commission and do not (and indeed could not) represent Government policy. Nevertheless, I would hope that it will be possible to make significant changes in the draft.

3. I understand that there is a suggestion that this document should be published. There are serious problems about the provision of paper and HMSO are likely to be exhorting Departments to economise in the use of paper, particularly during 1979–80. It is, therefore, for consideration whether this document of 60 pages – which reproduces in shriller tone what has already been incorporated in the Commission's annual reports for 1975, 1976 and 1977 – should be published at the taxpayers' expense. In particular, I would have thought that your Ministers would wish to consider whether the attack on this Government's social policies, as expressed in the comments on the level of social security benefits, housing policy, and employment measures, should be published in this form.

The letter continued in this vein, followed by two pages of more detailed comments. ("Paragraph 3.19: before saying unemployment is growing, they should check the statistics. 3.21: who says standard of living of families on supplementary benefit is unacceptably low?", and so on.)

Most of this we disregarded, but we rephrased passages wherever we could do so without changing what we had to say. Our Ministers would have agreed to publish what eventually became a forty-two page pamphlet. But by the time it was ready the government's life was running out. If we wanted a new government to listen to us, it would be wiser to wait and consult whoever was in power after the election before publishing our 'Response to "Social Assistance" '.

What had we learnt from the whole exercise in open government? The meetings, the publications and the sifting and summarising of public feeling had taken a great deal of expensive time and energy. Had they been worth it? The most important lessons we learnt were unspoken. Poor people do not describe themselves as poor. But you cannot meet claimants week by week over a long period without recognising that life is really hard for a lot of them: their faces, their gait, their clothing all show that. Local office staff know this, particularly if they go visiting. But civil servants at headquarters, however humane they may be, do not have this knowledge imprinted in their bones unless they meet and talk with their customers regularly, and seem them not as statistics but as living people. They still have to recognise that there are economic or political limits to what can be done for them here and now. But they will not ask in lofty tones: "Who says standard of living of families on supplementary benefit is unacceptably low?"

We learnt things about the workings of the scheme and the feelings of the people involved in it, some of which led to important changes in the original proposals for reform. The review team's short-term claims scheme for the unemployed would clearly have to wait till we made some progress with housing benefits – as I shall explain. The unemployed, accounting for two-thirds of the claims dealt with each year, were the least well represented of our customers. Other users of the social services who are scarcely ever heard from came to public meetings and spoke up. The lady representing the 'prostitutes' collective' was one of them. And at meeting after meeting we heard from pensioners, the disabled, lone parents and students. The prejudices of many social security staff against unemployed claimants emerged as a formidable problem. Perhaps we should have more frankly explained to critics complaining about the threatened curtailment of discretionary benefits that one reason for reducing discretion was that our staff, sharing many of the attitudes of the rest of the population, were simply not equipped to use such powers fairly.

We gained a clearer understanding of the impact which some of the team's proposals would make in different parts of the country. People on Tyneside and Clydeside, where families are large and unemployment is high, were understandably angry about the plan to postpone unemployed school leavers' entitlement to benefit till the end of their last school holidays.

But elsewhere in Britain there was less opposition to the proposal. (Coupled with the prolongation of child benefit and other dependants' allowances for all parents over this last holiday period, the proposal would distribute roughly the same total sum, but to a slightly different group of families.)

We gained confidence in much of the review team's basic philosophy. The great majority of people wanted to get rid of the scheme's vaguely defined discretionary powers and to rely instead on clear-cut rules. Many also favoured a radical simplification of housing benefit for people with low incomes.

More interesting, perhaps, were the divisions of opinion, not the majorities: on discretionary benefits, for example. Summarising crudely, it seemed that the unemployed wanted jobs, not benefits, and were suspicious of discretion; the pensioners and the disabled most wanted better insurance benefits as of right, without discretionary extras. It was the one-parent families, who could see no hope of an insurance benefit, who fought hardest for the extras.

We were able, by making the whole debate public, to hold open a few doorways to reform which other people were trying hard to close: the doorways to more rational systems of housing and fuel benefits, obstructed by the Departments of the Environment and Energy, for example; and the doorway to equal treatment for married women which the Treasury and the social security managers wanted to close. Civil servants gained a lot of useful experience, too. I particularly recall Michael Partridge, convincingly confronting the television cameras (to his permanent secretary's horror, I suspect); a visit to Plymouth where people were still talking about the lively performance which Evelyn Stewart (a review team member in her mid-twenties) had put up at a big meeting a year before; and the hard-pressed social security office in Willesden, where key staff had taken a day off (they caught up with all the work later) to study 'Social Assistance' and discuss it with local social workers and welfare rights workers whose views, often contrary to their own, they conscientiously presented to me when I came to see them. There were many more incidents of this sort.

There were mistakes and disasters, too. From these we often learnt more than from success. We learnt a good deal, for example, about how to conduct public meetings. You should decide early on whether you want a small, closed, expert meeting, or an open meeting. Each can be useful, but don't confuse them. If it's to be open, make it wide open; advertise it well in advance, and only exclude people if the hall is plainly full. If properly accredited spokesmen of claimants' organisations (themselves living on supplementary benefit) have to travel a long way to the meeting, pay their expenses – on the spot. Make proper arrangements to note and report all the main views expressed at the meeting, and explain clearly what these arrangements are, who is doing the job, and to whom his report will go. Keep the personal problems and complaints of individual claimants out of the meeting by making proper arrangements in advance to deal with these more privately immediately afterwards. Frankly recognise the errors, injustices and muddle of your service where they are real. But explain the difficulties of the staff too. However successful your meetings, remember that the greast majority of people never come to them. If they hear about you it will be through their newspapers, radios and television. So talk to the media and do not be afraid of them. Local papers and radio stations will usually report you more fully and fairly than their national colleagues do – particularly if you discuss a local issue of some sort. (The opening of a new shelter for homeless men, a cold winter and its impact on fuel bills, the threatened closure of a local factory: find out what the issues are.) Meet the journalists well before their deadlines (after 5.00 p.m. is no good); answer the silliest questions particularly carefully; and put the main things you have to say briefly and simply in writing. Don't assume anyone has shorthand. Get to meetings early. If their organisers intend to put you on a platform far above your audience or behind a table at the end of a long hall, re-organise things. Don't mind their feelings; it's the participants who matter. Get down on a level with your audience on the long side, not at the distant narrow end, of the room. Treat everyone – particularly the more irritating people – seriously and courteously. Encourage the staff to talk (civil servants are usually reluctant to do this unless they are union representatives.) Show the public that they too are human beings, who do not all agree with you or with each other. Be honestly angry if that seems fitting. But, whatever you do, keep your sense of humour. All very obvious advice. Would that I had always followed it myself.

Finally, and more generally: remember that open government is all of a piece. You cannot be open and honest with the customers unless you start with the staff. And you cannot be open and honest with staff in general unless you treat your secretary and your closest colleagues in the same way. Whatever happens in future to the DHSS's relations with the public, we left staff throughout the supplementary benefit service with expectations about the contribution they can make to discussions of policy and procedure which will be hard to brush aside completely in future. Remember, too, that open government is a long distance event, not a sprint. It's about credibility. That is something which has to be laboriously earned. If the service you work for has a history of centralised, secret decision making and its procedures are incomprehensibly complicated, why on earth should anyone believe you when you say you want to simplify, clarify and publish everything, and to consult them about your policies? They will only believe you as you begin, and keep on, doing it. It may take years to convince them. Better start now.

The Approaching Election

In the autumn of 1978 we were working on our own proposals for reform, and facing an unpredictable future. We expected an election in a few weeks time. At the end of the year the appointments of five of the Commission's eight members would run out. All of them could be replaced, and their successors would probably be chosen by a Conservative government. There were rumours that our chief officials might be moving too. Sir Alec Atkinson, the second permanent secretary, was due to retire. He was responsible, at the top level, for the social security side of the Department's work. If Geoffrey Otton succeeded him we would get a new Chief Adviser who might well be less effective than Geoffrey. But if he didn't, that could be worse still if the new permanent secretary was unsympathetic to us and Geoffrey was later moved elsewhere. There were rumours too that other Departments were hoping to capture Michael Partridge, the under secretary who was the driving force behind the supplementary benefits review. A team as able as the one we had assembled is always beset by such rumours. Only the plodders stay put for years. We were aware too that there were powerful people who felt that the Commission was getting out of control and should be reined in. It was going to be a worrying year.

Yet this is how social reform normally proceeds. It's like staging a play in which the author, producer and cast may be changed at any moment, or required to rewrite half their lines on the eve of the first night. Neglecting many other things which were going on at the same time, I will briefly tell in the next two sections how we got new Commissioners, new Ministers and new advisers.

Already by the beginning of 1978 the Labour Government had been running out of steam. There was no money for major new projects and, having no reliable majority in Parliament, Ministers were reluctant to introduce new measures lest they be crippled on their way through the House by some unholy alliance of back-benchers. David Ennals, our Secretary of State, was not robust and had been quite seriously ill during the previous autumn. On the evening of 18 January 1978, I attended a meeting of DHSS Ministers, their special advisers and top officials, to discuss the expenditure they would be bidding for in the next budget. We gathered in one of those drab, ill-lit rooms in the basement of the House of Commons. Spirits were raised by the scent of battle ahead, for everyone expected this to be the last budget before the election; always a good time for getting a little more social expenditure. The talk was mainly about tactics. Ministers agreed to give top priority to hospitals (Labour MPs in declining cities were worried about hospital closures) and to child benefits which they hoped to push up in April and then again in November. They could leave their colleagues in the Cabinet to insist that the annual £10 bonus for pensioners should be added to this shopping list. (The bonus was expensive, and always disliked in the DHSS where people would have preferred to use the money for other things; but it was far too popular to be abandoned.) They noted that to the usual political arguments supporting these bids they must add the new plea that much of DHSS expenditure (on hospitals, for example) would create jobs and reduce unemployment.

Ten days later I was speaking at the annual conference of the Conservative Political Centre in the Festival Hall. As usual, at this time, I focused particularly on the needs of the unemployed. In the discussion which followed I was attacked by two ladies in twinsets who held me personally responsible for seducing men from work with the generous benefits we offered, and for teaching youngesters in State schools ("to which, I am glad to say, my own children do not go") to live on social security rather than look for jobs. Senior Tories on the platform obviously found these women about as distasteful as I did. Patrick Jenkin, shadowing David Ennals in the House at this time, had to offer some distinctive Conservative alternative to Labour policies which would be more constructive than this without committing his Party to spending more money. In his speech he focused on 'the family' and discussed proposals for setting up some sort of Family Commission.

Our Ministers got the most important things they wanted in the Budget on 6 April, including the two increases in child benefit. But we again failed to win higher long-term rates of supplementary benefit for unemployed claimants although Ministers had bid for them. At the very last moment the Treasury tried to shave a percentage point or two off the benefits for claimant's dependants – mainly children – in order to recover expenditure they had been compelled to concede for other purposes. Our officials were unable to repulse this attack, and David Ennals had to go, only a few hours before the Chancellor was due to make his speech, to persuade Joel Barnett, Chief Secretary to the Treasury, to put things right. He succeeded. But it was a vivid example of the way in which the Treasury could ambush a weak Minister and discredit him in his own Party and throughout the country if he failed to fight them off in the few hours available.

Ministers held a conference that spring to introduce the new pension scheme – their Party's last major achievement in the social security field. Then, on 5 July, they staged a gathering at Lancaster House to celebrate the thirtieth anniversary of the measures often described as the founding of the 'welfare state'. It was a strange occasion. Posters had been distributed all over the country. Journalists, senior civil servants, trade unionists, academics, leaders of charities and pressure groups – the whole welfare 'establishment' – were invited. David Ennals was ill again, but Stan Orme made a speech. Then the Prime Minister addressed us, recalling in glowing words the achievements of the Attlee government. It was a great manifesto for the 1950 election. Nothing was said about the future.

If you re-read the newspapers and speeches of 1948 you will find that everyone in those days thought that the advance in social security was the great step forward they were taking. They talked mainly about the National Insurance Act and the hopes for the future held out by Beveridge, and also about the National Assistance Act and the abolition of the poor laws. Much less was said about the national health service and the personal social services.But Jim Callaghan's speech that day dwelt, like the posters, mainly on the NHS and the personal social services. History was being rewritten. Labour had lost its convictions about poverty and the redistribution of incomes. Or perhaps the voters at large had lost those convictions, and the Labour Party was afraid to remind them. No-one mentioned Jenny Lee, Aneurin Bevan's widow, who was standing on the edge of the crowd.

A few days earlier we had been talking with our Ministers about the forthcoming publication of the review team's proposals for reforming the supplementary benefits scheme. They were increasingly jumpy as the election approached, fearing that our usual plan for prior discussions with journalists would lead to embarrassing leaks. We went ahead regardless, knowing that our problem would not be over-exposure but how to get sufficient public attention for the ideas we were advancing. Then, after the September meeting of the TUC, when everyone was ready to go into battle, Callaghan called off the election.

Our Ministers, their advisers and top officials gathered again on the evening of 24 October for another 'forward look' meeting – this time in David Ennals' room at Alexander Fleming House, headquarters of the DHSS. They were tired, cynical, and still waiting for the election which should have happened that month. They considered how to manage or postpone public discussion of potentially embarrassing things such as their policies for the elderly, the review of the supplementary benefits scheme and the Merrison Report on doctors; and how to cope with industrial action in the hospitals. A reply to current Tory campaigns to 'cut the dole' and 'crack down on fraud' was planned – to be kept in reserve for the election campaign. As for 'the family', it was agreed to 'keep level pegging with the Tories in public', but to 'drop it' for practical purposes. A 2 per cent rate of growth in public expenditure was assumed and priorities for the use of this money were discussed. That, I calculated, would mean about £40 million extra each year for supplementary benefits, which in time could give us most of the things we were hoping for within the scheme. Reforms outside the scheme – of housing benefits, for example – would have to be financed in other ways.

The prospects for achieving any changes in our field were still very uncertain. At Christmas time I was invited, as usual, to the party given by the National Union of Teachers at their headquarters, just off the Euston Road. My 'ticket' for this party had been acquired a dozen years earlier as a member of the Plowden Committee, which reported on primary schools, and then as chairman of the Public Schools Commission. It was always the biggest and booziest of the many Christmas parties to which I was invited. But what an occasion! Politicians national and local, teachers, civil servants, inspectors of schools, chief education officers, professors of education, trade unionists, a big crowd of education correspondents – all the old war horses of this industry come, along with the Secretary of State for Education who makes a speech on behalf of the NUT's guests. They have jousted with each other for years. Yet together they constitute a sort of movement: for they all care about education, and they know the score – all the arguments and counter-arguments, all the facts, figures and people. The tides of battle swing back and forth from year to year. But some issues get resolved (comprehensive education steadily gains ground), others (such as the abolition of public schools) are abandoned, and the outcome is slightly less capricious and ill-informed, thanks to the movement which assembles on occasions such as these. Social security is different. And the DHSS bears some share of responsibility for the hazards of the political environment in which it operates. Things might be better if policy debates in this field had been more open, if more and better research had been published, if social security administrators had gained greater professional confidence and a wider circle of friends, and if journalists, pressure groups, academics and other outsiders had been treated with less suspicion.

We had been waiting for a new government before seeking decisions about appointments to the Commission. We needed caring people, prepared to grapple honestly with problems as members of a working team; but they must also be trusted by our Ministers. The postponment of the election meant that we had now to go ahead and seek decisions about the five Commissioners whose appointments were coming to an end. Officials, I knew, would be suggesting names, so I talked with them, made enquiries in various quarters, and put my own proposals to Ministers. Getting someone who cared about social security and also had first-hand experience of running a big service industry was not easy. (We found him in Harry Shepherd of Marks and Spencer.) Getting Ministers to accept candidates who really understood the claimants' point of view was not easy either. (Henry Hodge, until recently a lawyer at the Child Poverty Action Group, came as near to filling that bill as any of us.) Getting even the most robust pensioner accepted proved impossible — although more than half our customers were pensioners.

The new Commission assembled for the first time, without officials, over breakfast before our main meeting began on 28 February 1979. We arranged these breakfasts from time to time to give us a chance of talking more freely than the pressures of a crowded agenda and a bigger meeting would allow. We held a residential meeting during the first week of April at Worthing, where we got together twice a year in the Warnes Hotel. There it was clear that we had the best Commission yet.

Our previous team of Commissioners had been good people – experienced and humane – yet together we lacked aggression and creative tension. The chairman of such a body must give leadership. But he must know that the rest of his team have minds of their own and will intervene – and in the last resort resign – if they feel that things are going wrong. He works so closely with officials, because he devotes most of his time to the job, that he may not trust his own judgment if he gets into conflict with them. The rest of the Commission, being less involved in the work from day to day, can help him to hang on to his sense of direction in difficult times. I was to need that before long. At our meeting in Worthing we had three friendly but forthright arguments with officials – to the delight of those among them who enjoyed seizing the opportunities which our aggressive questions offered. I was reminded again how heavily we depended upon these reforming spirits to grasp the openings which we provided and develop them in ways which went well beyond our knowledge and capacities.

Meanwhile time had at last run out for the Labour Government. Stan Orme had 'played to the whistle', battling for us to the end – and in smaller things battling very successfully. One of these was the crisis over Iranian students for whom the Foreign Office eventually agreed to assume responsibility after we had supported them for months, on cruelly low rates of benefit, when their funds were cut off by the revolution in Teheran. We could fight off our critics more effectively if it was clear that there were diplomatic reasons for helping these young people. Then, on March 28 1979, the Government was defeated in a vote of confidence and the election was called.

Tension rose among the politicians. But for officials at our headquarters, some of them close to breaking point after contending with staff cuts, the SBC's next Annual Report and months of grinding work on our review – the election provided a breathing space. They read the manifestos, followed the debate, and prepared papers for their next Ministers: two separate sets, one for a Labour Government and one for the Conservatives. ('His' and 'Hers' they were sometimes called.) Those concerned with the review team were busy preparing and costing various proposals for reforming the scheme.

Labour's manifesto was depressing. Supplementary benefits and social security were barely mentioned. Successes in this field, the government evidently feared, would be as unwelcome as failures. Even the belated attainment of a more generous rate of child benefit was regarded as a 'loser' on the hustings and almost hushed up. The Tory manifesto promised simplification of social security, more generous support for the family, restoration of respect for work, and the imposition upon trade unions of greater responsibility for supporting strikers. Patrick Jenkin had told me that they would study the proposals emerging from our review, but do no fresh research of their own on supplementary benefit. That was good: if they won they would be able to look at the evidence without prior commitments before deciding what to do.

Just before election day the Commission went on a long-planned visit to Northern Ireland. Geoffrey Otton came too. He said, joking-serious, that he and his colleagues were anxiously waiting to see whether the Commission's chairman would feel compelled to resign if the Tories won. I replied, not joking at all, that if it did come to that I did not intend to go by myself. The possibility of losing the whole Commission had obviously been prepared for. "If that happens," said Geoffrey, "we've decided to get ourselves appointed to keep things running while Ministers look for a new Commission."

New Regime

The election brought the Conservatives to power with the biggest turnover of seats since 1945. Yet the Labour vote held up reasonably well. Indeed, some of the Labour MPs who lost their seats won slightly more votes than in 1974. But there was a bigger turn-out, and the third-party vote – Liberal, Nationalist and Fascist – collapsed. Labour lost no ground among the middle classes, and in Scotland they even gained a little. It was the midland and southern English working class – 'middle England' – who put Margaret Thatcher in power.

We were all waiting to see who our new Secretary of State would be. Patrick Jenkin was no surprise: he had led the Opposition's attacks on David Ennals for years. But we had expected Lynda Chalker, his hardworking second-in-command who had shadowed Stan Orme, to become Minister of Social Security. Instead we got Reg Prentice, who combined the jobs previously done by Stan and Alf Morris (Minister for the Disabled) but without a seat in Cabinet. Lynda became Parliamentary Secretary – the more junior post which Eric Deakins had previously held.

That evening, 8 May, there was a farewell party for David Ennals and his closest officials and advisers in Alexander Fleming House. It was a small wake, held below stairs while

the new masters of the house were celebrating their victory on
a floor above. David had been though a crucifying time, frequently in pain, and constantly vilified by the doctors, the
health service trade unions, the anti-abortion lobby, the pressure groups and the press. He seemed relieved to be out of it,
and said very simply that he had got through the last few
months by telling himself that he could do no more than his
best, whatever that might be. Pat Nairne, replying, said how
grateful he and his colleagues had been for the unfailing good
humour and kindness he had shown to all of them. An honest
and fitting farewell.

Geoffrey Otton meanwhile had become second permanent
secretary — next in line to Sir Patrick Nairne, *the* permanent
secretary. That was encouraging. It meant that Pat and others
at the top of the civil service approved of him and we would
have a friend highly placed in this court. He would become 'Sir
Geoffrey' in time — and did in the New Year honours of 1981.
During the election the top brass picked the man who succeeded him as our Chief Adviser.

During their first days in office new Ministers are surrounded
by a vibrant bush telegraph, their every move observed,
reported and appraised. The courtiers — their closest officials —
have studied their speeches and their Party's manifesto in
detail. They have seen them on television, and those whose
work took them to the House of Commons have seen them in
action there — often criticising the Department they are now to
lead. But, unless Ministers have held office in the Department
before, officials have never met them privately. Now, to serve
their princes effectively and defend the causes for which the
Department stands, the courtiers must get to know these
people very well. What do they want to do, and to be
remembered for? Do they *know* what they want? How do they
learn? By reading (like Keith Joseph)? By dispute (like Richard
Crossman)? Or by sizing people up and sensing whether they
seem trustworthy or not (like Stan Orme)? What kind of
people *do* they trust? And, most important of all, can they get
their way when it comes to a show-down in Cabinet or committee? The Prime Minister knows her team very well: they've
worked together for years. If she sends you one of the toughest
kids in the Parliamentary playground, that means she wants

your Department to win a few battles in the Cabinet. If she
sends you a loser, that tells you something about her attitude to
the whole Ministry.

Officials are going to have to work desperately hard for their
new masters in all sorts of situations. They are going to have to
explain complex issues and draft speeches for them. On their
behalf they will have to get exhausted people, stupid people
and people who serve the rival princes in other Departments of
Government to act, or to refrain from action. They will have to
reassure their own man in moments of panic, cope with his
rage, and comfort him in adversity. And all this will go on at all
hours of day and night, in the office, in trains and cars, on
public platforms, in broadcasting studios and committee
rooms of the House of Commons. If their prince is charming,
that will be nice. But if he knows his mind and can get his way
they will work their hearts out for him and be content to see
him garner all the credit at the end of the day whether they like
him or not. If that is not enough for you, then you had better
not be a courtier.

Officials who can do this job well and survive, without
growing tired or cynical, must at bottom be prepared to accept
their own countrymen, to respect the prejudices and the leaders which boil to the surface of a Parliamentary democracy
from year to year, and to subordinate their own interests and
aspirations of those of the disparate, changing team which
makes up a Department of Government. It's a great system of
values when it works for you; but it's pretty ruthless when you
come into conflict with it.

I met Patrick Jenkin a few days after the election, in the room
where I used to meet David Ennals and Barbara Castle before
him. The picture of Nye Bevan had gone – to be replaced by
one of Iain McLeod. He told me I was his first non-official
visitor. Reg Prentice and Lynda Chalker saw me during the
next few days. I had checked the latest gossip with Pat Nairne
and Geoffrey Otton before these meetings, telling them that I
intended to discuss the role of the Commission and our next
annual report (already nearly complete), to express concern
about next November's uprating of benefits (due to be announced very soon in the government's first budget) and more
generally to press for action on the review of the supplement-

ary benefit scheme. Our own response to the review was ready to be published as soon as Ministers had time to look at it.

I also intended to press gently for the appointment of special advisers to replace those we had just lost. Tony Lynes, David Metcalf and Malcolm Dean of the Guardian (along with Brian Abel-Smith, Malcolm's predecessor, who moved to work for Peter Shore at Environment a few months before the election) had together been one of the best teams of outsiders assembled to advise any Minister. For the future I had my eye on two excellent people who had been working on social policies in the Conservative Central Office, and was pleased to find that both permanent secretaries seemed to support the idea. Pat particularly valued the help advisers can give in redrafting speeches and articles for popular consumption – a task which civil servants were not particularly good at, he said. I had other tasks in mind too: the maintenance of Ministers' links with their own Party and with outsiders of all sorts who might have useful ideas to offer, and the contribution of a few fresh thoughts to the work of the insiders who sometimes get to know each other a little too well and find it difficult to remember the longer-term aims beyond the crises to be surmounted each day.

Pat Nairne reminded me that we had already been through one round of staff cuts in recent years. If Ministers were determined to keep to a 2 per cent cash limit and rely on staff cuts to pay for the rest of the fairly generous salary award granted by their predecessors during the election, then there would have to be real cuts in services to the public.

Patrick Jenkin was not interested in special advisers: nothing I said could shift him. He listened courteously to what I had to say about upratings, staff cuts and the review. He was encouragingly determined to go for a major reform of housing benefits which he had already discussed with Michael Heseltine before the election; but ominously concerned about 'incentives' and the 'why work? syndrome'.

I had been prepared to rebuild the Commission's political credibility from scratch. But all three Ministers accepted the conventions we had built up over the years with their predecessors. They expected us to go on publishing independent annual reports. And they would all meet me regularly and come to

Commission meetings occasionally – quite often, as it turned out. That was a tribute both to the advice they must have been given by officials, and to the regular meetings we had held with them when they were in opposition. Open government had paid off.

Budget Day, on 12 June, showed that Ministers had failed to get any increase in child benefits for the following November, and were going to break the 'double link' which had tied long-term insurance benefits to earnings or prices (whichever was the more favourable). The upratings promised in insurance benefits seemed so generous, owing to the massive rate of inflation expected,that journalists failed to spot that they were not in fact sufficient to keep pace with the rise in prices since the previous year. Even when they were alerted to this, there was little public concern. Labour leaders seemed to have been right in assuming that increases in social security benefit had become a losing, not a winning, issue. But a week later, when we published our Response to the Review, we got good coverage in nearly all the newspapers for this, our most radical and far-reaching statement of policy.

These were desperately active weeks, filled with debate, inside and outside the bureaucracy, about benefit 'upratings', fuel benefits (a lost cause rescued at the last moment by the Prime Minister's own intervention), the reform of housing benefits (put firmly under Treasury leadership – which would at least prevent Environment from killing the idea), the forthcoming social security Bills and the future of the Commission. For me there were meetings with pressure groups, speeches at various annual conferences, renewed uproar about the London reception centres for homeless men, uproar with staff trade unions about our attempt to get the 'A' Code of instructions for social security staff rewritten in plain English, and much else besides. It seemed impossible at times to cope with one more thing.

The main threads in this story were brought together again at an 'end of term seminar' held for all our Ministers at Sunningdale from lunch time on Friday, 27 July, till lunch time on Saturday. I was invited, along with about two dozen of the Department's top officials – all keyed up to serve their new masters. It was a blazing hot weekend. We sat in our shirt sleeves and dripped, as the government's strategies for the DHSS unfolded. I had brought with me the crucial opening chapter of our annual report – the one I always wrote myself – to leave with Patrick Jenkin who wanted to read it before going on holiday. It must have seemed like a voice from another world. We learnt that explicitly reactionary steps which would hand public services over to commerical operators were to be reserved for the national health service. Voluntary bodies should be induced to do more in various fields. How was not very clear. In the social security services the road to a comprehensive system of tax credits should be kept open; but, with no money to spend, there was no hope of going down it. Further work on a general-purpose benefit for the disabled was called off, but everyone was at a loss to find social security benefits which could be abolished. (They picked on the earnings-related supplements to short-term insurance benefits later.) Meanwhile the breaking of the 'double-link' with earnings and prices as a basis for uprating pensions would be social security's main offering on the altar of public sector cuts. Everyone knew, however, that the broader pattern of government policies would not reduce but increase social security expenditure because the numbers out of work were going to rise.

Meanwhile attention was sensibly focused on operational issues. The Department's massive but increasingly old-fashioned computer system would have to be replaced before long. That could transform the task of management, the work done by the staff, and the quality of service to the customers. (I did my best to warn that, unless deliberate action was taken to correct it, this would indeed be the order of priorities: managers would certainly get a more efficient system, but the staff might end up with more boring jobs and the customers with a service no better than before. It had happened before when unemployment benefits were 'computerised'.)

The supplementary benefit scheme was to be reformed, but without spending any more money on it. The SBC's discretionary powers would be abolished or drastically reduced. That would pose questions about the future of the Commission itself. Would a Commission be needed at all? Patrick Jenkin made it clear that he would want strong arguments to convince him that it was. (I said that the SBC was now working

out its own views about its future: on this point I had come to
listen, not to offer any conclusions. We presented our conclusions a few days later, as I shall tell.)

Tired though they already were by late-night sittings and
pressures of work, Ministers were still untarnished by the
erosion of hope and principle which sets in later. They were
buoyant, too, with the assurance that they had the voters
behind them. Patrick Jenkin was very much the head boy, loyal
to his headmistress. Still harking back to the days when he had
been a Minister at the Treasury, he was at his best on financial
questions – still rather too reluctant to do battle with Treasury
Ministers on behalf of DHSS causes. Reg Prentice was unclassi-
fiable: in most ways the arch-conservative, opposed to benefits
for strikers' families, opposed to giving the higher long-term
rates of benefit to the unemployed, and opposed to giving
representation to claimants. Yet he was an advocate of child
benefits and more open government. He was also unwell, and
too slow moving to contribute very effectively. His main political function was perhaps to demonstrate that Margaret
Thatcher would reward defectors. Lynda Chalker, best-
informed of all about social security (having shadowed Stan
Orme for the last few years) and the most progressive member
of the team, was too junior to wield much influence yet. But
before long she was taking over half Reg Prentice's work and
enjoying it: a humane, honest, hard-working manager, rather
than a formulator of new policies.

The most important thing to emerge from this meeting was
not the decisions taken but a sense of the political climate in
which we were operating. Barbara Castle's concept of the
'social wage' – the contribution of the social services to living
standards – had not been grasped by the voters. It was now
being quietly buried. The new statistical measure of living
standards which the Government was introducing, the tax and
prices index, would help to nail down the lid of that coffin
because it recorded movements in earnings, prices and taxes –
but not in social benefits. Thus if benefits were cut, living
standards would appear to improve because only the resulting
reduction in taxes would show up in the index. (Since then the
T & P Index has recorded larger rises than the old Retail Prices
Index and been quietly buried in its turn.) There was no more

talk about the redistributive effects of Government programmes or about the numbers of jobs which public services might
create or preserve: these factors were no longer to be considered when the government took decisions.

Previous Governments had made their cuts too, but always
in fear of the storm of rage they would evoke from their Party
and the pressure groups. The new team had shed the burden of
social conscience. Their confidence was founded on their discovery that the most effective way of dealing with the poverty
lobby was to tell it to go away. For the moment that was close
to the truth: the government was armoured against moral
pressure. The only people who could penetrate that armour
would be their own back-benchers – many of them newcomers
to Parliament, as I had discovered a little earlier when I met
some of them in the House on 10 July. The world of the Tory
back-bencher had not been much cultivated by the poverty
lobby. All this was depressing but not unexpected. More
surprising was my discovery that our new Chief Adviser
neither conveyed the Commission's views on important issues
to Ministers nor warned me that he would be taking an
altogether different line from ours.

Changing the Law

We had survived a change of Commissioners, a change of
government, and a change of Chief Advisers, and we were still
afloat. But in a different world. Were we still on course for any
destination we wanted to reach? We had a new government
with a large majority in Parliament and a commitment to
rethink policy in our field. The Department of Health and
Social Security had put some of its ablest people onto this job
over the past three years, formulating proposals for change
and publicly committing itself to getting something done.
Local authorities, pressure groups, trade unions, journalists
and academics had all been involved in the debate and were
expecting that something would now happen. Thus the lumbering vehicle of reform had been set rolling. A lot of people would
be disappointed, powerful men would look silly, and expensive time and effort would be wasted if the whole cartload sank
into the bog and was abandoned. We had an opportunity to

get something done which might not come again.

The government decided to reform our scheme with a two-part Bill. The first part, brief but contentious, would change the rules for uprating long-term contributory benefits. Pensions would henceforth keep pace with prices, not, as hitherto, with prices or earnings, whichever moved up faster. The unforseen 'ratchet effect' produced by that double link meant that pensions were moving up slightly quicker than earnings in the years when prices moved ahead faster. It was only a matter of time before some government would try to escape from the arrangement.

It was a pity, we felt, that the double link had to be broken so soon. Believing that poverty means exclusion from the living standards of the ordinary wage earner, we argued that if the double link had to be broken now, pensions should be hitched not to prices but to earnings. Instead, the Government had chosen what was usually the less generous link with prices. I think the Cabinet felt that by taking this unpopular measure through the House Patrick Jenkin had earned the right to do what he wanted with supplementary benefits in the second part of his Bill, provided it didn't cost anything. But this is to look ahead. At the beginning of August 1979 we had a few days in which to tell Ministers what we thought about the future of the Commission itself, before they went off for their holidays. That was not the first question we would have chosen to tackle, but fate does not feed questions to you in a logical order. Commissioners insisted that we work out an answer by ourselves, without officials.

If we got the sort of reform we were hoping for, abolishing the Commission's executive powers, there were three policies which could make sense. (1) Abolish the SBC, regularly publish all the facts required for well-informed public debate, and leave the pressure groups to get on with it. (2) Abolish the SBC and the National Insurance Advisory Committee (known as NIAC) which deals with contributory benefits, and set up instead a social security advisory committee to offer advice about social security programmes of every kind. (3) Enlarge the SBC and turn it into a poverty policies committee to advise about the whole confusing array of means tested programmes for poor people – not only DHSS benefits but also rent and rate rebates, fuel subsidies, clothing grants, free school meals and many other smaller benefits. Our Commission, centrally concerned with poverty, had already backed option (3) in their Annual Reports. But it was clear that the new Government was not interested in that idea. Option (1) – leaving it to the pressure groups – would be better than setting up the tamely ineffectual advisory body which some people had in mind. If a new Committee worked like NIAC it would be a body largely nominated by the CBI and the TUC; it would hold no regular meetings, and have no regular staff and no permanent office. It would make no Annual Reports to Parliament, do nothing unless invited by the Government, and then confine its advice to the specific question it was asked to consider. In short, it would be useful for delaying action ('the government have referred this question to the Advisory Committee and can do nothing until they have reported and the observations of all concerned with the matter have been considered'). But it would be pretty toothless.

We prepared a draft statement setting out the options, and discussed this at a private meeting with three people: Tony Lynes, Ruth Lister and Andrew Rowe from Conservative Central Office. It was the Tory who gave us the shot in the arm we needed. He reminded us that there was a responsible, compassionate tradition within the Party to which we must boldly appeal if we wanted to be heard. We wrote a new statement for our Ministers. In it we reminded them of the things which an authoritative and vigorously independent body could do – such as setting the review of the supplementary benefit scheme on foot, and opening up debate about housing benefits, fuel benefits and other major questions which were difficult for a Departmental Minister to take up. We pointed out that with rising unemployment and unpopular decisions ahead the government was going to need a body, believed to be independent and fair-minded, to which it could refer controversial questions – as its predecessors had done when they sought our help in dealing with striking firemen, cohabitation rules and other bitterly contested issues. We traced our ancestry back to the justices of the peace and the first poor law authorities – symbols of a tradition which, despite its failings and brutalities, represented some puiblic commitment to the protection of the oppressed. In the turbulent times ahead that tradition and its symbols should not lightly be thrown away. We concluded by listing the basic requirements for an effective advisory body. It should be entitled to pose and pursue its own questions, to have direct access to Ministers and officials and to publish independent reports. In fact we wrote a classic statement of liberal philosophy.

Early in the summer Michael Partridge, who was responsible for the forthcoming Bill, had to arrange with the Department's lawyers for Parliamentary Counsel – one of the few government lawyers trained and authorised to draft a law – to fit this work into his programme. Could we get the man we wanted? Would he prepare the shining new Act we needed, or only an amending Act which tinkered with all the previous legislation (more easily prepared, but incomprehensible to everyone except the experts familiar with these laws)? Would he get the job done in time to publish a Bill and the explanatory papers accompanying it by December? That was the most important question of all.

By the beginning of September preparations for the Bill were well under way. Michael had got the under secretary in Parliament who arranges the time-table for government business to book provisional dates for the second reading of our Bill (the main debate on policy) in mid-December, followed by committee stage (when the details are thrashed out clause by clause), report stage and third reading (when the Bill comes back to the whole House which reconsiders it, as amended in committee, and approves a final version). It then goes through the same procedure in the House of Lords and is finally brought to the Queen for royal assent, which makes it an Act of Parliament. That was planned for 24 May 1980. By then officials would be drafting the regulations to be made under the Act which would later be brought, sheaves at a time, to Parliament for approval. Each step in the time-table was crucial. If changes in the law were to be brought into effect when the annual upratings in benefits took place in November 1980, the staff would have to follow the new rules from the beginning of June when local social security offices start work on the upratings. So the measure had to get to the Queen by the end of May. (One day, when supplementary benefits are handled by computers, the calculation of new benefits can be left till much later in the year. Meanwhile the job still has to be done with pen and ink.)

Many other things had still to be fixed. Vital and time-consuming decisions about the content of the Bill had to be made by Ministers and got through Cabinet committees, and for that the way had to be cleared by negotiations with the Treasury, the Civil Service Department and other branches of government. There was haggling with the CSD, the DHSS establishments officer and the unions about the staff needed to get the new scheme going. Promises of action had to be extorted from the hard men who manage the Department's operations: men contending with a lot of other demands – staff cuts, strike threats from the unions, pressure for tougher action on fraud, a go-slow which had produced a breakdown in the administration of child benefits, and crises of every sort. Instructions and leaflets had to be rewritten and new training had to be organised for staff and tribunal members. Explanations of the Government's intentions had to be given to back-bench MPs, pressure groups, tribunal chairmen, social workers, local authorities, journalists and others. There were times when several senior officials were off sick at once – largely because of the strains imposed on them during this period. All this, you may say, is what courtiers are picked and trained for. But only a few senior officials have the special mixture of intelligence, aggression, integrity, generosity, patient good humour and capacity for grindingly hard work which makes a good reformer. They may or may not be radicals: these talents are related only dimly to ideology. They are the most precious members of any bureaucracy, and we were lucky to have several of them working on the Bill.

The Commission glimpsed all this back-stage work from time to time, but could only help with some of the more political front-stage activities.

First, however, we had to decide whether we *wanted* to help. It was clear that the reform now being mounted would only achieve whatever could be done without spending more money or recruiting more staff. That gave us a lot of things we had been asking for, as I shall explain. But within the supplementary benefits scheme we were not going to get our own first priority – higher long-term rates of benefit for the unemployed – or the twice-yearly lump-sum grants for all claimants which would make a drastic reduction in discretionary payments tolerable. Outside the scheme the real value of other benefits was to be reduced. Child benefits, which were our own top priority in the whole social security system, suffered a particularly severe cut in real value. Looking further afield it was clear that nothing would be done to increase opportunities for work. That had long been our first priority of all. But unemployment was now widely regarded as a solution, not a problem: no-one really cared about it any more. And it was not at all clear what sort of body the new Social Security Advisory Committee, replacing us and NIAC, was to be. What should we do?

We faced the usual dilemma of reformers: would this half loaf be better than no bread? In 1979 it was not yet clear that under this Government a 'nil-cost' reform would soon be regarded as a progressive triumph. We talked among ourselves and with Ministers, and decided that if they would make it publicly clear that they regarded this Bill as no more than a start on a longer-term programme of reform – a programme which would eventually call for some increase in expenditure – then we would publicly support the Bill. And if they made it clear that they wanted an independent and effective Social Security Advisory Committee we would back their plan to abolish us and NIAC. That is roughly what happened.

Patrick Jenkin quoted our support for the Bill inside and outside Parliament, and made it clear that he hoped for something more 'when resources permit'. (No Minister can promise action which calls for expenditure until the Cabinet has approved it.) Meanwhile we talked with staff up and down the country, with MPs concerned with social security on both sides of the House, with the TUC, the civil service unions and the pressure groups. We issued press releases, and I wrote articles and contributed to public debates of all kinds. Each time we argued for bolder action, but supported this measure as a reform worth having. I think we did right. But no-one can yet be sure.

The sudden decision to grant independence to Zimbabwe postponed the opening debate on our Bill and it looked for a few days as if we were going to miss the bus. Christmas was approaching and on the evening of 19 December the private offices serving DHSS Ministers had their annual party: wine and cheese, and young executive and clerical officers performing songs and sketches. It was all rather medieval: servants licensed to poke fun at their masters once a year. I recalled an exchange from the party held a couple of years earlier when one bright young EO asked another: "And how does Alf Morris's secretary keep him so busy – *all day?*" "By writing 'P.T.O.' on both sides of a blank sheet of paper" came the reply. Sensing perhaps that Ministers were not in a mood to laugh at themselves, the performers this year were a little more cautious. Patrick Jenkin had on his mind the opening speeches he was due to make on our Bill and the National Health Service Bill. Lynda Chalker talked amidst the din about her own anxieties. I spoke with each of them about potential candidates to chair the Social Security Advisory Committee which would replace us next year.

Three evenings later, on 22 December, Patrick Jenkin stood up to introduce the Social Security Bill in the Commons. His opening speech still contained an assertion that he regarded this as only the starting point for a longer-term programme of reform, but the final revisions imposed on him by the Treasury had deleted his hopes about future expenditure and the vigorous part an independent Social Security Advisory Committee would play. I had done some 'phoning earlier in the afternoon to MPs who might interject questions which would enable him to put these sentences back into the record. But when the questions came he ploughed loyally on, refusing to respond to them.

Stan Orme replied – as ever, less at home in opposition than in government. Throughout the evening there were friendly references from both sides of the House to me and the Commission for 'bringing the supplementary benefits scheme out of the darkness'. Far more important was the fact that it was a serious debate constantly returning to all the issues we had been discussing for years: child benefits, housing benefits, fuel benefits, equal treatment for women, and so on. At least the ground for further action had been prepared. Later, as numbers dwindled towards supper time, the new boys were allotted their opportunities to speak. Frank Field, recently Director of the Child Poverty Action Group, was better informed than anyone else – wittily combative too. The old hands seemed to regard him as a little swot, rather too clever for his own good. The chamber began to fill up again after supper with an increasingly alcoholic and chatty crowd of members. Reg Freeson, winding up for the opposition, conveyed an earnest asperity which quickly lost him this difficult audience. He ended by reading his speech into the record through a hail of interuptions. Reg Prentice, concluding the debate for the government, was heckled from the start. He responded by deliberately provoking uproar – "A Labour Party which Clem Attlee and Ernie Bevin would not have recognised: Dad's Red Army!" He ploughed on through the din till the Speaker called the vote. Impassively behind him on the narrow bench reserved for officials sat Michael Partridge, Alan Palmer, John Westbey, a lawyer, a finance man – as able a bunch of social security experts as you could find anywhere in the world. A day or two later they persuaded Reg to write, rather reluctantly, to his hecklers, using the replies they had prepared for each one who had posed serious criticism or questions about the Bill. As the division bells rang, more members rushed in to vote. Among them was Sir Keith Joseph who asked one of the officials whom he recognised (they had all worked for him when he had been Secretary of State for Social Services in the Heath Government) if this was a vote to abolish another of his creations – the over-elaborate administrative structure of the NHS. "No" was the reply, "*Another* of your creations: the double link for pensions. This is the Social Security Bill".

The Committee stage followed in February. Reg Prentice urged that a time limit be imposed from the start, which horrified officials. They actually wanted a thorough debate to check over the Bill for weak points; and they got their way. Night after night the opposition conducted a filibuster, provoked by the pensions clauses, which prevented government back-benchers from saying anything. If they were tempted into doing so, despite the warnings of Tony Newton their Whip, that gave each member on the Labour side the opportunity of making yet another speech in reply to whatever they said. So they sat through the nights, answering letters from their constituents, reading papers and magazines or just dozing, while Lynda Chalker, exhausted but unfailingly good-tempered, carried on the argument for the government.

Officials sat on the hard bench alongside her, preparing notes on every clause and amendment – Michael occasionally composing bawdy limericks to cheer her on. I sat on the public benches along the other side of the Committee room whenever I could get there. After dinner on 19 February Margaret Thatcher came in, very elegant, flanked by her Chief Whip, Parliamentary Private Secretary and a Private Secretary, to see how her troops were performing. You could feel the tension rise as power came among us. Stan Orme immediately took the opportunity of complaining about the absence of Reg Prentice who left the Committee each evening about 6.30 p.m. on grounds of ill-health which the opposition plainly regarded as spurious. The next session, beginning on 21 February, went right through the night into the next day – the debate rambling boringly and pointlessly on for twenty-six hours with fifteen-minute breaks every three hours.

A few evenings later, after nearly 100 hours in Committee, Reg got his guillotine at last. He gave notice to the Committee that the government would take the measure back to the House to impose this time limit on further discussion. Stan Orme and Reg Freeson, the opposition's main tacticians in this committee, immediately dropped out, and back-benchers – Andrew Bennett, Frank Field and others – took over the running. Tory back-benchers got into the act too, and the whole discussion became more productive. A sensible agenda for the rest of the debate was sorted out over supper between Tony Newton, Andrew Bennett and two of the more experienced people on the public benches – Tony Lynes working as a freelance with the Labour Party and Paul Lewis representing the National Council for One Parent Families. Reg had been right after all: provided time is not too short, Parliament works better when limits are imposed on its debates. The guillotine motion went through the House on 25 February with about fifteen members present on each side for most of the time and 560 coming in to vote at the end of the evening.

Committee stage is crucial, even when it brings no change in the Bill. This Bill consisted of a mass of amendments, incomprehensible to all but a few experts who were familiar with the legislation. Members of Parliament, who may only have had a few hours sleep snatched at odd moments, came to the Committee clutching the Bill, an explanatory red book prepared by the Department, a constantly changing sheaf of amendments, and a paper listing the clauses and amendments to be dealt with each day. In short, they needed help. Anyone can walk in and offer that help. But only a few people know how to do so. You must get the necessary papers, understand what they mean, and know how to prepare amendments to a Bill. You must be able to find your way around the enormous gloomy building, and follow the proceedings of the House so that you can get to the right committee room at the right time. You may have to stay there most of the night. You sit on the hard, narrow public benches within a few feet of the members, with officials on similar benches the other side of the room. If you signal or pass notes to any of them you will be turned out. But they may come and speak to you or invite you to come outside and talk in the corridor. (On this occasion, as a result of protests from the opposition, the chairman allowed Tony Lynes to pass notes discreetly to members: an unprecedented concession!)

Most of the amendments and speeches made by the more serious critics of this Bill were prepared with the help of experts in the poverty lobby: Tony Lynes, Paul Lewis, Nick Beacock for the Campaign for the Homeless and Rootless, and John Wilson speaking for the disabled. It is equally important to note who was not there. A mass of material was prepared by groups representing pensioners and brought to the House just after the clauses about pensions had gone through: a complete waste of time. No-one came specifically to represent unemployed claimants, although the Bill included clauses on registration for work and other matters which were very important for unemployed people. No-one came from the TUC, although we prepared lots of briefing for them, met their officials before Christmas, and took a strong delegation of Commissioners and officials to their Social Insurance Committee on 9 January. They knew their way around the House well enough because they sent a large team to the Committee, two doors further down the same corridor, which was discussing the Employment Bill. But pensioners and the unemployed are of less interest to them. Thus legislation evolves, moulded by organised public pressure on behalf of different issues and interests.

Since all this activity made little impact on the Bill it may seem pointless. But not quite. Every Minister taking a Bill through the House likes to give away a few concessions to show that he is taking the Committee seriously. Concessions were given, in this case, about Parliament's right to scrutinise the regulations made under the Act, and about some of the provisions to be included in regulations. Moreover the assurances given by Ministers when they fight off amendments are recorded in Hansard and can later have an important effect on the interpretation of the law. In this case Ministers repeatedly said that they wanted the new Social Security Advisory Committee to be an active and independent body – "no tame poodle". They promised that the SSAC would have an adequate staff, direct access to Ministers and every opportunity to write and publish their own reports. The third and final reading of the Bill, debated in the House on 18 March, went over this ground again. Thanks to these assurances the SSAC, which had begun with a most uncertain role when the Bill first appeared, ended up with a more authoritative invitation to be effective than the SBC had ever been given. They will be turning up those columns of Hansard in future if powerful people try to censor what they want to say.

The Lords' debate came later. These are more light-hearted affairs. Officials knew that their old friend Tony Lynes was writing speeches, very good ones, for Lord Wells-Pestell the opposition's principal spokesman. They were dismayed to find that Lord Cullen, their own man, tended to read out his whole brief, including the confidential warnings they gave him about the line which the government's critics might take. They had to rush round to the Hansard office next morning to get these out of the record before it went to press. (They may not have realised that the two Lords, whether in government or in opposition, had long shared the briefs given them by officials and pressure groups. Each would have thought it very unsporting to behave like the professional politicians in the Commons.)

The Bill finally received royal assent on 24 May, the date planned nearly a year before. By then the first batches of regulations to be made under it were already being drafted. Work on the uprating of benefits due in November began in local social security offices a few days later. A great deal remained to be done. But the vehicle of reform, though it had shed so many of the hopes originally loaded onto it, was still lumbering forward.

Parliament, it may seem, is little more than a sausage machine through which such a Bill has to be pushed, its product wholly predictable. In this case, with a new government backed by a large majority, that is not far from the truth. Legislation is vital, for without it nothing happens. But the Act does little more than register the intention to change things, providing a licence for the work of those who must then bring about change. What actually happens depends mainly on earlier phases of the drama, when reforms are formulated and got into the Government's time-table, and on later phases when they are put into practice.

What was Achieved?

What difference will it all make to the people who really matter? Will a deserted wife looking after two young children on a Stockport housing estate notice any changes? Or a sixteen-year-old boy leaving school in Paisley without much hope of getting a job? Or an elderly widow living by herself in a back street of Margate?

Whether they notice or not, the new scheme will have some effects on all of them, both good and bad. When they first claim benefit they will get, without having to ask for it, a written notice explaining how their money was calculated or why it was refused. And the rules of the scheme are laid out more clearly – at least for those advised by people who know their way around the regulations.

But will they get any more money? That's what matters most to them. It may be true, but it is certainly not sufficient, to say that even to preserve the real value of their benefits these days is an achievement. The money they get has changed a little. The deserted wife and her children do best – and in up to five different ways. All the short-term rates of benefit have gone up slightly, and she will get the higher long-term rates after one year instead of two. The five different rates previously paid for children have been reduced to three: if hers fall into the right age-groups she will get a little more for one or both of them. If one of her children is under five she will still get more money as an automatic addition paid to help meet the extra heating costs she is likely to have with a child at home all day. And if she can get a part-time job she will be able to keep a good deal more of the money she earns. It is equally important that all these extras come as a right, without having to ask for them or seek any favours. If she wants discretionary extras on top of these regular weekly payments she should find it a bit easier to get help in buying things which the weekly payments are clearly not intended to cover – a new pram or bed, or a second-hand replacement for her cooker, for example, or the costs of moving to a cheaper or more convenient home. But she will find it harder to get grants for shoes and clothing and other things which her weekly benefit is supposed to cover. If she gets a job, supports herself and remarries a man who cannot work (or who chooses to go back to college or to stay at home looking after the children) she will be entitled to be treated as the breadwinner of the household – but not until 1983. She will then also be able to get family income supplement for the children if her wages are low, and supplementary benefit for the whole family if she loses her job and cannot get another.

Things have worked out less well for the widow in Margate. Because all the long-term rates of benefit have been reduced a bit, hers has probably fallen slightly in real value. The increases gained by people such as the lone mother in Stockport have been paid for by smaller reductions in the benefits of much larger numbers of pensioners. However, if she is over seventy she will automatically get an addition to her weekly benefit, a good deal larger than the one she was probably getting already, to help meet the costs of heating. That is extra money put into the scheme as a fuel subsidy, not just a redistribution of funds. She faces the same changes in the rules about discretionary lump-sum-grants as everyone else.

The school leaver in Paisley will be affected too. He used to be able to claim as soon as he left school. Now he must wait until the end of the holidays. If his family are living on social security benefits they will not be greatly affected because his parents can go on drawing child benefit and dependants' allowances for him under insurance or supplementary benefits until the end of the holidays. But if his father is working they will only have the child benefit to help them out. They will retain that, however, till the end of the holidays even if the boy gets a job.

If any of these claimants face special difficulties, they ought henceforth to get a bit more help in sorting out their problems. Suppose the mother in Stockport was left in chaos by her departing husband – beset by arrears of rent, unpaid fines, and letters threatening to cut off her electricity and repossess the cooker and the TV set, and unsure which of these debts she is responsible for or where to turn for help. The local social security office now has someone on its staff called a 'special case officer' who has a little more training and a good deal more time than anyone had before to help her sort things out and 'phone the Housing Department and the Electricity Board. (The savings in staff made by postponing payments for school leavers were in effect used to make this possible.)

What these claimants may not appreciate is that the whole legal basis for decisions about supplementary benefits has changed. Henceforth these decisions are to be taken by staff in local offices, following regulations which are difficult to understand but at least cannot be secret because they are laid down by Parliament. The staff are no longer acting, as they were in the past, as agents of the Commission, relying on guidance from the SBC which even to the end was never wholly published. As 'supplementary benefit officers' they take decisions in their own right – with advice from the Chief SBO in London (Alan Palmer, who led the review team). Claimants who appeal against these decisions will find that the tribunals have a simpler job to do. They must decide whether the regulations were properly applied to the case and they have much less discretion than hitherto to interpret and vary the policies of the scheme. The tribunals should work a bit better too: as a result of other reforms, outside the new Act, they have a few full-time chairmen, more lawyers, full-time and part-time, and a good deal more training. If the claimants or the DHSS do not like the tribunals' decisions, they can appeal to an experienced lawyer specialising in supplementary benefits work – the Social Security Commissioner – instead of having to use the more cumbrous courts to which scarcely anyone resorted. For that claimants can get free legal advice, but not free advocacy. On a point of law they can still pursue their appeal beyond that, all the way to the House of Lords. And in Parliament there is now a standing committee which keeps an eye on the DHSS. They could do a good deal, if they choose, to make the new scheme work well and keep the momentum of reform rolling.

To sum up. The scheme has been slightly but significantly shifted. It is a bit simpler than it used to be. Its rules are clearer and more public. It offers people rather more rights and relies less on discretion. Critics will say it has become more 'rigid'. Decisions about the discretionary benefits which remain are based to a greater extent on facts, and rather less on judgments about 'welfare' and 'need' which sound benign but are too apt to go wrong. And the distribution of benefits has been shifted in favour of people with children, largely at the expense of old people.

Similar attempts have been made in the past to simplify social assistance and cut back the tangle of discretionary benefits which always grows up around the scheme. But complication and discretion burgeon again, more quickly each time. Democracy, bureaucracy and pressure groups together tend to produce that result. Is there any reason to believe that we shall not re-enact the whole rake's progress yet again? The more clear-cut basis for decision making, based on the new legal structure, the more consistent appeals system, and the special case officers who should be able to use discretion more humanely and confine it more closely to the small minority of cases in which it is really needed – all these should help to stabilise things. Previous attempts to reform the system lacked these elements and were not followed up with effective action as this reform should be.

But this is only a beginning. If the impetus for change peters out here and no more is done, those who worked for this reform will have failed. It is outside the supplementary benefit scheme that action is now most urgently needed. Action to get unemployed people back to work, to raise the incomes of low-paid workers with children to support, to sort out the confusion of housing subsidies for people with low incomes, and to create a fairer system of fuel subsidies – these come top of the list. They would in turn make bolder reforms of supplementary benefits possible. With better child benefits to raise the incomes of the working poor it would be easier to gain the higher long-term rates of benefit for the long-term unemployed. With a comprehensive system of rent subsidies administered by housing authorities for everyone with low incomes, whether in or out of work, it would be possible to get rent payments out of the social assistance scheme and greatly simplify the elaborate means tests now imposed on people who are out of work for a few days or weeks.

I shall say more about this unfinished business in the following chapter. In doing so I shall also touch on questions of style, management, and relations with the public which are as important as the rules, benefits and administrative machinery. Whether this modest start on reform ultimately works for good or ill will depend very heavily on the leadership given by Ministers, the back-bench MPs who should be keeping a sharp eye on the scheme, and the officials who manage it.

My hopes for the future have led me to give an optimistic view about the scope for improving things. A more pessimistic interpretation of events is equally plausible. As the living standards of the poor fall, as unemployment rises and cuts are made in the public services, there will be turbulent times ahead. The social assistance scheme, to which more and more people will have to turn for survival, is a potential flashpoint for disorder. The reform of supplementary benefits was not conceived simply as a way of bringing a sensitive sector of government under control. But that is how it could be interpreted. Simplification would then become a way of means testing more and more unemployed people without commensurate increases in staff. The new decision-making system would be a way of transferring powers from the SBC – a body which could at least be exposed to public pressure – to the Chief Supplementary Benefit Officer who is safely insulated from the public. Reforms of the tribunals might become simply a way of making them appeal-proof. Special case officers may only be used to process the more harrowing cases without too much scandal and protest. And the Social Security Advisory Committee may turn out to be a respectable front office for a service whose function is to divide the poor from the working population and keep them docile. Although things need not work out like that, these are possibilities we have to look at more seriously. But first I want to consider some of the unfinished business left on the agenda.

The next chapter deals with housing costs, fuel costs, and the quality of service to the public. After that, I return to the story of events before drawing conclusions from the Commission's whole experience.

CHAPTER 7

Unfinished Business

The fourth act in the drama of social reform had been completed. In the first we posed the main problems to be tackled; in the second we explored solutions and identified those contending for them; in the third we assembled a package of attainable goals; and in the fourth those of our hopes which had not been jettisoned along the way were carried through Parliament and passed into law. What actually happens depends on the fifth act of the drama in which the new law and regulations are put into practice. My story stops short of that crucial phase. There may then follow a sixth act in which the ideas and initiatives developed thus far are taken further. It is to this unfinished business, potentially more important than anything achieved earlier in the drama, that I now turn. I deal only with a few of the things which ought to be done.

However hard you try to avoid it, any public service designed specially for poor people is apt to become a poor service. If Britain is to be a tolerable country to live in, we should turn away from policies which rely increasingly on means-tested benefits. It will take a long time to achieve that. But a great deal can be done meanwhile, without transforming the whole system, to make policies for the poor work better. Provided we never relapse into believing that this is all that's needed, we should be pressing for reforms of this kind.

Housing Costs

The government's proposals, published in March 1981, for an altogether new system of housing benefits for tenants with low incomes could be an important step forward. Although this is the first official commitment to do anything about these problems, it is only the latest act in a much longer story which may be worth telling some day as a drama in its own right. The Supplementary Benefits Commission got into this act towards the end of 1975 when we first began looking into possibilities for reforming our own scheme. Housing costs and subsidies, it soon became clear, lay at the heart of some of the most chaotic tangles of that chaotically tangled system. There must be something wrong with arrangements which seemed to cause more work and were the source of more mistakes than any other feature of the scheme. I began to understand why prominent members of the government's advisory committee on rent rebates and allowances had privately pressed us to look into this can of worms.

In an attempt to sort things out as best we could for our own customers the Commission had already asked social security staff to go through about one million files to check whether claimants were getting the right housing benefits. That laborious exercise eventually transferred 90,000 claimants from supplementary benefits to housing rebates and allowances. We believed that there were three times as many people drawing housing rebates and allowances from local government who would have been better off with us. But nobody was telling them. Meanwhile there were many others who were entitled to one or other benefit and getting neither. Later we estimated that about 400,000 people were failing to get the housing benefits to which they were entitled. That was no way to run a public service.

Incomprehensibility and deprivation of rights were not the only problems this system posed. It created enormous quantities of work for local government and social security staff who had constantly to be recalculating payments and sending papers back and forth to each other. Nearly one in ten of the 30,000 people administering supplementary benefits in local social security offices were required to deal with the housing elements of this system alone.

Even when these arrangements worked properly they were often unfair, and widely resented. People who had carefully worked out which scheme would be the 'best buy' for them found that new benefits – fuel payments, free school meals and so on – were soon added or subtracted on one side of the scales or the other, and that their calculations turned out to be wrong. Because supplementary benefit can pay the whole of a tenant's rent and rates, while the maximum rebates are less generous than that, people living on similar incomes were treated differently – those out of work doing better than those in work. To sum up: we needed a scheme which would be easier to understand, which would achieve a better take-up of the benefits people were intended to receive, which could be administered less laboriously and inefficiently, and which treated people more fairly – giving them help according to their needs, not according to their status with the social security system.

For a while we pinned our hopes on what was still being called the Housing Finance Review, then going on at the Department of the Environment. If it was intended to sort out the 'dog's breakfast' of housing subsidies, to use Anthony Crosland's words, then this particular mess must be high on the DOE's agenda. We were soon put right about that: there seemed to be scant concern about the poor among those responsible for the housing review and no radical drive coming from the top. Instead we had to rely on a study group on poverty, chaired by a Treasury official, which was looking into many issues, including rents and housing subsidies. (Throughout this affair we found ourselves in the unfamiliar position of gaining support from the Treasury. It almost made me wonder whether we had got it all wrong! But any department concerned with good housekeeping – the Civil Service Department was another – had to share our concern about these problems.) Useful though this study group was, they proceeded slowly and secretly, and never published any reports. Like all groups of officials, they could analyse the problems pretty well, but they were not going to start a public debate or generate any pressure for reform.

When the DOE eventually published what had by then become a general review of housing policy we were quite relieved to find that they had nothing to say about subsidies for the poor. At least they had left us a clean slate. Although the technical volumes published with it were fascinating, their Green Paper of 1977 was a most conservative document – quite Baldwinesque in tone.

Meanwhile, for lack of a better vehicle on which to launch a public debate, we began discussing housing subsidies in our Annual Reports, starting with the second, published in 1977. We proposed that the whole confusing array of payments designed to help poor people pay for their housing should be swept away and replaced by a single, unified scheme. Given the necessary resources, we would be prepared to help in administering this through social security offices. But the housing authorities were plainly the best people for the job. Householders would rather go to the town hall than a social security office for help over housing. (That was why there were three times more people getting the 'wrong' benefits from town halls than from us.) And housing staff were better equipped to make calculations about rents and rates than our staff were: they were doing it all the time. These ideas were seriously discussed in leaders and feature articles of *The Times* and other posh papers. But ours was a wholly 'unofficial' contribution to the debate, and it evoked no response from local government. Local authorities would not take the idea seriously unless 'their' Ministry – the Department of the Environment – gave them a lead.

Discussions continued interminably in an interdepartmental working party of officials. The DOE resisted action: they opposed DHSS proposals, responded reluctantly to Treasury requests for counter-proposals, sent representatives to the meetings who were more junior than the spokesmen sent by other Departments, and dragged their feet all the way. If it had not been for Geoffrey Beltram, our under secretary working on the problem, the whole idea would probably have died at this stage.

The DOE had one very good reason for opposing reform. The means tests for supplementary benefits, rate rebates and rent rebates were different. That was why they were such an incomprehensible mess. The 'tapers' – that is to say, the speed at which the benefits are withdrawn as incomes rise – were much more gentle for rent rebates, and particularly for rate rebates, than they were for supplementary benefits. The poorest of the people not on supplementary benefits were treated less generously than people with similar incomes who were on supplementary benefit. But other less poor people, with incomes well above supplementary benefit levels, were getting quite a lot of help: these were mainly pensioners with rate rebates. Therefore any reform which was to treat equal needs equally would probably cost a good deal of money in order to increase benefits for the poorest people outside the supplementary benefit scheme; otherwise it would not be 'saleable' to politicians. The only other way of increasing benefits for these people would be to scrape some money down to them from slightly less poor people getting rate rebates. That could be done by making the 'taper' applied to a new, unified benefit a good deal steeper than the present tapers for rebates. But there was no point in asking a government which was already losing its nerve to take money away from a lot of elderly ratepayers. Thus a single, comprehensive scheme of housing benefits for people with low incomes would either be expensive, or there would be too many 'losers' and not enough 'gainers' to make the idea politically saleable. Either way, the DOE and its Ministers would get the backwash that followed. No wonder they opposed reform.

We saw the force of these arguments. That was one reason why we wanted the government to go the whole hog and bring owner occupiers as well as tenants into the new scheme. Tax relief for house buyers is completely out of control, increasing in value every year with indefensible results which give most generous advantages to the richest people. Sooner or later a Chancellor of the Exchequer will have to make sense of these reliefs. They are now worth £1,500 millions a year: £50 million – no more than the small change to be shaken out of a reform of these reliefs – would pay for an acceptable scheme of benefits for the poor. We had other reasons, too, for wanting to bring the owner occupiers in. More and more of them are turning up among supplementary benefit claimants. Any reform which left them out would leave the social security system still wrestling with some of its most difficult calculations of housing costs.

Other objections to reform coming from the DOE were less convincing. The government, they said, must retain a rate rebate system as a publicly presentable protection for poor ratepayers in the years when sharp increases are expected in rates. (Since a new benefit replacing rate rebates must in any case have the same effect as these rebates, the argument was not about realities – only about how to present them to the public.) The local housing authorities, they said, would hate the whole idea. And anyway, they were not capable of handling the new scheme proposed. (Since they were already handling far more complicated schemes covering two-thirds of those who would be involved in the new one, that too was an unconvincing argument.)

We decided that we had better find out for ourselves what the housing authorities really thought. So we started consulting housing directors and their committee chairmen up and down the country, beginning with Bristol in September 1978. I talked at Shelter's annual conference and at other public meetings, and wrote articles about our proposals for rationalising housing benefits. Local government's response was clear. Provided the extra expenditure imposed on the authorities by a unified benefit, together with any extra administrative costs involved, was borne by the central government and not loaded onto the rates, and provided that they were properly consulted and given time to make sensible arrangements, they were prepared to take on a scheme of this kind. Indeed, most of them welcomed it. It would make life easier for them by simplifying their administration and solving some of their most difficult cases of rent arrears. There would no longer be any need to collect individual rents or rates from tenants living on supplementary benefit: the whole job could be done through one payment made by central government each month to local government. As for the loss of rate rebates – although we repeatedly asked whether that would make difficulties for them, no-one was much bothered about that. We had discovered, yet again, that you do not have to dig very far into the grass roots to learn more about what goes on at ground level than Whitehall knows.

Meanwhile, as we looked more deeply into the supplementary benefit scheme which was now being reviewed from top to bottom, it became increasingly clear that we could only achieve a radical simplification of our own system if we first got housing payments out of it. While it continued to be the main instrument for meeting the housing costs of the poorest people, everyone who claimed the benefit – even for a day or two – had to be put through an elaborate means test, a central purpose of which was to pay for their housing. If that problem could be solved in other and better ways, 130,000 people could be got off supplementary benefit altogether. These were the claimants whose benefit was no more than their rent. In future they would do as well by relying instead on the new housing benefit and their old age pensions or whatever other income they had. Every other householder left on supplementary benefit could then be given a simpler means test. But to overcome the political inertia which blocked progress, money would have to be found to reduce the numbers of people likely to lose from the change. The big problem then would be a technical one. Could the housing authorities get the new benefit into householders' pockets quickly enough to prevent people with high rents who fall out of work suddenly from getting into serious difficulties? Some authorities which had installed efficient computer systems could already do that. But many still took weeks to provide rent rebates and months to provide rate rebates. That would not be good enough.

We had reluctantly to abandon the hope of bringing the owner occupiers in from the start of a new scheme. It was going to be difficult enough to cope with tenants. But if we could get a scheme off the ground for them, home owners might be brought in later. Without the owner occupiers and their tax reliefs, however, it would be harder to get the money needed to bring the numbers of losers down to a politically tolerable level.

After repeated attempts by DHSS officials, warmly supported by their Ministers, to get some proposals for action published, we had to recognise that the Labour government's capacity for getting anything done was ebbing away. We would have to wait for the election and hope it produced a government with a majority in Parliament and the will to act. It did. But the prospect of a Conservative reform of housing finance was frightening to anyone concerned about the poor. The new regime might be too little concerned, rather than too obsessed, about potential losers.

I met Patrick Jenkin a few days after the election. I had often talked to him and his colleagues when they were in opposition about a single, comprehensive housing benefit for people with low incomes, and was encouraged to find that he had already discussed the idea with Michael Heseltine who seemed interested. Heseltine was now Secretary of State for the Environment. Support for a unified housing benefit at the DOE would be something new. Meanwhile the Government was determined to reduce the numbers of civil servants, and before long Patrick Jenkin was giving private assurances that he would achieve that. The only way in which DHSS could cut staff on a considerable scale in supplementary benefits – the most labour-costly part of its services – was by getting rent payments out of the scheme. That saving would be partly offset by what looked like being small increases in staff which local authorities might need to administer the new scheme. But in social security it would open the way to further simplification and staffing economies in future. The civil service unions might not like the prospect of all these cuts, but before long it was clear that the Government's economic policies were going to lead to such a drastic increase in unemployment that there would be more social security staff, not less, at the end of the day – paying money to people out of work. (A mad world: but we had better seize any opportunity it gave us for making a bit of progress.) Ministers set up a study group to work out proposals for a unified housing benefit. It was placed firmly under Treasury leadership, and even the DOE began to make positive proposals for action. At last we seemed to be getting somewhere. But where?

The proposals published about eighteen months later show where the government are heading. The DOE officials responsible for the publication must still have regarded them with some distaste. They declined to publish a simplified popular explanation of them, or to discuss them at a press conference, or to give the specialist correspondents a detailed background briefing about them – as you must do if you really want to explain things to the public. Not surprisingly, people like David Hencke, *The Guardian*'s specialist on housing, unable to believe anything good of Michael Heseltine, attacked the proposals even before they were published. As I write, local authorities are being asked to comment on them. These proposals could in fact prove to be a real break-through. They are, in a somewhat battered form, the new scheme we have been seeking all these years. And they could be made better still.

Local housing authorities will administer the new scheme, which will look to the public much like rate rebates. The new benefit will replace rent rebates and the housing payments for tenants which now come through the supplementary benefit scheme. Thus council tenants living on supplementary benefit or with earnings no higher than supplementary benefit levels will not be asked to pay any rent or rates. Cash allowances serving the same combined purposes will be paid to private tenants by the local authorities. Above the supplementary benefit level of incomes, the benefit will taper off at a speed rather faster than the present rebates. The Exchequer will meet in full the extra costs of this benefit and its administration which would otherwise fall on local government. Some of the bigger housing associations may be given the same powers which local authorities will have to act for their tenants.

But owner occupiers will only be brought into the scheme for their rate payments. And because the government have proposed a 'nil cost' reform, they expect 2,150,000 people to lose from it and only 810,000 to gain. The great majority of losers – 1,700,000 of them – will suffer a cut in income of less than 50 pence a week. But 50 pence could amount to two pairs of shoes a year. And now that rents and rates are to rise there will in fact be still more losers and fewer gainers. That has already provoked a lot of protests from the pressure groups. The Government will find it worthwhile to buy off some of these critics with a more generous scheme. The savings they will make on staff, estimated at £17 millions a year, will cover much of the cost of doing that. Later, if the reform enables them to simplify the whole supplementary benefit scheme still further, there will be even larger savings to be made. The Government rightly expect that a single, simpler benefit will achieve better rates of take-up as more people come forward to claim their rights. But their nil-cost rule means that the extra money paid out for this purpose will have to be found by reducing the benefits which go to those already claiming. It should be a proper obligation of the taxpayer to provide the money required for benefits which Parliament already intends people to have. In these ways the numbers of losers could be greatly reduced.

After that, there will be administrative problems to tackle. Some local housing authorities are already very efficient; but others will need a bit of prodding and a good deal of practical help if they are to pay the new housing benefits quickly enough. Householders who can now appeal about rent payments to the supplementary benefit tribunals must in future have some other way of gaining redress for their grievances. The rent tribunals seem to be the obvious body to take on this job.

More fundamentally, the basic aims of this reform must not be forgotten. It should not be designed just for the bureaucrats – to save staff for the DHSS, to provide a cheap way of reducing rent arrears for the housing authorities, and to give the DOE the political protection of a benefit which looks like a rate rebate. The aim must be to give poorer people prompt and effective help in meeting their housing costs, and to bring all the relevant branches of Government more efficiently to bear for this purpose. If that is attained, other reforms will be easier. One of them could be a new benefit for the people who have most difficulty in paying their fuel bills – a benefit which could be distributed to householders already identified by a properly organised rent subsidy.

Fuel Costs

Early in 1979 I was out visiting in bitter weather with a 'TEO' – a territorial executive officer – from one of the south-east London social security offices. We were working among the towering flats of a council estate. It was the sort of neighbourhood from which anyone with young children tries to escape: the sort of neighbourhood to which they send mothers who need a home urgently when their marriages break up. Many of the calls the TEO made in these blocks were prompted by trouble over fuel debts.

We rang the bell at a door on the ninth floor. A tense looking woman opened it to us and we explained that we were from social security and had come in answer to her letter. Sitting in her living room we began to understand why she was so anxious. First she had got behind with the rent. Now she was behind with the electricity bills too. Everything in these flats works by electricity: there's no fire-place and no gas. The

Electricity Board had cut off her supply, and through the worst weeks of a bad winter she had survived with the help of a paraffin stove and candles. Each day when her daughter came home from school they went out to fish and chip shops or Chinese take-aways: it was an expensive way of eating, but at least they kept warm for a while sitting in these places. She had asked the council months ago to move her to a house where there would be an open fire and a gas cooker (unaware that they do not transfer tenants with rent arrears). Eventually she found a man who illicitly reconnected the electricity for her. That must have cost her something too: ten pounds, perhaps. (On Merseyside there's a lady from the Salvation Army, known as 'Screwdriver Lil', who reconnects the poor for nothing. A modern Robin Hood: they never catch up with her.) But this woman was sure that the Electricity Board would find her out and send her to prison. We took a look at the reconnection to see whether it was obviously dangerous. It looked like a professional job, and we told her that we would not report her. But she would have to own up about it if we were to help her in any way with the bills. Meanwhile we would do our best to sort things out for her with the Electricity Board. We left and went on to see another woman in a rather similar plight in the next block.

With the help of some good people in the better Gas and Electricity Boards our officials got arrangements set up which now generally prevent supplementary benefit claimants who have children, pensioners or disabled people in their families from being cut off. Instead, the Boards' staff ask these customers to get in touch with DHSS staff if they fall behind with their payments. Deductions are then made from their benefit and sent direct to the Boards. That eventually gets fuel bills paid. But too often these arrangements only transform the problem; they do not solve it. For the problem is usually poverty, not poor housekeeping. And it is not confined to people living on supplementary benefit: the working poor need help too. Neither is this problem going to go away: indeed, it will grow worse.

Labour and Conservative Governments alike have expected the price of energy to double in real terms – in relation to the price of everything else, that is – between 1978 and the year

2000. That increase will not come smoothly: prices will take unforseen jumps from time to time and a lot of vulnerable people will be in trouble. The Government are gradually finding ways of helping some of these people, first by increasing supplementary benefit for claimants who have children under five, or elderly or frail people in their households, and for those whose homes are particularly difficult to heat. Now they are also subsidising the insulation of homes, and doing that more generously for people with low incomes. But it is still the poorest people who are most likely to live in poorly insulated homes and in housing which depends entirely on the most expensive forms of central heating – electric night storage and underfloor systems, for example. The rich are more likely to use gas. Meanwhile prepayment meters which enabled people to control their fuel costs are disappearing. And the tariffs for gas and electricity still charge more, per therm, to the small consumer than the large consumer. Thus cases of the sort that I have described are likely to grow more common in future as energy prices go on rising.

We need four kinds of action: first to make it easier for us all to use energy more efficiently and economically (with better insulated homes and work places, more efficient cars, and so on); second to raise the incomes of the poorest people (by enabling them to get jobs, providing more generous pensions, and better benefits for children and for larger families on low incomes); third to make it easier for poorer people to manage their fuel consumption and pay their bills (for example, by reorganising the tariffs so that small consumers are not so unfairly charged, by installing meters for those who want them, and making other easy payment methods – now rarely used by the poor – more attractive); and fourth to subsidise the poorer consumers. That is the line of action I want to explore here, but the other three must not be forgotten.

Subsidies for poor consumers have been opposed by officials in the Treasury and the Department of Energy who seem to regard them as another expensive welfare programme advocated by bleeding-hearted liberals. If so, that only shows the ignorance of the critics. Until new energy sources and technologies are developed, fuel is going to be increasingly scarce. Energy-using industries and activities throughout the world are growing faster than the supplies of conventional fuels. The real price of energy must therefore rise fairly sharply. Indeed, if it did not do so we would never organise ourselves to achieve the greater efficiency in energy use which is now urgently needed and readily feasible. But the higher prices which the mass of consumers should pay for fuel cannot be charged without constant uproar and political set-backs unless the poorer consumers are first protected from the consequences. Thus fuel subsidies to protect the poor are no more than an act of political realism. The funds to pay for such a subsidy are ready to hand. The pricing policies now being imposed on the energy industries confer enormous profits on them. It is high time we established that a sort of commission must be charged on such profits made by monopoly suppliers of an essential resource. A modest percentage levied directly on them or on the taxes they pay would cover the costs of subsidising poorer consumers. That is no more than socially responsible and politically competent management of public enterprise.

As the review of the supplementary benefit scheme got under way it became clear that a comprehensive, simpler and fairer system of housing subsidies might be the most important thing we could achieve. For a couple of years we focused a lot of effort on that. Then, as our hopes for a unified housing benefit grew, we turned our attention to fuel benefits. I went with Stan Orme and our officials to meet Tony Benn, Secretary of State for Energy, John Cunningham his Minister, and Frances Morrell, their special adviser, on 21 November 1978. The energy Ministers promised to work with us in formulating a national fuel discount scheme. But there was no enthusiasm for the idea among their top officials and nothing came of it. We met the fuel pressure groups privately, and then in a bigger seminar at the National Council of Social Service on 8 December. Everyone there agreed about the urgency of the problem, but not about the action to be taken. Then, after the election, all proposals for fuel subsidies were abandoned. But Margaret Thatcher and some of her senior Ministers recognised that, with further increases in fuel prices on the way, this would be politically damaging. So just before Parliament rose in the summer of 1979 these proposals were rescued and a more generous set of fuel benefits invented. But they were confined to people living on supplementary benefit. It's always easier and cheaper to use this scheme as a passport to any new benefit for poor people.

The specifications for a fuel subsidy should be much the same as those for a housing benefit for the poor. It should be focused on needs, and must not be confined only to people living on supplementary benefit. It should be easy to understand and simple to administer: there's no point these days in calling for a scheme, however good it may be, that will require lots more civil servants to run it. It must be distributed in ways which will not humiliate anyone or deter people from claiming their rights. And it should leave them with some incentive to use fuel economically: it would be wrong simply to pay the bills, whatever they come to. The public would rightly resent that.

These specifications lead to a scheme that rides on the back of other benefits which already reach the poorest householders: we should not be inventing yet another means test. The new unified housing benefit should serve that purpose for tenants, and the fuel subsidy could be distributed to them by the Housing Departments. Rate rebates and supplementary benefits would identify the owner occupiers entitled to help. Until the new housing benefit is working, the supplementary benefit scheme, coupled with the present housing rebates and allowances, will do as passports to fuel subsidies. Together these schemes reach about six million householders who might be ranked into different bands – perhaps three – according to the amount of fuel subsidy they would be entitled to. The subsidy itself could be given in the form of fuel stamps if the various fuel boards would in future agree to use the same stamps. Before long, coal and paraffin could be brought into such a scheme too. Customers for any kind of fuel would then present stamps when paying their bills and no-one would know whether they had bought them for themselves or been given them by the Department of Energy.

Better schemes will in time be devised, but this one shows what could be done quickly. Progress towards a scheme of this sort has been held up – but not only by reactionaries in the bureaucracy. The pressure groups concerned with 'fuel poverty' bear some share of the responsibility too. Some of them are prepared to back a simple but workable scheme of this sort. Others demand a more elaborate scheme which takes more precise account of the customers' needs, and will settle for nothing less. Meanwhile, Members of Parliament contributing to debates on this topic hesitate to commit themselves to any firm programme until the pressure groups have reached pretty close agreement about what ought to be done. Politicians rely on these people to advise them, help them prepare speeches, and conduct campaigns in favour of any Bill that is to make its way through Parliament. Once united, the pressure groups wield considerable power: while they remain divided they obstruct progress.

It's high time the Department of Energy took these problems more seriously. In doing that they would be helping to establish the principle that every Minister – and not only the Secretary of State for Social Services – has obligations to poor people. It is always easier for Departments of Government to focus on perfecting their products and forget the customers. That way they can concentrate single-mindedly on providing good hospitals, schools or housing, or developing efficient fuel industries. But if they claim to be public services, not merely technological enterprises, each Department must also make certain that people with low incomes are not excluded from the service for which it is responsible – be that medical care, education, housing or a fuel supply sufficient to keep their homes warm through the winter.

The Quality of Service

Ever since I got involved with government, I have heard the same *cri de coeur* from civil servants: "If only they'd stop changing policies, we could produce a really top-class service" Well . . . their chance is coming.

Existing programmes may be axed. But once the cuts have been made, things are likely to settle down. There will be nothing to compare with the reorganisation of secondary schools, the slum clearance programme, the new pension scheme, the great tax credit scheme which fell by the wayside – the constantly changing demands of a growing economy which have for so long made the lives of public servants exhausting but exciting. Whoever is in power, economic stagnation will see to that. For innovating spirits, this will be a time for getting out of the backroom study groups which used to draft proposals for reform and into operational management – wherever the quality of existing services needs improvement. For that is where most of the action will be for the next few years.

But what does 'the quality of service' mean? It's intangible, yet unmistakable. Working for the Plowden Committee (on primary schools), the Public Schools Commission and the Supplementary Benefits Commission, I have visited well over 100 social security offices and scores of schools and hotels in several different countries. You sense the quality of the service they provide within a few minutes of entering. *What* you sense in the good ones is much the same in any service and any language.

Take the twelve-year-old boy who was the first person you met in a school playground. Whether in uniform or an old pair of jeans, he seems at home in his clothes – takes some care of them and of himself. Realising that you're a bit lost, he confidently asks "Can I help?" and takes you to the headmaster's office, chatting along corridors which are shining clean yet full of human interest. The pictures, you feel, were painted and the plants tended by the pupils. Or take the girl at the hotel's reception desk: she's neat, brisk, and pleased to see you. "Would you like some help with your bags? . . . a morning call? . . . tea? . . . newspaper? Dinner will be ready from seven o'clock." There are flowers somewhere, and an ashtray on the counter, regularly emptied.

And what about the good social security office? The man waiting to greet you at the entrance is neither obsequious nor offhand. He's welcoming and alert. He stops to have a word with a bewildered old lady and explains which waiting room she should go to before taking you up to the manager's office. (The customers are more important than the chairman.) The floors are clean; there's a rack of leaflets, placed under the eye of a member of staff where people can pick them up for themselves. Already you sense that the girls on the switchboard will be business-like but friendly, greeting callers with "Social security – good morning!" The food in the canteen will probably be good too. The toilet is clearly signposted; the posters on the walls are up-to-date; the chairs in the waiting rooms are not screwed to the floor. Barriers between staff and the public, if they exist, are not obtrusive. (London offices may not believe it, but there are offices with no barriers at all in some of the roughest parts of Clydeside – in neighbourhoods where the drink shops are barred from counter to ceiling.) When you reach the manager, he and his team will tell you their priorities for the coming year. They know their opposite numbers in the social work, housing, employment and fuel services by name. Pretty soon they hand you over to junior staff, some of whom are critical about features of the service they're providing, and not afraid to say so. Their trade union representatives are robust but cheerful. Staff interviewing claimants explain why they have to ask so many questions. If a payment is to be made, they say how and when the claimant will get it. And they are not afraid to give their names.

Everything about these services conveys the same messages. Their staff know what they're supposed to be doing. They care about their customers and treat them with respect. And they have pride in themselves and their work. That's partly because their managers care for *them*. They clearly explain what's expected of their staff, give them time and training for the job, make demands which are challenging but never impossible, and look after them if they get into real difficulties. This account of good practice will provoke cynical snorts in many quarters. It describes what could happen, and generally does, in places such as Falkirk, Ebbw Vale and Worthing, where there are good managers, and the staff and their colleagues in neighbouring services stay in the same place for years – as do most of their customers. But what about social security offices where there's *never* time to cope with all the customers' demands, or even to find out which are the most urgent; where turnover is high, most of the staff are inexperienced and managers find it hard to get to know them; where errors abound and no-one uses or understands the official codes of instructions? In such offices, where staff work in an anonymous, tumultuous urban world, fraud and abuse are easy – and resented. People run out of compassion on both sides of the counter. If some claimants are too ignorant or too exhausted to claim their rights, if files get lost, and if switchboards get too jammed to carry the traffic of incoming calls, those are no longer perceived as problems. They are solutions, giving the staff a respite to cope with other work.

As unemployment rises still higher and insurance benefits are cut back, there will be more and more social security customers, and more of them will have to claim the more complicated and contentious means-tested benefits. If, on top of this, there are cuts in staff, then poor service and anger on each side of the counter are bound to grow more common.

What can the reforming administrator do in the face of these trends? He can press for simplifications which would ease pressures of work. I have already shown that there is really no need to run three separate means-tested schemes for rate rebates, rent rebates and allowances, and supplementary benefit rent payments – all for the same purpose: to help poorer people pay for housing. Other long-overdue simplifications would be possible once we get this one adopted.

Technology can help too. As bus fares and postal charges rise and telephones grow relatively cheaper, the opportunity should be taken to reduce the queues in the waiting rooms by using telephones more efficiently. Two-thirds of the people in these queues are not making a claim – only seeking or giving information. This could often be transacted more simply on the 'phone. But the telephone service would have to be improved first. Properly organised, it has the advantage that it can connect you to the specialist who really knows the answer to your question. The one or two receptionists facing the queues in the waiting room can never know all the answers to the questions which are put to them. So they have to leave their posts and go looking for the specialists, or give the wrong answers – or they try to deter people from asking questions in the first place.

The social security computers at Newcastle and elsewhere – one of the biggest systems in the world – are going to be replaced over the next few years. Next time round, the supplementary benefit scheme will be brought into the system too. Reformers should seize the opportunity to make the scheme more efficient and more humane. By the end of this decade it will be cheaper to hold information in words, on-line in a computer than to keep it on paper. The costs of doing this have already fallen by nine-tenths over the last few years and that trend will continue. Soon there need be no files to get lost: the data on each case could be called up instantly from a central store on a visual display unit – *and* checked by the customer. No longer need anyone worry about keeping the code books up-to-date: again, every rule could be called up on the visual display unit and shown to the customer. Leaflets and forms, already much improved, could be made still simpler and clearer.

Routine interviewing, in cases which present no special problems, could eventually be done by machines. And the machines don't have to be placed in a social security office: they could be in the citizens' advice bureau or the public library. We already know from medical research that a well-programmed computer can elicit more information more willingly, even on the most sensitive topics, than a doctor or a nurse. In banks people now queue to use the cash dispensing machines, even when tellers are free to serve them. For routine business most people prefer machines. That could free the staff for more demanding and interesting work. But thus far, when computers have been introduced into the social security system, they have made things better for management, not for the staff or their customers. Management gets fewer errors, better statistics, less internal fraud, closer control and lower labour costs. But the customers do not get their benefits any quicker or receive clearer explanations of their rights; and the staff have more boring, less responsible and less well paid work to do.

In future the customers could be paid in any way they choose: many would prefer a credit transfer to a bank, a building society or post office savings account. Fewer giros would then be lost in the post. Indeed, the lost giro, the lost file, the over-loaded switchboard, the unanswered questions, the secret codes – all the things which provoke most exhaustion and anger in social security offices – could be largely abolished. And thanks to advancing technology that could be done without spending a lot more money. Freed from its load of mechanical work, the local office should then be given more opportunity to experiment. Many of the improvements so far made in the quality of the service – such as payments by giro and interviews by appointment – were first invented in local offices. But civil service traditions make local innovations of this sort far more difficult than they ought to be.

A headmaster, like the head of a clinic or a social work area office, is regarded as captain of his team. If members of the team develop a successful innovation, they write articles about it and speak at conferences, they attract students, foreign visitors and able recruits from all over the country, and they gain promotion. But the grey anonymity of the civil service works against all that. Too often local office managers merely manage resources over which they have no control. Innovation seems risky. They are not allowed to choose their own key staff; and their regional controllers exert only a little more influence in choosing them. (So much depends on seniority and the candidates' claims to 'local connections'.) They cannot reward their staff with pay or promotion. They do not even control their own accommodation.

Somehow the social security service must be made more accountable to its customers. The mass of statistics which a local office collects deals mainly with the volume of work processed. By this means, the manager can defend or increase his complement of staff. But these figures tell nothing about courtesy, kindness, the length of the queues in the waiting room, the general accessibility of the service or the satisfaction of its customers. The DHSS has no regular, continuing programme of market research. Any company with a turnover one-tenth the size of the social security service's would spend a lot of money every year on this kind of research. When the SBC persuaded the Department to launch a nationwide study of this kind it was blocked by trade union opposition.

Even without research, commercial organisations know pretty well what the public thinks of their service. People who work in a hotel quickly learn if the customers are dissatisfied: vacant rooms and an empty bar tell them. And soon they get a new manager. The civil service tells its managers if they are not satisfying their regional controller. But no one really knows what the customers think about the service they are getting, or tries to find out. No effort is made to discover, on a local or regional scale, how many people actually get the benefits to which they are entitled. Even on a national scale there was no regular study of the take-up of benefits till the Commission asked for one – and cuts in Government research mean that there is no assurance that this will continue.

After lengthy research and negotiation, the Commission proposed that one or two social security offices might experiment by setting up local liaison groups representing the people using their services, together with local managers and the civil service unions. In a world in which most other public services have gone a good deal further in representing the people whom they serve, that did not seem a particularly bold idea. Nevertheless, it was killed off; by trade union opposition.

Some offices already have pretty close working relations with the communities they serve. I recall good examples in Ebbw Vale (where everyone knows everyone), in the Falls, Belfast (where government offices which lose the confidence of local people get burnt down or blown up) and in Handsworth (thanks to some lively spokesmen of local immigrant groups and a responsive management). There must be many others. But they are still the exception, not the rule.

This is a plea, not simply for better public relations, but for a break-out from deeply-rooted civil service and trade union conventions. Central control and nationwide uniformity, not local innovation or local accountability, have been the aims of management and unions alike. It's no good simply asking local office managers and their staff to meet the public and respond to what people say. They must first understand the policies and dilemmas of their service, and be given greater responsibility for running their own offices in their own way, subject only to general assessment of the efficiency and quality of the service provided. The civil service constantly forgets that the principals who now head the increasingly large social security offices it has created have the rank of colonels in the army. Corporals on the streets of Belfast have more training in dealing with the public, and a more demanding tradition of looking after their own men in the field than the DHSS's local office managers are given. Social security staff do not have to reveal their names to their customers, or even to sign letters legibly. (I was fascinated to see the script which a recently recruited executive officer had already perfected to make the name Jones unreadable.) If somebody lashes out at an interviewing officer, the normal response is not to find out why, but simply to build bigger barriers. We are unlikely to make the service more accountable to its customers unless they are given, or demand, a voice which has to be listened to. Otherwise, when hard choices have to be made – about the new computers, for example – management will always tend to protect the bureaucracy rather than improve the quality of the service.

To tackle these problems, the civil service will have to face up to its trade unions. Their right to defend the legitimate interests of the staff must be respected, and they should be consulted about every change in working procedures and conditions. But management must resist the temptation to buy peace with the unions at the expense of the public. The staff and their unions are going to need the public support which a first-class service can help to mobilise for them. During my time with the Commission the unions prevented us or the DHSS from making a national study of customers' attitudes to the service, from devolving responsibilities for management more completely to local offices and junior staff, from experimenting with ways of representing and consulting the users of social security services, from giving the difficult and delicate task of dealing with 'living together' cases to a properly trained specialist in each local office, and from doing research designed to enable us more quickly to identify which customers are most likely to suffer if the flow of social security money is temporarily disrupted (by a strike, for example). They made difficulties, eventually resolved, about our attempt to rewrite codes of instructions in simpler words; and they opposed proposals for improving opportunities for experienced staff to work part-time and return to full-time work after a break in their employment. Several of these were flagrant abuses of power, shameful to good trade unionists.

This is a bad time for civil servants, and particularly for those who work in the social services. Many people, including some leading members of the Government, are frankly hostile to them and to the public services to which they devote their working lives. If, in this discouraging climate, they can nevertheless bring about real improvements in the quality of public services, they will have done something far more important than filling in time till opportunities for more dramatic reforms return. They will have helped to restore public confidence in government, and to give Britain the time and good temper she needs to solve more fundamental economic and political problems. But if the quality of these services grows still worse that will be one more step towards a breakdown of civilised order.

Watershed

The climate of opinion has been changing yet again. From time to time in the course of its history a nation crosses a watershed in its political journey – a point at which the whole landscape of popular assumptions and aspirations seems to change. It may be long after the event that the timing and meaning of these changes becomes clear. But not this time. The crest of the watershed we have just crossed was so clearly marked that I almost heard the crunch as we passed over it. To be precise, it was at about 3.00 p.m. on 26 March 1980 – Budget Day.

During the weeks leading up to the Budget I had, as usual, got wind of some of the battles, first between officials and then between Ministers, which raged around the formulation of plans for social security. Supplementary benefit rates were to go up sufficiently to keep pace with inflation. The safety net would hold. Family income supplement for poor working families would increase quite a lot. But the earnings-related supplements to insurance benefits were to be abolished. Child benefits, although they were to go up in money terms, would fall quite sharply in real value, for wages and prices were going ahead much faster. And powers were being taken to reduce insurance benefits for the sick and the unemployed – all the short-term rates – by 5 per cent in each of the next three years. That, they said, was a way of taxing these benefits until the Inland Revenue perfected methods for taxing them properly along with other income at the end of each year. We agreed they ought to be taxed, but suspected, because the Government would give no promise that the 15 per cent lost by 1983 would ever be replaced, that this was a smooth way of making a straight cut in all the most widely used social security benefits, and putting people on means tests instead.

Underlying these measures were far more fundamental shifts

in policy. Every government since the second world war, no matter which Party was in power, had claimed that they wanted to support the family, to maintain – or return to – full employment, and to get people off means tests by enabling them to earn their own living and giving them adequate insurance benefits when they could no longer do so. What governments actually *did* was often very different. But those which moved in the opposite directions explained their actions as regrettable and temporary deviations from the road towards the old unchanged goals. In their rhetoric, at least, they held to the doctrines which the British had learnt in the 1930s and 1940s, in depression and war. Political speeches were littered with symbols of that doctrine – memories of the Clydeside and Jarrow hunger marches, of the hated poor laws and their means tests, and all the hopes for full employment, adequate benefits as-of-right, a free national health service and generous support for the family.

Mrs Thatcher's government too had come to power with a manifesto which relied heavily on the old rhetoric, promising more generous support for the family, more opportunities and incentives for work, and a tax credit scheme that would ultimately replace most of the social assistance system. But things were now changing. They were proposing quite deliberately to increase a rate of unemployment which was already rising disastrously. After handing out tax reductions to the rich and preserving the real value of tax allowances which mainly benefited people without children to support, they were cutting the real value of most of the benefits for working families. For not only child benefits but free school meals, educational maintenance allowances, grants for clothing and other benefits mainly aimed at families with low incomes were falling in real value. And by cutting contributory benefits and relying increasingly on supplementary benefit they were deliberately resorting to means tests to support more and more of the growing numbers who would be out of work. Those who were paying the heaviest price for these policies were working parents with modest wages raising one or two children. Many of them were the very people whose votes had put Margaret Thatcher in power.

Whether you believed in these policies or not, they clearly

amounted to a fundamental break with the past. Support for the family, jobs for workers, getting people off means tests – all had been cast aside, or relegated to the status of longer term, not immediate, priorities. Ministers and Treasury officials were well aware of that. In the battles leading up to the Budget it had been pointed out to them that there were some things they could not do without courting disaster. The last time a social services Minister – Keith Joseph in the Heath Government – had announced what amounted to a deliberate cut in his Department's benefits he had been unable to make himself heard in the House for several minutes. The last time – fifty years earlier – that benefits for the unemployed had been attacked the government itself had fallen.

As usual, I had been invited, along with others, to discuss the Budget on television as soon as the Chancellor sat down. I went to the little studio the BBC sets up for these occasions just opposite the Houses of Parliament, knowing only what was to happen to social security benefits. Sitting with other contributors to the programme as the long speech unfolded through our headphones, I realised that Sir Geoffrey Howe was spelling out the practical implications of a whole new politics.

We went into action as he sat down. Our chairman called first upon a spokesman of business and a politician from a Labour local authority to comment. Then I was told by a production assistant in an apologetic whisper that I would not be needed. Instead, they invited some character to make an impassioned appeal for the right of smokers to pursue their addiction untaxed. A political watershed had been crossed and the transition was not even worth discussing. I cycled back towards Aldwych through Parliament Square.

The point I am making is not about a wasted afternoon, or about the tawdry values of the BBC. It is that in terms of the immediate concerns of Londoners, which are a national journalist's first test of news values, *the BBC was right*. There were no angry or anxious crowds in Parliament Square. The Chancellor, and next day Patrick Jenkin announcing the social security measures in greater detail, were interrupted by no more than a ritual protest. The public opinion polls showed that, unpopular though the government were, the Budget had gained, not lost them support; and their plans for social security were by no means the least popular part of their programme. Later, when the Social Security No. 2 Bill enacting some of the main changes went through the House, a leading opposition spokesman sent telegrams to the leaders of every major trade union inviting them to say something – anything – about the measure. No-one replied. They were not misjudging their members' feelings: the TUC's 'day of action' against the cuts was a flop.

Things may change again. But for the moment at least the boundaries which divide what is politically thinkable from the unthinkable have been significantly shifted. And the wolves in the Treasury, always ranging abroad in hopes of bringing down a social benefit, learnt their lesson and have since come back for more. Meanwhile, although the main structure of our own scheme remained intact, we were already feeling the bite of the new wind blowing through Whitehall. Allegations about social security fraud had been bandied about a lot at the general election and the government were going to have to show that they were doing something about it. In February 1980 Reg Prentice did his best to gain some political mileage out of the issue by launching a big campaign. Officials had argued that the most effective way of saving public money was not to put all their efforts into pursuing fraud but to try harder to get unemployed claimants back to work and to make sure that absconding husbands paid their wives the maintenance ordered by the courts. Thus most of the extra staff brought to bear were in fact devoted to 'unemployment review' and 'liable relatives' work, and not to fraud prevention. Sensible though this decision was, it was not widely explained to the public.

The Supplementary Benefits Commission always took fraud seriously. It discredits an essential service whose customers are in the great majority of cases perfectly honest. They are more likely, every study shows, to be getting too little, rather than too much, out of the system. Fraud also sours the morale of social security staff and their relations with the public. But we usually left it to Ministers to make public statements about it; partly because they, and not we, were actually responsible for dealing with fraud, and partly because we did not want to encourage the already widespread belief that 'scroungers' are always supplementary benefit claimants, never the people who claim the remaining 85 per cent of social security money. So our contributions to debates about fraud were mainly conveyed in private, and mainly designed to reduce hysteria and spread a realistic sense of proportion.

The Commission discussed the whole subject with the assistant secretary responsible for dealing with fraud: a clever, obsessional man who was apt to remind you that he had himself lived on national assistance as a boy and knew supplementary benefit claimants could perfectly well manage on much less money than they were getting.

"What is the most common form of fraud?" we asked.

"Working and drawing benefit at the same time."

"So there will usually be an employer involved somewhere, who must be getting something out of the deal through evading insurance contributions, tax payments or the payment of legal minimum wages?"

"Yes – but it's almost impossible to prove complicity."

"You don't *have* to prove complicity," we said. "All you have to do is to enforce compliance with the law over the payment of national insurance contributions, tax and the proper wages. Then working and drawing benefit will be very difficult because the social security system will throw up two cards for anyone who is doing both. And employers will have nothing to gain from employing defrauders instead of legitimate workers."

"Well it's not quite as easy as that."

"You've put 1,200 extra staff onto all this work. Have you put an extra man onto investigating employers?"

"No"

"Has the Inland Revenue?"

"No."

It was clear that he was labouring at the politically necessary job of showing that the Government were 'doing something' about fraud, without upsetting ordinary voters who, as customers, workers or employers, often participate in fraudulent transactions. While unemployment continued to rise his efforts could not greatly affect the total amount of fraud. For, like the old fashioned rat catcher who always left a healthy breeding pair of rats in any building he searched to make sure that he'd be called back to do the job again, the assistant secretary was careful to leave the root causes of the problem undisturbed.

We intervened more forcefully with Ministers over proposals they were discussing to recover over-payments – even those which were due to innocent errors, rather than fraud – by making drastic deductions from benefits. We did not succeed completely, but at least we helped to fend off some of the most punitive proposals which were being considered. We also wrote and spoke to Ministers and protested publicly about proposals for cutting out the provisions which enabled us in cases of really urgent need to pay benefit to single people involved in industrial disputes. In the small minority of disputes in which anyone gets supplementary benefit the money normally goes only to workers' dependents: thus the single get nothing unless they're starving. Henceforth, even that provision will be abolished. On that we failed. And sooner or later there will be a tragedy and a scandal.

The sums involved in these arguments were trivial – not to the claimants, but in relation to the total flow of benefits we were dealing with. Yet the principles were momentous. Every time we erode the public assumption that social assistance payments represent the minimum standard of living which Parliament regards as tolerable, and the assumption that in the last resort everyone in this country (no matter who he is or what the cause of his plight) can at least be sure that he will not starve, we tamper with the foundations of a tolerant and humane society which have been patiently built up since the days of the Tudor poor laws. These assumptions guide social security staff in their work. Every exception made to them poses the question: "Who's next?" If it's all right to cut the benefits of the fraudulent, the forgetful and the ignorant well below Parliament's guaranteed subsistence levels, then why impose any limits on the amounts of benefit to be deducted in payments for rent arrears and fuel debts? If it's all right to let single strikers starve, how about claimants suspected of fraud? Or recently arrived immigrants? Or men who are insolent to their employers?

This change in the political climate was not suddenly brought about by an autocratic and unfeeling government.

Some Ministers did indeed welcome a tough line. Reg Prentice explained frankly that if you are convinced that the only way to solve the country's problems is to offer greater rewards for success, that means making the rich richer. And if the national income is static or falling, that can only be done by making the poor poorer. But other Ministers were as disturbed as we were about these trends. And all responded promptly enough to a surge of public opinion sufficiently powerful to worry their own back benchers.

Proposals for drastic cuts in free transport to school were quickly dropped when the rural lobby and the church schools made their protests. A few months later, a team of officials working with Sir Derek Rayner (brought in from Marks and Spencer by the Prime Minister to eliminate waste) were planning more efficient ways of distributing all kinds of social security benefits. They proposed to give people the choice, if they preferred it, of having their money paid into a bank, post office savings, a building society or any other account, instead of having to collect it from the post office. That might have saved about £50 millions a year in charges now paid to the post offices. But if you suggest any major saving you will soon find out where the money is going. This proposal was deliberately published in the most provocative fashion by the head of the Post Office. Within days rural post-masters and post-mistresses staged a march on London from the Tory shires and so beseiged the Secretary of State that for two weeks he could do virtually nothing but placate all concerned.

The new tides of political feeling are far more fundamental than a change of government. They were already flowing strongly under Labour. The reluctance to tell people the truth about the fundamental character of the economic crisis this country faces and the difficult choices we have to make; the simulated but ineffectual distress about rising unemployment; the reliance on phoney stop-gap measures for concealing the numbers out of work; the concealment of the few mildly egalitarian reforms which were achieved, lest these excite anger somewhere in the electorate; the abandonment of any serious attempt to create a new and better society; and the adoption of a self-interested politics of the market place – "Vote for us and we will administer the slump more smoothly, disturb you less, and keep the world safe for conservatives in the intervals between Conservative Governments" – this was the regime to which we had already become accustomed before the election.

Where will these trends lead? To break out of them will call for more fundamental changes which will threaten powerful interests in all classes. That will only be possible as people become convinced that present policies can no longer be tolerated. War, a collapse in the birth rate, a significant drop in living standards, or fairly widespread public disturbances: these have in the past been the triggers for major changes in policy. Some of them now loom as real probabilities.

At such a time, radicals too often assume that events will play into their hands, leading the nation leftward in reforming directions. On the contrary: it has more often been the Right rather than the Left which gains strength from political turbulence. For the disorder encouraged by rising unemployment and falling living standards is always associated with other problems – with racial conflicts, religious bigotry, political extremism or more trivial nastiness: drink and football hooliganism, for example. It is these factors to which the government and the news media attribute the trouble when it comes – always with sufficient justification to confuse the issues. That leads, and is intended to lead, not to a recognition of fundamental economic and social problems but to a punitive, 'crack-down' response, to the training of special police forces, the banning of political demonstrations, the bringing in of the army, and eventually the conscription of the unemployed. We have already gone far down that road in Ulster. We are moving in the same directions in Britain. Time is not on the side of the humane forces in this country. They will have to learn and think and organise if the drift towards increasingly brutal social division and disorder is to be arrested. "For evil to triumph," as Edmund Burke said, "it is only necessary for good men to do nothing." This is the setting for any conclusions we are to draw about policies and politics.

CHAPTER 8

Conclusions

It is time to draw some conclusions from this story, first about the way in which policies are made – the politics of poverty – and then about the policies themselves.

The Politics of Poverty

I have told what the Commission sought to achieve, and how far we got within five years. It was not a long way. Yet significant changes were made in the provisions, procedures and style of a major public service which had changed very little over many years. Movements for change extending well beyond the social security services into housing, energy policies and other fields were set on foot or carried forward, and the impetus for reform has not been exhausted. Whether the ultimate effects of all these changes are good or bad will be for others to decide. A lot of people are already doing research to find out. (That so much independent research should have been launched by a Department which hitherto kept its distance from academics working in the field of social security is itself a big change.)

In this last chapter I shall reflect first on how these things happened and who brought them about – the drama and the cast in this story of the politics of poverty. It is important to understand these things. So many of the people I met – claimants, social security staff, politicians and others – recognised the problems I have discussed but felt unable to do anything about them. They had good reason to feel helpless: by himself even the Secretary of State is incapable of getting anything done. Yet together, if they know what they want and how to set about it, the same people can shift apparently immovable institutions. And if enough people start doing that the political climate itself begins to change. I shall describe first the acts of the play, and then the actors.

Stripped to its essentials, the drama of social reform has six acts. In the first, questions are posed and the issues to be considered are defined and located on the political map. Barbara Castle's invitation to the Commission to make independent annual reports to Parliament; the appointment of a new chairman, new Commissioners and new senior officials, most of them unfamiliar with this field of work and thus without prior commitments to particular interests or points of view within it; the breaking open of the issues, first in response to the Child Poverty Action Group in the columns of *Social Work Today,* and then in speeches, articles and the Commission's first Annual Report: these were the first act of the drama. Excessive complexity, poor take-up of benefits, poor morale among staff, confused relations with neighbouring social services, the misuse of discretion, and the danger of a general breakdown of the system – these were the main issues posed.

To gain attention, the questions must be urgent, practical and easily understood. They must also be defined in broad enough terms to be capable of re-interpretation and development as unforeseen things happen. The impetus for reform will have to be carried forward through changes of Minister, economic cuts, scandals real and imaginery, general elections, and whatever else time may bring. We focused on rather too many issues. But at least they were genuinely important questions. That was because we were constantly meeting claimants and the staff of local social security offices and trying to understand what was really happening to them. Other people were trying at the same time to focus the debate on altogether different issues – on 'scroungers', incentives to work, the plight of particular types of claimant and so on. We had to explore each of these seriously if we were to demonstrate that they were ill-founded.

Although there was widespread dissatisfaction with our service, we lacked the support of any organised public movement for reforming it. Neither was there any flagrant incident capable of dramatising our problems and focusing public attention upon them: we had (thank God!) no equivalent to the death of the O'Neill boy which led to the Children Act of 1948, the great smog which led to the Clean Air Act of 1956, or the Rachman scandals which led to the Rent Act of 1965. Thus we had to 'start from cold' – but at least with a clean slate.

In act two of the drama all the potential solutions for the problems posed in act one must be flushed out into the open for inspection, along with their advocates. The appointment of the review team and their steering group of senior officials representing different Departments of Government; public and private consultations with staff, claimants, pressure groups and neighbouring social services; the Commission's next Annual Reports and the chairman's articles and speeches; the publication in *Social Assistance* of the review team's analysis and proposals, and the public discussions which followed: these were our second act.

The review team and the Commission did their best to take a fresh look at the problems and design solutions for them – each of us inevitably confined by our rather different assumptions about the scope of these issues, and the range and quantity of the resources which might be brought to bear upon them. But most of the solutions presented at this stage are ready-made – waiting to be offered to anyone with a problem to which they can be applied. Whatever question you ask of the Child Poverty Action Group, bigger child benefits will be part of their answer; just as more interesting and less stressful work for civil servants will be part of the answer given by the civil service trade unions. That is normal and proper. In act two of the drama the reformer always finds himself surrounded by interests trying to capture and interpret for their own ends the issues posed in act one. (The problem, he may be told, is about hypothermia and the elderly, about cohabitation rules and the rights of women, about computers and the mechanisation of administrative routines. . . .) Each formulation of the issues should be seriously considered. For at this stage the game must be kept as open as possible.

Means must also be found to consult important groups whose voices would otherwise go unheard. We did our best through our own and other people's research to explore the needs of unemployed people. Although their claims furnished most of the work done by the service, and their needs were often the most urgent of all, they were least likely to gain for themselves an adequate hearing.

In act three a winning consensus must be assembled round a set of proposals which will attract as much support and provoke as little opposition as possible. Steps must also be taken to mobilise supporters and reassure or isolate potential opponents. It is rather like the process of 'compositing' resolutions at a Party conference. Continuing debate, public and private, with pressure groups, trade unions, professional associations and local authorities; consultations with Ministers, opposition spokesmen and back-bench groups of MPs; the discrediting of Iain Sproat and others who sought to fan hysteria about 'scroungers', the publication of the Commission's response to the review: these were among the events which constituted our third act, leading us through a general election and the appointment of new Ministers, Commissioners and senior officials to the decision to legislate.

The political climate had been changing. At the start of act one, many people were still saying that the benefits were too low. By act two, more of them were saying that they were too high. Now, in act three, they were saying that it took too many staff to administer them. Simplification became the central theme, and restraints on public expenditure. At least we fended off pressure for cuts in benefits. We also found, and helped to build, increasing support among politicians and officials for publication of our rules, and for a system based on ascertainable rights rather than discretion. And we gained a government with the will to act and a majority in Parliament. That opportunity might not come again. But it might be destructively used.

In act four the decision to change things is formally registered and legitimated. In our case this meant that a Bill had to go through Parliament. This had first to be agreed by our Ministers and then approved by a Cabinet committee. Next came the preparation of a Bill and a timetable which would achieve royal assent in time to get the new system working next year, and weeks of debate on the Bill, in and around Parliament. Since most members of Parliament do not have time to get a grasp of complex legislation (and this was a very complex amending measure) officials briefing Ministers, and pressure groups briefing the opposition each played vital parts in staging the debate on the Bill. Once again, the dogs which did not bark – the missing spokesmen of the pensioners and the unemployed, for example – were as important in shaping events as the dogs which did bark.

The law by itself does not change things very much: it provides little more than a licence authorizing those who must get things done to start work. Implementation is act five of the drama. It may be brief or it may go on indefinitely. Officials began preparing voluminous regulations to submit to Parliament before the Bill had become law; then they were redeploying staff, writing instructions for them, and training them; they explained the new system to social workers, pressure groups and members of appeals tribunals; they prepared new forms and leaflets for the public, helped Ministers to pick a new Social Security Advisory Committee, and got the whole scheme working. Crucial at this stage were the new rules about discretionary benefits, plans for the new 'special case officers', (viewed at first with some suspicion in the local offices in which they were to work), and the jobs to be done by the Chief Supplementary Benefits Officer, who interprets the regulations for local staff and advises them how to deal with difficult cases, and the four new full-time chairmen of the appeals tribunals. Together they will go a long way to shape the character of the new scheme.

Act six is optional; it may never follow: this is the drive for further reforms developing the ideas and initiatives already set on foot. It is too early to say what will happen in this case. But action already taken by the Government on fuel benefits, proposals they have made for a major reform of housing subsidies and rate rebates, Parliament's recent discussions about child benefits, the decision to give older unemployed claimants the long-term rates of benefit, and plans now being prepared for the reorganization of social security operations and the introduction of new computer systems all show that the impetus for change has not been exhausted. Some of these things would have happened in any case, but all bear the marks of the review and its aftermath.

If these are the main acts in the drama, who are the actors? Because I have told the story from the standpoint of the Commission I have inevitably exaggerated the importance of that body. Although our contribution was vital, it was strictly limited. We had very little power. But we were able to pose questions which officials and Ministers, confined by their Departmental responsibilities, would have found much harder to ask publicly. We opened doorways to change and suggested the directions in which people might go through them. But other people had to pass through these doors, and do the work and take the risks which ultimately led to action. All our main proposals affected other groups and interests with good reasons for defending existing arrangements. Thus someone always tried to close any door we opened. In private discussions and persistent public argument, we were able to keep some of them open long enough to preserve opportunities for reform which would otherwise have been lost. We did that for several years almost unaided over rents and housing subsidies. We also helped to do likewise over fuel subsidies, over the publication of social security rules and policies, and over the provision of written notices explaining for all claimants how their benefit is calculated. The Commission also had a lot more work to do in keeping the system running. Only by doing that work well could we learn enough about the system to play an effective part in reforming it.

The essentially political job of launching the debate which may eventually lead to reform can be done in all sorts of different ways. It may be secret or well publicised; it may originate with a Minister, or he may pass the question to a Royal Commission; or it may be forced by events upon a reluctant government. But nothing happens until large enough questions – questions which cannot be satisfactorily answered within the confines of present arrangements and assumptions – have been convincingly and publicly posed. Posing those questions was the Commission's main contribution to the drama. Equally important was the task of getting the right officials to work on the reform. Officials close to Ministers – the courtiers I called them – often bear the main responsibility for analysing the problems which have been posed, for formulating solutions and appraising their costs and benefits. Much has been written about that in text books, but far less about their equally important task of negotiating a potentially winning consensus. In this case that called for discussions with their colleagues in other branches of government and with local authorities, professional bodies, trade unions and pressure groups. Officials with sensitive political judgment, negotiating talent and the capacity to collaborate with reforming spirits outside the bureaucracy play a crucial part in this act of the drama. They may be frowned on by more cautious superiors for risking embarrassment to their political masters. Yet any attempt to launch a reform within central government which did not begin by recruiting some of these innovators would get off to a bad start within the informal but well-informed 'club' of Whitehall courtiers.

I have stressed the crucial parts played by good civil servants in the drama of reform. It follows that a sufficiently senior official who is unsuited for the task can be a disastrous obstruction. He may be an able administrator. He may even, on other occasions, have been an effective innovator. But if he is out of sympathy with the aims and ethos of this particular reform and has difficulty in working harmoniously with other members of the cast he must be removed. Other officials, senior and junior, will be most reluctant to do anything to bring that about. To outsiders this closing of the Whitehall ranks in defense of a colleague looks like a conspiracy. Some ex-Ministers have said as much. But they are usually wrong. What the outsiders are up against is a protective code of behaviour imposed on civil servants by the knowledge that when the outsiders have come and gone officials will have to go on working alongside each other for many years to come. For the same reasons, prisoners do not 'grass' on each other, and boys in boarding schools do not tell tales about each other to their headmasters. Shifting a senior official in these circumstances therefore becomes a political act: an act, that is to say, which may have to be brought about by compelling the very top brass to recognise that the alternatives will be even worse. Outsiders can only pull that off if they are, in the last resort, capable of doing without the official in question and more valuable to the government than he is. If they fail, that is due to their own political weakness within the apparatus of government.

Beyond the officials most closely involved stand many other interests capable of playing a part in the drama. They range from those who can prevent reform if their concerns are not satisfied, through those likely to gain a hearing of some sort in the debate, to those so inarticulate that you have to hunt them out. The Treasury, the Civil Service Department and the civil service trade unions rank in the first group – the people who have to be consulted because they may be able to veto action. A few back bench MPs may wield similar power if the government has a small majority in Parliament.

The more effective pressure groups stand in the second rank among the people who will in any case gain a hearing of some sort. To be effective these groups must do good case work on the problems the service is dealing with, and they must also be capable of collating the evidence derived from that work and presenting it convincingly to journalists and government back-benchers. That way they will gain a hearing which compels officials and politicians to listen to them. Academic researchers with similar qualities may also be found among this second group – people with challenging ideas who are doing good empirical research which reveals what's really going on, and who also communicate their ideas convincingly to audiences extending well beyond their students and academic colleagues.

No matter how many people the reformers consult, most of those who hear about the issue will learn of it from newspapers, radio and television. Thus journalists, and particularly the expert specialist correspondents and broadcasters working in the field concerned, play a crucial part in the drama. Whether they favour the reformers' proposals or not is less important than their capacity to focus and sustain public interest in the relevant issues. Gaining the sympathy of these correspondents is not essential for success; but to embark on reform without first establishing your credibility with them is like starting an old-fashioned battle without first securing command of the air. Foolish.

I have left Ministers till the last. They are the most important actors, and they have to take the biggest risks. Officials whose efforts misfire may blot their records and spoil their careers, but they still have a job and a salary. Ministers may put themselves and even their Party out of power. They have a peculiarly complex role. As democratic politicians they depend entirely on their Party for the opportunity to play any part in public affairs. Yet as leaders of a Ministry they are trustees for major public interests – the interests of tax payers (as Treasury Ministers), students (as Education Ministers), or health service patients and social security claimants (at the DHSS) and the interests of the relevant staff. This means that they must be prepared to defend their Department and quickly identify a few of its causes on which they are prepared to stake their reputations in conflicts with their colleagues in Cabinet. A few causes, but not too many. They can't expect to win all their battles. Meanwhile if they want to achieve lasting reforms which leave a mark on their field of government they must also find ways of building a tacit consensus about important issues with their most bitter critics – the shadow ministers put up by the opposition to discredit and destroy them politically. There can be little satisfaction in taking a Bill through the House only to see it repealed with contempt after the next general election. Thus Ministers must be quick to choose the few problems to which they intend to give reforming attention during their term of office, but cautious about committing themselves publicly to solutions. To do that too soon will only compel their critics inside and outside Parliament to take a contrary line. But if public debate can be carried forward till a sufficiently convincing consensus has been formulated, their oppenents and their colleagues in the government (who will be competing for the same resources of money, manpower and Parliamentary time on behalf of their own projects) may be induced to support what will become a lasting reform. In our particular drama we did our best to generate interest in our proposals on both front benches while postponing specific commitments from either until we had a convincing prospect of getting a reform through Parliament.

These are the essential members of the cast. Others mentioned in this book may also play important parts in the drama – political advisers to Ministers, for example. Some will complain that the customers of the service have barely been mentioned. They may influence government in all sorts of ways, not only as claimants but also as constituents and voters, as tax-payers, as members of pressure groups, as appellants before tribunals, and so on. Riots, in which they may also play a part, influence governments too. But in a service as extensive as ours the customers rarely amount to a single, consistent interest. The Claimants' Unions do a valuable but sporadic and ill-co-ordinated job. Groups more closely united by common interests have generally been more effective. One-parent families, for example, have over the past decade won widespread sympathy which gained real benefits for them in this story. The disabled have gained a lot of ground too. Students can never be wholly neglected. But the unemployed lack the confidence and the political 'clout' which these groups have.

The most successful spokesmen of the poor gain support which is not confined to the poor but drawn from people in all walks of life. One-parent families, for example, include graduates and members of well-established professions. Even those who remarry do not altogether abandon the cause. And every Cabinet Minister must have some lone parent among his relatives or friends. But the ablest and most effective spokesmen of the unemployed, although they have been described as leaders of a 'conscript army', are always apt to desert to the 'enemy': they get jobs. For pressure groups representing the poor these realities have important implications. To gain a hearing they must make common cause, as spokesmen of the aged and the disabled have done, with interests and groups strongly entrenched throughout society.

The story of reform which I have told is a highly selective tale which omits most of the daily work of the social assistance service and the Commission that presided over it. That itself represents a point of view: the conviction that politics in general, and such a Commission in particular, should be centrally concerned with changing things. Not because change is good in itself – some changes should be fought tooth and nail – but because in this field so many unresolved problems cry out for solution.

The dramas of social reform are not so uniform nor are their acts so clearly distinguished as this simple account suggests. Yet something of this kind takes place when any major new initiative is launched in a large public service. Even in the most favourable political climate innovators rarely have more than a brief 'window' in time through which to 'process' reform. Ministers and their Parties cannot pursue a campaign, bureaucracies cannot concentrate talented courtiers, and journalists and their editors believe they cannot sustain public interest in particular topics for very long. Thus reformers have to do what they can when the time seems ripe for action, and then reformulate the issues or pick new ones. Within that time they have somehow to work through the processes I have described, and in much the same order. Royal Commissions, inter-Departmental committees, town planning inquiries and other operations of this kind are rituals or vehicles which society has invented for dealing with central phases of these dramas. The actors in the particular play I have described invented a new model which was designed to combine the advantages and avoid the disadvantages of previous vehicles for reform. Such vehicles can be used to mobilise and direct the impetus for change or to dissipate and obstruct it. Whichever your intention may be, you should know how these things work if you want to get into the act.

As they move forward, these dramas assemble commitments to act, and specifications for what is to be done. Politics is a learning process. Some accounts of it suggest that the logical way to go about it is first to specify with increasing precision what must be done, and only then to ask people to do anything. But in fact learning and action, specification and commitment, evolve together – in parallel not in series. People only devote time and effort to deciding what should be done as they become convinced that a commitment to action is building up. And they are prepared to commit themselves to action because they see more clearly what might be done. Neither process is a smooth one: each may be unexpectedly carried forward or set back as Ministers, Governments and senior officials change, as economic and political crises come and go, and other unforeseen developments take place.

The process of learning which politics consists of may operate at widely varying scales – on big or small things. The transformation of the legal structure of the supplementary benefit scheme, the redistribution of benefits in favour of claimants with children, the provision of written assessments for claimants which showed how their benefits were calculated, the appointment of 'special case officers' to deal with particularly difficult cases, important though they seemed to their advocates, were all small-scale tactical matters.

Strategic changes, of the sort that would be needed to bring about a big improvement in job opportunities for young people, or really generous child benefits for every family, will call for action on a much bigger scale transferring large volumes of resources from some people to others. To achieve such fundamental changes in policy calls for what amounts to a new set of moral values. That cannot be brought about by Ministers and officials alone, even with the help of belligerent pressure groups. New rights, to be secure, cannot be conferred from the top; they must also be taken by the people at the bottom. And that calls for a movement of some kind. For individuals, and poor people in particular, cannot demand new rights and impose new values on society single-handed, or even as members of groups speaking only for the poor. They need the support of a collective consciousness spanning a wider range of social interests, and the conviction, courage and influence which that can impart.

Social class and the loyalties and conflicts generated around it provide the best-known but by no means the only framework within which such changes can be brought about. Regional patriotism, concern about particular age groups – old or young – religious or ethnic loyalties and the women's movements have all at times provided a similar, supportive framework making larger changes possible. If the poor are to make advances in future, that is again likely to be achieved through the intervention of movements based on these larger interests and loyalties.

Policies

As supplementary benefits Commissioners we were the State's watchdogs on poverty, the inheritors of a tradition which went back 400 years to the parish overseers of the poor and the justices of the peace under whose general supervision they worked. It has always been an ambiguous tradition, concerned as much with the prevention of disorder and the protection of the comfortable as with the prevention of destitution and the protection of the helpless. How should that tradition now be interpreted? Indeed, does it any longer serve any purpose? Poverty of the sort the Tudors witnessed has disappeared. No-one starves. Very rarely does anyone freeze to death.

Supplementary benefit today is worth about twice as much as national assistance was as recently as 1948. So why worry about the poor?

Poverty means exclusion from the living standards, the life styles and the fellowship of one's fellow citizens. That exclusion is not experienced merely as a frustrating failure to keep up with the Joneses. The assistant secretary in charge of the campaign against fraud who believed everyone could manage perfectly well with an income equivalent to the national assistance rates of his boyhood on which his own parents lived had forgotten that they had an open fire and probably a cooking range which could burn all kinds of fuel. They were not compelled to live in a flat with one of the more expensive forms of central heating. They could probably grow vegetables in the back garden, and walk to the shops every day – little shops which would give you credit if you were short of cash. They had no need of a refrigerator for storing their food. They could hang out the washing in the yard and had no need of launderettes or washing machines. Since no-one had television sets their children would not have felt at a loss in the playground and the classroom for lack of what has now become most people's main window on the world – almost the only window for those who cannot afford to go anywhere.

We constantly manufacture new forms of poverty as we drive forward the living standards of the majority without thinking what we are doing to those who cannot keep pace. And we add humiliation. A mother left on her own with a couple of infants or an unemployed man who has run out of insurance benefits may live on cups of tea and get behind with the fuel bills in order to keep up their payments on the fridge and the TV set. If they ward off loneliness and depression with an occasional cigarette, we say they're 'bad managers'. If they go to the social security office they are directed to a more squalid waiting room than the one used by better-off people claiming insurance benefits. They usually have to wait there longer. They have to answer more intrusive questions about their incomes and savings and the people who may be living with them. And the world is more likely to call them 'scroungers'.

We create conflict as well as poverty, destroying people's

capacity to work together on the daunting problems which now confront us all. Government does that by handing out tax reliefs to the rich while putting more and more of the unskilled and the poor out of work. It does it by starving the State schools and hospitals of funds, while putting public money and tax benefits into private schools and hospitals. Trade unions get into the act too, negotiating escape routes from the national health service for their members with the help of private insurance. Government and unions alike turn their backs on the search for broadly acceptable policies for regulating incomes and prices, and rely instead upon 'free collective bargaining' – commercial and political power struggles – to settle some of the most fundamental decisions which any society takes about its character and future. Industry, commerce and the City of London do it when they invest the nations' resources in American shopping centres, in the Cayman Islands – anywhere but in the enhancement and productive use of our own peoples' capacities and skills. They do it every time they build into their new factories and offices the separate entrances, the separate eating places and separate lavatories for people of different status which I saw on my journeys up and down the country. And then they expect people who cannot even eat or pee together to get round a table and reach constructive decisions about new technologies, the future deployment of workers, and the distribution of their collective incomes. Universities play a part in the story too when they dignify all these arrangements by teaching their students that they are the outcome not of a man-made culture and its seedy moral values, but of impersonal and irresistible 'market forces'.

I believe that gross and persistent inequalities – inequalities which impoverish or enrich the same people over and over again in many different ways and are transmitted from generation to generation – destroy Britain's capacity for civilised human relationships, for tolerant democracy and for self-respecting productive work. But make no mistake, I would be no less disturbed about poverty if you could somehow demonstrate that I had got it all wrong, and that inequality serves to maintain order and increase our competitive strength. For I am moved most fundamentally of all by the plight of poor people, some of whom I have tried briefly to describe in this book. I am disgusted by the depression, deference, fear, jealousy and supercilious contempt – all the sick human relationships – which flourish and fester around poverty. And when the plight of the poor is contrasted with the wealth and the massive productive capacities which could so readily put things right I am enraged too. And so is everyone who has not lost the capacity for being shocked by injustice. The political reactionaries, the clever professors, the complacent people of middle England who contend, when they argue at all, against the social theories of committed egalitarians are aiming at the wrong target. It is experience, not theory, which moves us. They should instead get out and see the world for themselves. Then ask: "Is this a world I can feel at home in? Would I like *my* daughter to be raising children in these conditions? Would I like *my* son to be leaving school at sixteen in this city, with no prospects of a job? Would I like *my* father to die in this reception centre for homeless men?" If they do not like what they see, what are they prepared to do and how much are they prepared to pay to put things right? That is what poverty policies are about.

Several things follow. Although the condition of the poor is the most urgent concern of these policies, the unity of the nation and the capacity of each of us to respond to the needs of our fellow citizens, the resources of the economy, the examples set by the rich and powerful – all these are part of the agenda too. Poverty may entail hardship. But it is fundamentally about inequality, exclusion, powerlessness and humiliation. Thus although money is crucial, poverty is also a question of relationships and rights; a question of how people are treated by teachers, doctors, employers, landlords and the officials in job centres and social security offices. It concerns all of us, every sector of the economy and every branch of government.

The State has to play a vital part in changing these things. But it can only set the scene and give a lead. If people are still locked into hierarchies of status and dominated by relationships of authority and deference you can destroy the whole ruling class and transform the role of money and it will make little difference. Poverty and privilege re-emerge in new forms. (If we had forgotten that, a visit which some of us made to the Soviet Union would have reminded us.) Thus poverty policies have to evolve democratically. Like it or not, this must be a field of open government. For to succeed in these matters by fraud or repression without carrying the people with you would be to fail.

Every Department of Government – not only the social security ministry – must have a concern about the impact which its policies and programmes make upon the distribution of money, life chances, status and power. To load that responsibility onto the DHSS alone is worse than ineffective. It does little or nothing for people – full-time workers, for example – who are excluded from means-tested social assistance. It does little or nothing for people whose handicaps originate in other fields such as housing and education. And it means that one Minister, the Secretary of State for Social Services, has to fight alone in the Cabinet and in Cabinet committees for the poor, instead of every Minister (and particularly the Treasury Ministers) taking their proper responsibilities for policies in this field.

Hopes for the future which the British people worked out during the depression and wartime years – hopes for full employment, adequate support for families with young children, decent incomes paid as a right to those unable to earn their own living, a free health service and so on – all these are still basically sound. But with the economy moving towards collapse, and everyone encouraged to grab whatever they can for themselves by a government offering nothing higher to work towards, it is not enough to reassert the hopes of the Beveridge years. We must also work for more immediately attainable objectives. First priority of all must be given to getting more and better opportunities for people to support themselves. Rising unemployment is the crying scandal. It makes it harder to get sane policies adopted in every other field – from more ˙ flexible retirement ages to more equal opportunities for women, from more productive work for prisoners to the solution of demarcation disputes between trade unions.

Within the government's social programmes, first priority should be given to the 'working poor', particularly to men and women working for low wages and supporting a family. Thus higher child benefits should be the first priority within the social security system, coupled with other programmes which help working families: fairer systems of housing subsidies and fuel benefits, education maintenance allowances for youngsters from poor families who stay on at school, and so on. These families, bringing up children on modest incomes, have generally gained least and lost most over the last twenty years from changes in social benefits, in taxation and in prices. Their living standards and morale impose a political ceiling on what any Government can be expected to do for people who are not in work.

Within the social assistance services, the first priorities should be to eliminate discrimination against the unemployed, and to raise the benefits paid for children which are clearly too low in relation to those for adults.

Some of the steps I have called for will cost a lot of money. I have shown at various points in this book where much of this money could be found. The remainder is a modest sum in comparison with the funds transferred during the last two years by tax reductions and cuts in social service expenditure. The present government has proved that it is perfectly feasible to transfer resources on a scale that would put an end to most kinds of poverty. Meanwhile it would cost very little to give people living on social assistance payments firmer and more clearly understood rights. That will call for simplifications of some incomprehensibly complicated services, and for a determination to base decision-making wherever possible on ascertainable facts, rather than moral judgments. Discretion should be confined to its essential purposes; providing sufficient flexibility to meet urgent or really exceptional needs, and a means for responding to unforeseeable economic and social changes (from Dutch elm disease to the trebling of oil prices) in ways which ultimately confer more clearly defined rights.

The quality of the service given by the social security system – and hence the morale of the staff providing it – should be improved. That will call for a drive for greater accountability to the customers and the local community, and hence for some devolution of powers to local office managers and their staff, a more open style of government at all levels, an end to secret codes, and simpler, clearer leaflets, forms and posters. There must also be regular arrangements of some sort for representing the users of the social security services at a local level. These things will not be achieved without a reappraisal of the role of the trade unions representing the staff – recognising their rights in dealing with management, but protecting their customers from abuses of union power.

These have been the policy themes of this book. Meanwhile it grows clearer each day that the promise of minimal government which aims only to protect our property, reduce our taxes, and disturb us all as little as possible is a delusion. Whether in Labour or Conservative forms, it is leading to economic disaster, rising unemployment and violence in the streets. New and difficult decisions will have to be taken about investment, the distribution of incomes, international trade, the use of the oil revenues, the training and deployment of labour, the organisation of trade unions, and other matters which extend well beyond the sphere of this book.

As the turbulance associated with rising unemployment grows, we should welcome the fact that ethnic, local and other loyalties enable some people to reject the humiliations and the role of scapegoats which so many other poor people have had to accept. That in no way implies a welcome for the injuries which so many people have suffered. It is shameful that we have had to wait for this long-predicted violence to produce more action than years of rational argument have achieved. (A start is even to be made on giving unemployed people – those over sixty – the higher long-term rates of supplementary benefit.) These belligerent loyalties and the communities from which they spring should be recognised, not repressed. From such a policy there may emerge national and local programmes which help to establish the dignity of the unemployed and make them an effective political force. So long as the rest of us can afford to disregard what is happening to them, no fundamental reappraisal of policies will take place.

In every big city there should be local centres, not confined to the unemployed, where people can meet, seek advice, borrow tools for do-it-yourself jobs, find opportunities for training and for setting up their own enterprises, and organising political action. People out of work must play a central part in managing these centres. Local public expenditure – for the improvement of housing and its surrounding environment, for example – should be more imaginatively used to generate employment in poverty-stricken neighbourhoods. Outside the peak hours of public use, local authorities should offer unemployed people whatever resources they can provide – through the use of schools, concessionary fares on the buses, free access to swimming baths, sports centres and so on. Social security rules should be amended to enable people to use these opportunities without being threatened with the loss of their benefits because commitments to voluntary service or the setting up of new enterprises mean they are no longer 'available for work'. In areas with large black minorities there must be more effective action to prevent racial discrimination by employers and landlords; central and local government contracts should be withdrawn from any firm which does discriminate against black workers; and more convincing procedures, in which the representatives of local communities play a part, should be devised to investigate complaints about the police. These are only a few of the proposals for deprived neighbourhoods which have been discussed, and neglected, for years.

Such steps will not transform the lives of those who are out of work. But the struggle to get that much done may give people who are now without hope some attainable aims to work towards. The rest of Britain is now afraid lest the unemployed start mobilising for political action, but before long they may wish they had offered the workless such constructive and legitimate objectives to work for. If governments, Labour and Conservative, do nothing more effective on behalf of people who are out of work it will be their fault, not that of the 'agitators' upon whom they will seek to lay the blame, when streets burn and civilised order disintegrates.

Sources Quoted

The main publications mentioned or used in this book

Supplementary Benefits Commission Administration Paper (1976) No. 5, *Living Together As Husband and Wife*, HMSO.
———— (1977) No. 6, *Low Incomes. Evidence to the Royal Commission on the Distribution of Income and Wealth*, HMSO.
———— (1978) No. 7, *Take-up of Supplementary Benefits*, HMSO.
———— (1978) No. 8, *Social Security Users – Local Consultative Groups*, HMSO.
———— (1979) No. 9, *Response of the Supplementary Benefits Commission to 'Social Assistance: A Review of the Supplementary Benefits Scheme in Great Britain'*, HMSO.
Supplementary Benefits Commission Annual Report (1975) Cmnd 6615, September 1976, HMSO.
———— (1976) Cmnd 6910, September 1977, HMSO.
———— (1977) Cmnd 7392, October 1978, HMSO.
———— (1978) Cmnd 7725, October 1979, HMSO.
———— (1979) Cmnd 8033, September 1980, HMSO.
Department of Health and Social Security (1978) *Social Assistance: A Review of the Supplementary Benefits Scheme in Great Britain*, DHSS.
———— (1979) *Report on a Survey of Claimants' Attitudes to Central Issues of the Supplementary Benefits Review*, DHSS.
———— (1979) *Review of the Supplementary Benefits Scheme: Analysis of Views and Comments*, October 1979, DHSS.
———— (1981) *Supplementary Benefits Handbook, A Guide to Claimants' Rights*, (first published 1970, 3rd edn 1981), HMSO.
Department of the Environment Consultative Document (1981) *Assistance with Housing Costs*, March 1981, DOE.
Donnison, David (1975) 'Equality' *New Society*, November 20, 1975.

————— (1976) 'Supplementary Benefits: Dilemmas and Priorities' *Journal of Social Policy*, vol 5(4), October 1976.

————— (1977) 'David Donnison Replies' *Social Work Today*, (reprinted by British Association of Social Workers with five other open letters, edited by David Bull) vol. 8(32), May 17, 1977.

————— (1977) 'Against Discretion' *New Society*, September 15, 1977.

————— (1978) 'Feminism's Second Wave and Supplementary Benefits' *The Political Quarterly*, vol. 49(3), July–September 1978.

————— (1979) 'Social Policy Since Titmuss' *Journal of Social Policy*, vol. 8(2), April 1979.

Lynes, Tony (1981) *The Penguin Guide to Supplementary Benefits* (4th edn), Harmondsworth, Penguin.

Titmuss, Richard (1971) 'Welfare Rights, Law and Discretion' *The Political Quarterly*, vol. 42.

Index

Abel-Smith, Brian, 18, 24–5, 163
Adams, Barbara, 30
Age Concern, 106–7, 128, 130, 144
Anna, Sister, 103
Annunciata, Sister, 103
Assistance Board, 14
Association of Directors of Social Sciences, 31
Atkinson, Alec, 153
Attlee, Clement, 174

Barker, Paul, ix
Barnett, Joel, 155
Beacock, Nick, 176
Bedford College, 123
Bell, Kathleen, 45
Beltram, Geoffrey, 99, 187
Benn, Tony, 196
Bennett, Andrew, 175
Bernstein, Basil, 138
Bevan, Aneurin, 14, 156, 162
Beveridge, William, 6, 117–8, 146, 156, 229
Bevin, Ernest, 174
Boreham, John, 30
Boyle, Edward, 138
Brent Borough Council, 104
British Institute of Management, 64
British Leyland, 65, 78

British Medical Association, 36, 113
British United Provident Association, 87
Brown, Peter, 74
Brown, Ted, 50
Bull, David, 143, 147
Burke, Edmund, 213
Burt, Sir Cyril, 138
Byatt, Ian, 30

Cabinet Office, 30
Callaghan, James, 51, 52, 85, 156
    Labour Government 1976–79, 83
Cammell-Laird, 78, 81
Campaign for the Homeless and Rootless, 129–30, 176
Capital Radio, 116
Carmichael, Kay, x, 35, 71, 74
Castle, Barbara, ix, 24–5, 30–2, 34, 36, 40, 50, 52–3, 58, 65, 86, 90, 162, 166, 215
Catherwood, Sir Frederick, 64
Central Housing Advisory Committee, 19
Central Policy Review Staff, 32, 59, 135
Centre for Environmental Studies, 19, 139
Chalker, Lynda, 160, 162, 166, 173, 175

Chamberlain, Neville, 61
Child Poverty Action Group,
47–8, 85, 127, 130, 143,
145, 147, 158, 174, 215–6
Civil and Public Services
Association, 85
Civil Service College, 51
Civil Service Department, 55,
59, 142, 145, 171, 186, 221
Civil Service Union, 129
Claimants' Unions, 116, 128,
130, 145, 223
Collison, Harold, 16, 25, 28
Community Relations
Commission, 56
Confederation of British
Industry, 31, 73, 76–7, 169
Conservative Manifesto, 159
Conservative Political Centre,
155
Crosland, Anthony, 138, 186
Crossman, Richard, 54, 161
Cullen of Ashbourne, Lord, 177
Cunningham, John, 196

Davies, Sue, x
Deakins, Eric, 160
Dean, Brenda, 50, 84
Dean, Malcolm, 163
Deevy, Patrick, 66
Defence, Ministry of, 49
Devlin, Paddy, 37
Douglas, James, 138

Education and Science, Dept. of,
57, 59, 222
Employment, Dept. of, 57, 59
Energy,
Dept of, 151, 195–6, 198
Ennals, David, 73–4, 144,
154–6, 160, 162

Environment, Dept. of, 30, 52,
57, 59, 139, 151, 163–4,
186–8, 191
Equal Opportunities Commission, 120, 122
European Economic Commu-
nity, Commission and
Council of Ministers, 122

Family Commission, 155
Field, Frank, 127, 174–5
Finer Committee, 114
Foot, Michael, 52
Foreign Office, 159
Freeson, Reg, 104, 174–5
Freud, Sigmund, 136

General Electric Co., 22
Gingerbread, 116, 128
Glass, David, 138
Grunwick, 22, 84

Hall, Michael, 104
Halsey, A.H., 138
Hayes, Maurice, 37
Healey, Denis, 74, 155
Health and Social Services
Group (Labour Party), 51,
74
Heath Government, 174, 208
Hencke, David, 191
Heseltine, Michael, 139, 163,
191
Hobman, David, 106, 130, 143
Hodge, Henry, 158
Holtham, Carmen, 50
Home Office, 11, 36, 59
Housing Corporation, 104
Housing Finance Review (DoE),
186
Howe, Elspeth, 122
Howe, Geoffrey, 208

IBM, 83
industrial training, 86
Inland Revenue, 37, 42
International Monetary Fund,
   54
Islington Borough Social
   Services Dept., 99

Jaguar Motor Works, 78, 81
Jarmany, Bert, 30
Jenkin, Patrick, 155, 160,
   162–3, 165–6, 168, 172–3,
   190–1, 208
Joseph, Keith, ix, 18–9, 34, 161,
   174, 208

Kemp-Jones Committee, 123
Keynes, J.M., 24

Lee, Jenny, 156
LEFTA, 74
Lewis, Paul, 130, 175–6
Lister, Ruth, 127, 147
Local Government Board, 10
Lockwood, Lady Elizabeth, 122
London School of Economics,
   18, 20–1, 28
Lord Chancellor's Department,
   11
Love, Adrian, 116
Lowe, Anna, 28
Lynes, Tony, 18, 30–1, 127,
   163, 175–7

McKenzie, May, x
McLeod, Iain, 162
Manpower Services Commis-
   sion, 72–3, 83, 86–7
Marks and Spencer, 57, 87, 158,
   212
Marx, Karl, 136
Meacher, Michael, 37
Merrison Report, 157

Metcalf, David, 163
Milner Holland Committee, 19
Mind, 107, 128, 130
Morrell, Frances, 196
Morris, Alf, 50, 173
Moser, Sir Claus, 51, 138
Murray, Len, 73, 85

Nairne, Patrick, 49, 51–2,
   161–3
National Assistance Board,
   14–5, 25, 53, 130
National Campaign Against the
   Supplementary Benefits
   Review, 147
National Coal Board, 87
National Consumer Council,
   34–5
National Council for Civil
   Liberties, 47
National Council for One-
   Parent Families, 45, 127,
   130, 175
National Council for the Single
   Woman and her Dependants,
   128
National Council of Social
   Service, 196
National House Builders Regis-
   tration Council, 106
National Institute of Social
   Work, 46
National Insurance Advisory
   Committee, 168–9, 172
National Union of
   Mineworkers, 82
National Union of Teachers,
   157
Newton, Tony, 174

O'Brien, Richard, 72
O'Malley, Brian, 25, 29, 50–2,
   54, 57

O'Malley, Kate, 52
Orme, Stan, 57, 66, 73, 144, 147, 156, 159, 160–1, 166, 173, 175, 196
Otton, Geoffrey, 36, 49, 52–4, 59, 134–5, 141, 153, 160–2
Oxford and Cambridge Club, 51

Palmer, Alan,
 review team, 58–60, 122, 140, 144, 146, 174, 180
Pargeter, Frank and Doris, 105
Parker, Roy, 135
Parliamentary Commissioner, 47
Parry, Terry, 84
Parsons, C.A., & Co., 79–81
Partridge, Michael, 39, 147, 151, 154, 170, 174
'Patchwork', 100–1
Perkins, Alice, 29, 33, 36, 39, 57, 135
Plowden Committee (Central Advisory Council for Education), 19, 157, 199
Poor Law Commission, 10, 13
Prentice, Reg, 70, 160, 162, 166, 174, 175, 209, 211
Prime Minister's Policy Unit, 32
Public Schools Commission, 19, 157, 199

Rayner, Derek, 212
Right to Work March, 84–5
Robbins Committee, 138
Rodgers, Barbara, 35
Rothschild, Nathaniel Mayer Victor, 135
Rowe, Andrew, 169
Rowntree, Seebohm, 6
Royal College of Surgeons, 28
Russell, Margery, x

Salvation Army, 194

Scargill, Arthur, 82
Shelter, 47, 85, 128, 189
Shepherd, Harry, 158
Shore, Peter, 144, 163
Shotton Steel Works, 77–8, 81
Sinfield, Adrian, 52
Smythe, Tony, 47
Social Administration Association, 135
Social Democratic Party, 88
Social Democratic and Labour Party, 37
Social Science Research Council, 139
Social Security Advisory Committee, 172–3, 177, 183–218
Social Security Research Policy Committee, 134
SOGAT, 50, 84
Sproat, Iain, 57, 217
Stabler, Arthur, 50
Stationery Office, Her Majesty's, 144
Stewart, Evelyn, 151
Supplementary Benefits Handbook, 73–4
Supplementary Benefits Commission *Annual Report*, 32–34, 36, 58, 187
Supplementary Benefits Commission *Notes and News*, 35, 52, 57
Supplementary Benefits Commission for Northern Ireland, 37

Tanner, Bernice, 50, 67
Tanner, James, 138
Thatcher, Margaret, 85, 160–1, 164, 166, 175, 196
 Conservative Government 1979 –, 86, 207
Thomas, Ken, 85

Titmuss, Richard, M., 16, 18–9, 29
Townsend, Peter, 18
Trades Union Congress, 16, 31, 73, 84–8, 122, 156, 169, 172, 176, 209
Transport & General Workers Union Retired Members' Association, 107
Treasury, 12, 25, 30, 32, 42, 50, 54–5, 58, 59–60, 71, 82, 122, 142, 145–6, 149, 151, 155, 164, 171, 173, 186–7, 191, 195, 208–9, 221–2
Trew, Leslie, 52

Unemployment Assistance Board, 11, 15
University of Bristol, 143
University of Edinburgh, 46
University of Glasgow, 36
University of Nottingham, 132

Vaisey, John, 138

Walker, Peter, 139
Warner, Norman, 32, 36, 52
Weinstock, Arnold, 22
Wells-Pestell, Reginald Alfred, 177
Westbey, John, 174
Wheatley, John, 61
Wills, W.D. & H.O., & Co., 78
Wilson, Des, 47
Wilson, Harold, 36, 51
Wilson, John, 176
Wilson, Tom, 36
Woodman, Graham, 37–39

Young, Michael, 34, 138